Reading Shakespeare's Soliloquies

RELATED TITLES

Performing King Lear, Jonathan Croall
Emotional Excess on the Shakespearean Stage, Bridget Escolme
Shakespeare's Fathers and Daughters, Oliver Ford Davies
Shakespeare in the Theatre: Mark Rylance at the Globe, Stephen Purcell
Shakespeare in the Theatre: Nicholas Hytner, Abigail Rokison-Woodall

Reading Shakespeare's Soliloquies

Text, Theatre, Film

Neil Corcoran

Bloomsbury Arden Shakespeare
An imprint of Bloomsbury Publishing Plc
B L O O M S B U R Y
LONDON • OXFORD • NEW YORK • NEW DELHI • SYDNEY

Bloomsbury Arden Shakespeare
An imprint of Bloomsbury Publishing Plc

Imprint previously known as Arden Shakespeare

50 Bedford Square	1385 Broadway
London	New York
WC1B 3DP	NY 10018
UK	USA

www.bloomsbury.com

BLOOMSBURY, THE ARDEN SHAKESPEARE and the Diana logo are trademarks of Bloomsbury Publishing Plc

First published 2018

British Library Cataloguing-in-Publication Data
A catalogue record for this book is available from the British Library.

ISBN: HB: 978-1-4742-5351-2
PB: 978-1-4742-5350-5
ePDF: 978-1-4742-5353-6
eBook: 978-1-4742-5352-9

Library of Congress Cataloging-in-Publication Data
A catalog record for this book is available from the Library of Congress.

Cover design: Irene Martinez Costa
Cover image: Lucian Msamati as Iago. Photo by Keith Pattison © RSC

Typeset by Fakenham Prepress Solutions, Fakenham, Norfolk NR21 8NN
Printed and bound in Great Britain

CONTENTS

LIST OF ILLUSTRATIONS

PREFACE

When we took one of our sons, at the age of thirteen, to see his first Shakespeare play in Stratford he whispered to me, in awe, after watching someone perform a soliloquy, 'What confidence!' I agreed. This seemed an understandable response to an actor standing alone on stage reciting a lengthy speech from memory. I myself could no more do so than fly unaided to the moon. As a university teacher, though, I have lectured to audiences in various parts of the world over many years, which demands a certain theatrical skill and needs careful forethought and practice in the art of memory. But it's not the kind demanded by the delivering of a Shakespearean soliloquy on the stage of a theatre, in costume and usually under lights, and with the responsibility of keeping to marks and remembering all the things you have been told at the technical rehearsals, or by speaking into the lens of a camera on a film or TV set – a different, but almost certainly an equally taxing, art.

My own first encounter with a Shakespearean soliloquy in professional performance was also at the Royal Shakespeare Theatre. We went from school in 1964 and saw Peter Hall's *Richard II* with David Warner. I found his account of Richard's only soliloquy – 'I have been studying how I may compare / This prison where I live unto the world', in Act 5 – riveting. We were doing the play for A level, and I knew the soliloquy pretty well, or at least the words of it: I still do not think I 'know' it at all, and in places it's breathtakingly difficult. I had certainly been told about how Richard presents himself here as a kind of poet, appearing a bit like, say, John Donne elaborating a conceit in a seventeenth-century 'metaphysical' poem, and I was impressed by that. But I had never really thought about how the soliloquy might sound or look on a stage.

Nor had I at all adequately taken stock of the fact, savagely brought home by this production, that this was just about the last thing this man would do, and say, before he was murdered in his prison cell. The play on the page had encouraged me to ponder what it might be like for someone to 'study to compare'; on the stage, it made me realize, sharply, the impact of that other phrase in the soliloquy's opening lines, 'where I live', since this soliloquist in dank dungeon confinement had hardly any time at all left for living. Sometimes actors and directors are criticized for making Shakespeare a function of their own egos, and there are probably times when the rebuke is justified, but I am very glad indeed to have so often experienced what the egos of actors, so acutely necessary to get them up there in the first place, have made possible. Therefore I take much stock in this book, particularly in Part III, of how actors and directors understand soliloquy, and I frequently focus on its treatment on screen, which has been influential beyond cinema too.

In 2010 I published a book called *Shakespeare and the Modern Poet*, a study of the ways some poets respond to Shakespeare in their critical prose and absorb him into their poems. Frequently, these poets are drawn, as their Romantic forebears were also, to the soliloquies, and I decided to read a book about them. Only three exist (although there are of course many essays and book chapters on the topic): Morris Leroy Arnold's *The Soliloquies of Shakespeare: A Study in Technic* (1911), W. H. Clemen's *Shakespeare's Soliloquies* (1987) and James Hirsh's *Shakespeare and the History of Soliloquies* (2003).

Arnold's book is engaging and still worth reading for its taxonomies, but, inevitably, is dated. W. H. Clemen is one of those Shakespeare critics whose work, deriving from that of Caroline Spurgeon, traces patterns of imagery, or identifies 'image-clusters', as a means of interpretation. His book is patiently explicative, therefore, and insightful within the limits of its method, as he reads various soliloquies more or less independently of one another. However, the method omits contexts that now seem necessary to the study of Shakespeare and is too uncomplicatedly assured about the singleness of extractable meaning. As the consequence of all kinds of literary and linguistic criticism since Clemen wrote, Shakespearean language has come to seem more problematical, contrary, slippery and indeterminate than it does to him. James Hirsh's book is vast and full of detailed readings. Although many of these are of considerable interest, his thesis, much repeated, is resistibly doctrinaire, as I explain in Part II of this book. So there is scope for another and different contemporary study of soliloquy.

Some of the most prominent Shakespearean critical kinds of recent times, broadly new-historicist and poststructuralist, have not been much interested in, or have even been actively hostile to, form and psychology, both of which are vital to the consideration of soliloquy. Reading Shakespeare as a 'site of intersecting codes' or a 'set of social practices', some of this criticism has been more interested in context than text and some has placed the concepts of the 'individual', 'subjectivity' and 'interiority' under suspicion as constructs of liberal humanist ideology. I have myself benefited from a great deal of this criticism, and I expect this to be apparent in what follows. In Part II, considering 'soliloquy in theory', I take stock of some major recent statements about soliloquy, and elsewhere I hope I show an awareness of relevant context. But matters of form and psychology have never wholly disappeared from academic Shakespeare criticism either and such books as *Shakespeare Up Close*, edited by Russ McDonald and others in 2012, suggest that close reading of different kinds, some of it taking stock of context and theory too, is again assuming academic prominence. Matters of form and psychology, it need hardly be said, have always, of necessity, been of vital importance to actors and directors – and to audiences.

I should say something about how I have organized my material. Taking off from a close reading of a famous soliloquy in *Macbeth*, Part I offers examples of the kinds of thing Shakespearean soliloquy does on the page, stage and screen, marshalling a large number of examples under specific headings. The aim is to convey both the variety of its literary, dramatic and cinematic possibilities and the centrality of its usefulness and effect. Part II steps back from the specific to do several things: to illustrate the ways in which Shakespearean soliloquy has been understood and debated over the course of its history; to offer a sense of its permanent literary and dramatic influence by proposing that we inevitably understand it at least in part through the literature it has affected; to describe some of its historical contexts; to touch on how it has been pondered philosophically and theoretically; and to demonstrate some of its central thematic preoccupations and concerns. Part III consists of transcripts of interviews I conducted with eight outstanding Shakespearean actors, and I explain in an introduction to that section how I came to decide that it should form part of the book's structure. Part IV offers close readings of the soliloquies of four plays – *Richard III* (together with *Henry VI, Part 3*), *Romeo and Juliet* and *Othello* – with the intention of showing both how soliloquies work as individual speeches *and* how they work dramatically in their relationships with one another. *Hamlet* is not discussed here, although some readers might expect it to be. The play's soliloquies are given considerable attention elsewhere in the book, and my sense of how they have contributed to the understanding and reception of Shakespearean soliloquy more generally and to the history of literature itself will be clear. Faced with the necessity of choosing a few plays for close scrutiny in this section, though, I felt that I could say more interesting things about the soliloquies in those chosen than I could about the hyper-intensively discussed soliloquies of *Hamlet* itself.

All quotations from Shakespeare in this book are taken from the *Arden Shakespeare, Third Series*, which I nominate, as is customary, Arden 3. Where the Arden 3 edition of a play has not yet appeared, I use *The Arden Shakespeare Complete Works*, edited by Richard Proudfoot, Ann Thompson and David Scott Kastan (Bloomsbury, 1998; reissued with additional material, 2012).

I do not use footnote references in this book, since I intend it to be accessible to a general as well as to a university and drama-school readership, but all the secondary texts I refer to appear in my select bibliography.

In my introduction to Part III I thank the actors I interviewed. I am also very grateful to Andrew Murphy and Neil Rhodes, my one-time colleagues at the University of St Andrews, for generously reading and very helpfully commenting on earlier drafts of some of this material.

PART I

Soliloquies in practice

1. Is this a dagger?

In Act 2 Scene 1 of *Macbeth* the hero speaks one of the best known of Shakespeare's soliloquies. Macbeth has instructed a servant to ask Lady Macbeth to strike a bell to let him know when his drink is ready and then to go to bed. ('Lady Macbeth' is never in fact referred to like this in the quarto or Folio texts of the play and Arden 3 calls her simply 'Lady', but I use the long-sanctioned form for ease of recognition.) The anticipated bell sounds not long before the soliloquy's end, and the lines following it imply that this is the signal that it is now time for Macbeth to commit the murder of their king, Duncan, that we know he and his wife have planned together. Mention of the bedtime drink is one of those incongruously domestic details that recur in the play's representation of the Macbeths' marriage. Its apparent routine contrasts strikingly with the soliloquy that follows, which seems to erupt from another mode of being altogether:

Is this a dagger which I see before me,
The handle toward my hand? Come, let me clutch thee.
I have thee not, and yet I see thee still.
Art thou not, fatal vision, sensible
To feeling as to sight? Or art thou but
A dagger for the mind, a false creation,
Proceeding from the heat-oppressed brain?
I see thee yet, in form as palpable
As this which now I draw.
Thou marshall'st me the way that I was going,
And such an instrument I was to use.
Mine eyes are made the fools o' th' other senses,
Or else worth all the rest. I see thee still,
And on thy blade, and dudgeon, gouts of blood,
Which was not so before. There's no such thing.
It is the bloody business which informs
Thus to mine eyes. Now o'er the one half-world
Nature seems dead, and wicked dreams abuse
The curtained sleep; Witchcraft celebrates
Pale Hecate's offerings; and withered Murder,
Alarumed by his sentinel, the wolf,
Whose howl's his watch, thus with his stealthy pace,
With Tarquin's ravishing strides, towards his design
Moves like a ghost. Thou sure and firm-set earth,

> Hear not my steps, which way they walk, for fear
> The very stones prate of my whereabout,
> And take the present horror from the time,
> Which now suits with it. While I threat, he lives;
> Words to the heat of deeds too cold breath gives.
> *A bell rings.*
> I go, and it is done; the bell invites me.
> Hear it not, Duncan, for it is a knell
> That summons thee to heaven, or to hell. (2.1.33–64)

This is Macbeth's second soliloquy. He speaks one in Act 1 Scene 7, 'If it were done, when 'tis done ...', and, before that, in Scenes 3 and 4, he utters a revealing series of asides – one of them exceptionally lengthy (1.3.129–44) – when he learns that he has indeed been made Thane of Cawdor, in fulfilment of the Witches' prophecy earlier in the scene.

These asides have prepared us for the extreme state of mind apparent in this soliloquy. In one, Macbeth abstracts himself from the others on stage so noticeably that one of them, Banquo, comments on it ('Look how our partner's rapt') and Macbeth apologizes, as though he has committed some kind of faux pas ('Give me your favour. My dull brain was wrought / With things forgotten'). The asides let us know that he regards the terms of the Witches' prophecy 'As happy prologues to the swelling act / Of the imperial theme' – that is, that they have set in motion the drama of his own progress towards the throne. One of the asides also introduces both the word 'murder' itself – making Macbeth the first character in the play to speak the word – and the fact that he has 'horrible imaginings'. He says that these bring about a state of mind in which 'nothing is, but what is not'. This phrasing, pivoting around the dividing comma, is a form of antimetabole, the rhetorical trope in which the same words are repeated in inverse order. Here, it suggests a kind of internal chaos, as if Macbeth's consciousness itself is being sucked into the void between the phrases 'nothing is' and 'what is not', disappearing into the comma's trail.

Then, in the 'If it were done' soliloquy, Macbeth contemplates Duncan's virtues and anxiously ponders the 'assassination' and its potential 'consequence': that the murder may 'return / To plague th' inventor'. He also makes it clear that, as his kinsman, host and subject, he is more than usually obliged to protect Duncan. This soliloquy ends with Macbeth's insistence that he has no 'spur' to action other than his 'vaulting ambition' and that he has not yet decided what to do. But by the time of the 'dagger' soliloquy we have heard Lady Macbeth making plain in two soliloquies her intention to act as the spur he requires and have then seen her applying this spur by insinuating that the murder will prove his masculinity.

Even though these several soliloquies and asides prepare us relatively well for the feverish state of mind exhibited by the 'dagger' soliloquy, it still takes us aback. Macbeth's 'horrible imaginings' now become a form of delusion or hallucination, as a dagger he thinks he sees in front of him seems as 'palpable' as the one he actually possesses, which he will presumably use to kill the king. The hallucination foreshadows the banquet scene (3.4) in which Macbeth 'sees' Banquo's ghost, although no one else on stage can. Lady Macbeth – both psychoanalyst and literary critic – herself draws attention to the equivalence in that scene when she tells her husband that Banquo's ghost is 'the very painting of your fear: / This is the air-drawn dagger which you said / Led you to Duncan' (3.4.58–60). This lets us know too that Macbeth has by now confessed to her the terrors of his soliloquy, which is rich testimony to the deep, and deeply disquieting, intimacy of this marriage and also to Shakespeare's exceptional powers of rendering the social and psychological density of human relationship in the briefest of touches and with what seems an almost uncannily synoptic view of his text. Lady Macbeth's diagnosis marks a further stage in the increasingly hallucinatory solitude into which Macbeth is by then moving, and the 'dagger' soliloquy also presages the terrifying first scene of Act 4, in which Macbeth's encounter with the Witches culminates in his being visited by the three apparitions of armed head, bloody child and child crowned with a tree in his hand. In the 'dagger' soliloquy Macbeth says that Murder moves towards his design 'like a ghost'; one consequence of his own act of murder is that he does indeed see ghosts.

An actor's gestures will underline the effect of hallucination. In Orson Welles's expressionist film version (1948), for instance, Macbeth (Welles himself) clutches at the air, his fingers snagging on nothing, a gesture carried over from stage performance but enhanced by voice-over technique and lighting, which hits his face in close-up in the chiaroscuro of surrounding darkness. This renders the cinematic image of Macbeth with something of the striking intensity with which Macbeth himself appears to see the hallucinatory dagger. In Roman Polanski's film version (1972), however, the dagger actually appears on screen as an illusory special effect, brightly sparkling and moving forward out of Macbeth's (Jon Finch's) grasp as he reaches towards it. The consequence is that we, as viewers, do see the dagger, whereas we know that Finch cannot. This seems muddled and banal and even carries a hint of comedy, especially now that the effect itself appears dated. The movie is far better than this moment in it, but the contrast between the Welles and the Polanski is proof that in cinematic soliloquy, as in the theatre, suggestion can be far more potent than technological illusion. Justin Kurzel's screen version (2015) seems to include a sense of its own belatedness by handling the delusion quite differently from all received versions. Inventively transforming the soliloquy into something consistent with its portrayal of Macbeth (Michael Fassbender) as an emotionally damaged war casualty, the film presents him seeing the dagger held out towards him by the ghost of a boy he has previously encouraged into battle and subsequently helped bury. The ghost-boy leads him towards the tent in which Duncan lies sleeping and disappears as Macbeth says

'There's no such thing' – releasing him, we must assume, into culpability for his own murderous action.

In the speech as it's written, Macbeth's hallucination fluctuates as he concentrates his mind on it, and the dagger appears to acquire 'gouts of blood', as if the deed has already been done. Yet he is fully aware of the potential unreality of what he 'sees', realizing that this may be merely a function of his own consciousness, a delusion. He is self-reflective even while in a state of emotional and psychological extremity. Self-reflection is presented as a form of internal debate – in Macbeth's anguished questions to the object of hallucination about its own reality and in the desperate rapidity of his self-correction. The capacity for self-reflection is probably the single most impressive aspect of Shakespearean soliloquy. The great tragic soliloquists register their own states of mind with subtle discernment even as they endure extreme distress or are trapped in, and then gradually overwhelmed by, the plots which they themselves have set in motion, or which have been maliciously or accidentally set in motion for them. In their soliloquies, Shakespeare's tragic heroes and heroines seem to be, in the philosopher Hegel's great phrase, 'free agents of themselves', but in reality they are doomed by the dramatic plots in which they figure. Their soliloquies tend therefore to be inherently ironic. Strung between freedom, or the illusion of freedom, and necessity, the tragic soliloquist stages the encounter between his or her self-conception and the play's conception of him or her. That discrepancy produces our moral judgement – we may well, for instance, choose to read self-conception as self-deception. Even so, there are cases where it's plain that soliloquists can judge themselves more incisively than we ever can. Soliloquy is the site of both self-knowledge and self-delusion.

That Macbeth's soliloquy seems a form of self-communion is an impression conveyed partly by its prominent personal pronouns and possessive adjectives. Its opening three lines alone contain six in rapid succession (*I*; *me*; *my*; *me*; *I*; *I*). These are emphatically reinforced by the grammar of vocative address: to the imagined dagger; to the earth itself; and to the absent Duncan, sleeping somewhere close by. The soliloquy proceeds, therefore, as a kind of imaginative summoning, in which absent things are conjured into vivid aural presence by the rich intensity of the soliloquist's address. Such an exclamatory address is known by the rhetorical term 'apostrophe'. Frequent in Shakespearean soliloquy, even endemic to it, 'apostrophe' is usually to an *absent* person or thing – but not always, as we shall see below in Prince Hal's address to the crown in *Henry IV, Part 2*.

But the soliloquy is not merely self-communion because, whether as readers or audience members, we are given access to it. In the crucial paradox of soliloquy, *we* are part of this conversation that Macbeth is having with himself. It's a kind of dramatic irony formally inherent in soliloquy that, while soliloquists may not realize that an audience is present to their self-communing, the actors of course always do. A great deal, as we shall see, attaches to this. In the case of the 'dagger' soliloquy, the consequence of Macbeth's self-debate is that we 'sympathize' with him in the way Thomas de Quincey says we do in his essay 'On the Knocking at the Gate in *Macbeth*' (1823) – with 'a sympathy of comprehension, a sympathy by which we enter into his feelings, and are made to understand them, – not a sympathy of pity or approbation'. We experience Macbeth's agitated anxiety as he himself experiences it, and at the same time. The soliloquy therefore appears to give us privileged access to this character in the insecure process of decision-making and self-invention. We are drawn to the vulnerability of his anguish even as we are repelled by the decision itself.

This soliloquy also makes potential consequence almost as palpable as the hallucinatory dagger. When Macbeth says to the dagger 'Thou marshall'st me the way that I was going', he makes his own actions seem eerily compelled from without as well as initiated from within. In this, the dagger acts as the Witches do, guiding Macbeth on the path he may well have taken anyway, and they are sometimes represented theatrically or cinematically as Macbeth's hallucinations. The Witches' language seems to penetrate this soliloquy when Macbeth's 'it is done' echoes the first Witch's 'I'll do, I'll do, and I'll do' (1.3.10), and the words 'do', 'done' and 'deed' are pervasive in the play, even to the extent of echoing in some of its proper names ('*Dun*can', '*Don*albaine', '*Dun*sinane'). This makes Macbeth seem almost scripted by the Witches, driven by them in the very forms of his self-expression, and his first line in the play, 'So foul and fair a day I have not seen' (1.3.38), has already echoed the Witches' chant 'Fair is foul and foul is fair', which is also an example of antimetabole. As such, it's one of the play's many figures of repetition, echo, return and refrain. These unnervingly contribute to the way the language of *Macbeth* seems almost impacted, horribly turned in upon itself, doubled and duplicitous, notably so in the Witches' prophecy that Macbeth disastrously misunderstands: that 'none of woman born' can kill him.

When Macbeth refers to the murder of Duncan as 'the bloody business', it's also a repetition, since his wife has earlier called it ''this night's great business' (1.5.68). The hideous complicity of husband and wife seems an element of Macbeth's introspection itself. It's as though Lady Macbeth is, like the Witches, whispering inside his head. The phrases are euphemisms; both Macbeth and Lady Macbeth use other euphemistic phrases for murder too during the play. Macbeth's euphemism is in fact less euphemistic than his wife's, since it at least acknowledges that the business is 'bloody' rather than 'great', but their shared use of the word makes them partners in crime as well as marriage – 'business' partners, indeed, intent on upward social mobility. The euphemism also makes it seem that, in the same motion of mind, they withdraw from the crime even as they will it into being. Its 'consequence' therefore appears almost written into the language of its inception. When the euphemisms finally give way to the 'consequence' itself, Macbeth and his wife, Banquo and Macduff's wife and children are all violently dead, and the 'business' is revealed as indeed both great and extremely bloody. It's apt, therefore, that words associated with the murder repeated throughout the play – 'time', 'hand', 'blood', 'ghost' – also figure prominently in this soliloquy.

Its hallucinatory quality is intensified by the way Macbeth abstracts himself from his immediate situation to identify the 'half-world' itself – the hemisphere – as expressive of his own state of mind, seeing it acted upon by the nightmare personifications of Witchcraft and Murder and the mythological and semi-legendary figures of Hecate and Tarquin. When the wolf that is Murder's sentinel is said to move with 'stealthy pace', the blank verse of Macbeth's lines itself moves with a stealthy, insinuating, alliterative pace, as six 'w' sounds closely follow one another: '*w*ithered Murder, / Alarumed by his sentinel, the *w*olf, / *Wh*ose ho*wl*'s his *w*atch, thus with his stealthy pace ...'. This is the *OED*'s first citation for the word 'stealthy'; and although the recent development of databases for early modern words and texts has taught us to be sceptical about such ascriptions of 'first usage', it may not be too fanciful to think that Shakespeare has here invented the word out of his own need for it, discovering it in his versification itself. In Rupert Goold's BBC film version of the play (2010), Macbeth (Patrick Stewart) howls out the word 'howl's' as if he *is* momentarily a wolf, with terrifyingly appropriate effect.

Hecate is the goddess of the moon and also of sorcery, so the sense that Macbeth's imagination is subject to supernatural agency is reinforced; Hecate subsequently appears as a character on stage with the Witches in both Act 3 Scene 5 – sometimes thought to have been written by Thomas Middleton – and in the tremendous first scene of Act 4. These figures appear therefore to move in Macbeth's mind, and then out from it, like paradigms of perverse behaviour, almost like Freudian archetypes. Although the Freudian concept of the unconscious was obviously unavailable to Shakespeare, he certainly understood its workings, and Freud's psychoanalytical paradigms were themselves deeply influenced by Shakespeare (especially *Hamlet*) as well as by the Greek myths from which he derived his terminology. Shakespeare has himself been extensively read in relation to Freudian theory, and I cite an example relating to *Richard III* in Part IV.

The Tarquin who moves with 'ravishing strides, towards his design' as an analogy for the stealth of the wolf is the Roman rapist whose story Shakespeare had told in his long poem *The Rape of Lucrece* (1593–4). The allusion is therefore self-referential (and would probably have been recognized as such by at least some of the play's original audience) and so also a form of repetition. It offers a classical instance of human depravity as a shadowy presence behind what Macbeth calls 'the present horror' of the soliloquy's moment, the final one before he commits his own depraved act. The allusion also suggests a sexual element in this depravity. These intimations are made explicit in Justin Kurzel's movie, in which Macbeth and Lady Macbeth (Marion Cotillard) make love while she persuades him to commit the crime. Afterwards, in his apology to Macduff for killing Duncan's bodyguards, Macbeth describes the dead king's body almost as if its penetration has been sexual: 'And his gashed stabs looked like a breech in nature / For ruin's wasteful entrance' (2.3.114–15).

This soliloquy ends the scene in which it's spoken, as many Shakespearean soliloquies do, and, as many also do, it ends with a couplet, which is inherently more memorable, and more summative, than blank verse. When it ends a scene in this intensely memorable way, a soliloquy has an especially powerful kind of authority. The pause succeeding it impresses it on the reader's or audience's mind more than is possible for a soliloquy embedded in dialogue, and the stage picture of the soliloquist isolated and alone is framed more definitively. Macbeth's soliloquy is unusual in ending in fact with two couplets, separated by an unrhyming line, or, we might even say, in ending twice. In the first ('Whiles I threat, he lives; / Words to the heat of deeds too cold breath gives') Macbeth chastises himself for the delay this very soliloquy, with its many 'words', represents, just as Hamlet chastises himself in a soliloquy for his delay in killing Claudius. Then the bell sounds, interrupting the soliloquy, and in the following unrhyming line Macbeth notes its urgent 'invitation' to him. He then brings the soliloquy to what we might call a final end with his grim admonition to the absent king he is about to kill. This makes clear his dreadful knowledge that, in the Christian dispensation apparently accepted by the play, this action will have metaphysical as well as physical consequences. Macbeth fully understands that he may be eternally damning as well as murdering his victim: 'Hear it not, Duncan, for it is a knell / That summons thee to heaven or to hell.' That this soliloquy should end twice may be read as one final instance in it of echo, repetition and inversion as well as the conclusion of its strategy of postponement. It's as if Macbeth must work himself up to an ultimate verbal intensity at least once again before his very words themselves pitch him, persuaded at last by his own rhetoric, towards what has only now become inevitable action.

2. Attributes of Shakespearean soliloquy

Every soliloquy in Shakespeare is unique, both to the dramatic moment of its occurrence and to the stylistic habits and patterns of the character uttering it, although we can trace relationships among soliloquies too, and I shall be doing so in this book. In addition, the great Shakespearean soliloquies convey the linguistic, formal and metrical excitements of experimentation, plunging us into what the Chorus in *Henry V* calls 'the quick forge and working-house of thought'. They sometimes seem approximate, unfixed and hazardous, and their magnificent successes may come with all the raggedness of semantic risk. Pitched towards an ultimately revelatory form of articulation, some soliloquies may become, for several lines at a time, virtually unintelligible – which is why some lines in soliloquy have demanded so many acres of hopefully explanatory glossing.

A famous instance occurs in Macbeth's first soliloquy, in the astonishing lines

> And pity, like a naked new-born babe,
> Striding the blast, or heaven's cherubim, horsed
> Upon the sightless couriers of the air,
> Shall blow the horrid deed in every eye,
> That tears shall drown the wind. (1.7.21–5)

'The imagery is suggestive, rather than precise', say the editors of Arden 3, truly. So the diffident words 'may' and 'perhaps' are repeated, a little anxiously, in their glosses – but we are grateful for whatever glossing we can get. This is a notable Shakespearean crux, and the subject of a famous essay by Cleanth Brooks in *The Well-Wrought Urn* (1947), in which he says that these lines are 'as strained as [John] Donne is at his most extreme pitch'. If that is so, then we must wonder how any theatre audience might be expected to understand them as they are spoken, and there are passages in other Shakespearean soliloquies too that behave with comparably complicated linguistic energy.

William Hazlitt, writing in the early nineteenth century, was presumably thinking of such lines of Macbeth's when he said of the play's soliloquies that they are 'dark riddles on human life, baffling solution, and entangling him in their labyrinths'. And it's much to the point that one of William

Blake's great images, his colour print *Pity* (1795), derives at least in part from these lines, as though the great Romantic visionary was impelled into creative dynamism by the interpretative effort involved in responding to the furious dynamic of Shakespeare's own lines. In fact, Blake's image is the product of a misunderstanding: his horses are blind because this is how he understands 'sightless', whereas Shakespeare almost certainly meant 'invisible'. Even so, Blake's response is one indication of the way Shakespeare's soliloquies, prodigiously exceeding those of other early modern dramatists (notably Lyly, Kyd and Marlowe), invent a new poetic and dramatic possibility and, as Shakespeare proceeds towards his major tragedies, become more and more the vehicles of profound introspection. In these lines Shakespeare's language appears to push against all usual constraints in the effort to convey a specialized and richly individuated rhetoric of consciousness.

For all the experimental uniqueness of individual soliloquies, we can begin to identify some persistent attributes of soliloquy by generalizing from Macbeth's 'dagger' soliloquy. I do so in what follows, sometimes commenting at length – even to the extent of offering short essays – on attributes as they may be variously perceived and understood in a range of examples, and sometimes merely making brief identifications with a view to pursuing these attributes further as the book advances.

* Soliloquies are spoken by a character either alone or believing himself or herself to be alone on stage, or in the presence of another character presumed to be dead, unconscious or asleep.

While this might seem obvious, even axiomatic, it has been disputed. It's why the soliloquy is commonly thought to represent a voiced interior monologue, and why the soliloquist is considered to be articulating his or her inner thoughts. Being alone on stage speaking aloud to oneself raises literary, dramatic, philosophical, political and theological issues, all of which I survey in Part II.

* Soliloquies are usually spoken at a moment of heightened emotion or even in a state of extremity, except when they behave in a purely expository way to convey necessary information to an audience.

At the beginning of one of the first great soliloquies in Shakespeare, Richard, Duke of York, in *Henry VI, Part 2*, before setting off on the Irish wars that are part of his secret plan to gain the English crown, says, 'Now, York, or never, steel thy fearful thoughts, / And change misdoubt to resolution' (3.1.330). His forcing of the moment to its crisis is exceptionally explicit, but such moments constitute the essential dramatic life of many soliloquies. It's as though the time normally stretched out through the course of the play's action is being suddenly concentrated to a fine point of intensity. York is articulating the moment of psychological crisis itself, almost as if speaking the word 'resolution' aloud will render it performative, enacting what he desires – although in this case what he ultimately desires never in fact transpires. When a soliloquy is spoken by one of the main agents of a play's action, it may also constitute a critical moment in the plot. Lady Macbeth's first soliloquy, in which she reads her husband's letter telling her what the Witches have said, turns into an address to Macbeth himself when he appears on stage, and what she says then virtually defines this tendency of soliloquy. She tells him that his letters 'have transported me beyond / This ignorant present, and I feel now / The future in the instant' (1.5.56–8). Soliloquies can be the agency of such transportation, as their concentrated verbal power explodes into subsequent dramatic action.

* Mythological and legendary characters were not always treated reverentially by the Elizabethans and Jacobeans and were sometimes subject to ridicule – witness Shakespeare's own treatment of Helen and Achilles in *Troilus and Cressida*, for instance. Even so, the emotion in soliloquies may be heightened further by reference to major figures or analogous cases from myth, legend and literature. This sometimes invites ethical comparisons in which the soliloquist is in some way measured against the figure evoked.

Although the early plays flourish their classical references more than the later ones, probably the best known such analogy is Hamlet's in the 'O that this too too sullied flesh would melt' soliloquy when he compares his father to Claudius – 'So excellent a king, that was to this / Hyperion to a satyr' – and then brings himself into the range of analogizing by saying that Claudius is 'no more like my father / Than I to Hercules'. The former compares the Greek sun god to a figure of drunken debauchery; the latter offers us Hamlet self-deprecatingly measuring himself against probably the greatest of mythical heroes: Hercules performed twelve supernatural 'labours', whereas he himself has difficulty completing just one promised act.

A major instance of such analogizing is Richard of Gloucester's soliloquy at the end of Act 3 Scene 2 of *Henry VI, Part 3*, in which the future Richard III tallies those who stand between him and the throne, telling us how he intends to dispose of them. Its rhetoric rises to a crescendo as Richard's hyperbolic self-dramatization seeks out analogous instances before deflating into a rhyming couplet:

> I'll drown more sailors than the mermaid shall,
> I'll slay more gazers than the basilisk,
> I'll play the orator as well as Nestor,
> Deceive more slyly than Ulysses could,
> And, like a Sinon, take another Troy.
> I can add colours to the chameleon,
> Change shape with Proteus for advantages,
> And set the murderous Machiavel to school.
> Can I do this, and cannot get a crown?
> Tut, were it further off, I'll pluck it down. (3.2.186–95)

The soliloquy has previously made it plain that Richard is motivated partly by the corrosive sense of sexual disadvantage visited on him by physical deformity. Now he sees himself as he might appear in the flatteringly distorting mirror of mythical, heroic and political case history. He fantasizes himself into his future by conjuring himself into a competitively victorious relationship with heroic and superhuman figures from the literary and historical past. In the words 'play', 'deceive', 'add colours' and 'change shape', he also confesses his dissimulation in the language of *acting* itself. More than any other character in Shakespeare except Iago, Richard incarnates the etymology of the word 'hypocrite' – from the Greek: an actor on the stage, a pretender, a dissembler.

When Young Clifford comes across his newly killed father towards the end of *Henry VI, Part 2*, his grief-stricken speech culminates in a cry of vengeance on the house of York, which takes depth and complication from its references to Ovid and Virgil:

> Meet I an infant of the house of York,
> Into as many gobbets will I cut it
> As wild Medea young Absyrtus did.
> In cruelty will I seek out my fame.
> Come, thou new ruin of old Clifford's house;
> [*He takes him up on his back.*]
> As did Aeneas old Anchises bear,
> So bear I thee upon my manly shoulders;
> But then Aeneas bare a living load,
> Nothing so heavy as these woes of mine. (5.2.57–65)

Medea's extreme cruelty to her brother Absyrtus combines with the image of Aeneas carrying his father from the burning city of Troy, almost the archetype of Virgilian *pietas*, to underline very powerfully Young Clifford's baffled feelings when confronted with his murdered father. His sense that his misfortune outdoes Aeneas's own resembles Richard's advertised superiority to his analogues, but to quite different effect. Where Richard's analogizing is designed to bolster his self-assurance, Young Clifford's renders him pitifully abject.

In quite a different – comic – vein, a prose soliloquy of Armado's in *Love's Labour's Lost* attempts a definition of love but becomes entangled instead in love's contradictions, just as the play's plot itself does:

> I shall be foresworn, which is a great argument of falsehood, if I love. And how can that be true love which is falsely attempted? Love is a familiar; love is a devil. Yet was Samson so tempted, and he had an excellent strength. Yet was Solomon so seduced, and he had a very good wit. Cupid's butt-shaft is too hard for Hercules' club, and therefore too much odds for a Spaniard's rapier. (1.2.163–70)

Armado's initial analogues for being wholly overcome by love – the cases of Samson and Solomon – have biblical provenance, which would seem to lend them dignity and propriety. So Armado is encouraging himself by the consideration that, although they were overcome, Samson was noted for his strength and Solomon for his wit. This attempted propriety collapses, however, when the biblical analogues give way to a classical one, in which the competition between Cupid's arrow and Hercules' club appears to secrete – but not very secretly – a bawdy meaning in which the 'butt' insinuates the buttock, and the 'shaft', 'club' and 'rapier' the penis, so that 'love' is made to seem very close kin to lust. The soliloquy offers a kind of struggle between biblical and classical reference, with the latter undermining the former in a mode wholly appropriate to a play in which undermining and self-undermining form a large part of the plot.

Mythical analogizing is also crucial to soliloquies by, among others, Romeo, Juliet, Falstaff, Timon and Antony – some of which I discuss later in this book – but we might consider here one further remarkable instance. In Act 2 Scene 2 of *Cymbeline*, Innogen goes to bed at midnight, asking her maid (anachronistically) to mark her place in the book she has just put down. She then asks the gods to protect her 'from fairies and the tempters of the night' and sinks into a deep sleep. Iachimo has hidden in a trunk in her bedroom so that he can describe the room to Posthumus, with the intention of convincing him that Innogen has been unfaithful. While she sleeps, Iachimo climbs out of the trunk and utters a lengthy soliloquy.

At its opening, he compares himself to Tarquin ''ere he wakened / The chastity he wounded'. As I explain above, Tarquin, the Roman rapist, figures in Shakespeare as a character in *The Rape of Lucrece* and in an allusion in *Macbeth*. Iachimo calls him '*our* Tarquin' because he is also Italian, and he addresses the sleeping Innogen as 'Cytherea' – as Venus, that is, the goddess of love – and, thrilled by the idea of her virginity, calls her a 'fresh lily'. So, for an anxious audience, it seems entirely possible that he is on the point of raping her. However, although he does appear to kiss the 'rubies unparagoned' of her lips, in the event no rape occurs.

Even so, Iachimo behaves as an alarming voyeur, literally writing an inventory not only of the bedroom but also of Innogen's body. He employs a classical analogy as he removes her bracelet – 'As slippery as the Gordian knot was hard', where 'slippery' might suggest an unfaithful woman and the knot that of virginity – and lewdly takes stock of 'a mole cinque-spotted' on her left breast. Finally, he notices her book and tells us what it is:

> She hath been reading late,
> The tale of Tereus: here the leaf's turned down
> Where Philomel gave up. I have enough:
> To th' trunk again, and shut the spring of it.
> Swift, swift, you dragons of the night, that dawning
> May bare the raven's eye. I lodge in fear;
> Though this a heavenly angel, hell is here.
> [*Clock strikes.*]
> One, two, three: time, time! (2.2.44–51)

This lets us know that Innogen has been reading Ovid's *Metamorphoses*, a work crucial to Shakespeare's imagination. One of its more frightful transformation tales is that of Philomela, who is raped and has her tongue cut out by her brother-in-law Tereus. Philomela and her sister Procne exact revenge by serving Tereus a meal of his young son whom they have murdered. Tereus's subsequent frenzied pursuit of the sisters culminates in the metamorphosis of all three into birds. Shakespeare refers to this story extensively in *Titus Andronicus*, whose plot runs parallel to it.

Here in *Cymbeline*, something remarkable is happening. Iachimo's soliloquy finds at its beginning and end legendary and mythological analogues for the act of rape by which he is clearly tempted but in which he does not actually indulge, and we judge him by the analogues he offers us. He is repulsively voyeuristic, yes, but he is not culpable in the way Tarquin and Tereus are. Ethical scope is left therefore for what happens later in the play when he apologizes and sets out on the path of reformation.

The allusions in this soliloquy are also more complexly involved in the play's texture than is usual in soliloquies containing analogies. Iachimo adverts to the tale of Tereus and Philomela only because Innogen has been reading it, and he tells us that she stopped reading at exactly the point at which the rape occurs ('Where Philomel gave up'). It's almost therefore as if Shakespeare is showing his hand here – since it's he who has read Ovid so that he can have Innogen read Ovid and then have Iachimo point out to an audience that Innogen has been reading Ovid, in the vertiginously allusive play of this dazzling soliloquy. And then Shakespeare crowns it all with yet another allusion – to his own contemporary, early rival and possibly co-writer, Christopher Marlowe (the *New Oxford Shakespeare* published in 2016 and 2017 proposes that Marlowe co-wrote the *Henry VI* plays with Shakespeare; obviously, the editorial and critical reaction to this proposal is not yet apparent). Iachimo's concluding lines, together with the striking of the clock, echo Faustus's final soliloquy in *Doctor Faustus* even while reversing its terms: 'Swift, swift, you dragons of the night' in Shakespeare, '*Lente, lente, currite noctis equi!*' in Marlowe, quoting Ovid's *Amores* I.13, in which the post-coital lover pleads with the horses of night to delay the sun's rising so that he can stay in bed with his lover. At the end of Faustus's speech, as midnight strikes, the devils come to take him to hell; Iachimo's 'hell is here' has a metaphysical implication too, as well as simply meaning that he fears being caught in the bedroom as night advances. The devil Mephistopheles in *Doctor Faustus* says 'Why this is hell, nor am I out of it', meaning that to be a devil is to make everywhere you are a kind of hell. Seeing Innogen as a heavenly angel, Posthumus nevertheless knows his true place.

Marlowe may well have entered Shakespeare's mind here because of his association with Ovid. He made a version of Ovid's *Amores* and wrote the Ovidian narrative poem *Hero and Leander*, to which Shakespeare alludes in *As You Like It*. Iachimo's soliloquy is therefore the tracing of a pattern of literary interconnection in which the new work advertises its indebtedness to the old works in a form of ongoing literary and dramatic creativity. It pointedly and elegantly includes, as an element of its dramatic representation, the act of reading by which it came into being. But, bringing a new work into being, the act of reading is competitive too, and the allusion to Faustus's final soliloquy in Iachimo's reveals a Shakespeare gracefully willing to acknowledge that he has absorbed Marlowe but possibly also implying that he has superseded him.

* Soliloquies let us know things we would not know otherwise; they convey information; they are always to some degree expository, even when they have other, more complicated things in mind too.

Hamlet's first soliloquy ('O that this too too sullied flesh would melt') tells us complex things about his state of mind while also conveying the vital information that his mother has married his uncle within two months of his father's death. Many other soliloquies also convey information necessary to the play's plot.

Soliloquies can, more obviously, identify characters, both by name and by state of being or condition. Edmund, in his first soliloquy in *King Lear* ('Thou, Nature, art my goddess'), lets us know that he is a bastard. He defends the condition and then tells us that his name is Edmund by saying, in an apostrophe to his absent brother Edgar, 'Our father's love is to the bastard Edmund / As to the legitimate' (1.2.17–18). This is a relatively sophisticated introduction of the necessary information, but Shakespeare can be surprisingly (or challengingly?) crude in his expository means even in the late plays. Autolycus in *The Winter's Tale* introduces himself forthrightly, while still, like Edmund, letting us know something of his nature: 'My father named me Autolycus, who being, as I am, littered under Mercury, was likewise a snapper-up of unconsidered trifles' (4.3.24–6). Belarius in *Cymbeline*, in the soliloquy in which he lets us know that Polydore and Guiderius are Cymbeline's sons going under assumed names, bluntly lets us know that he does so too: 'Myself, Belarius, that am Morgan called' (3.3.106). When characters go in disguise in Shakespeare, they sometimes make sure we understand this by means of soliloquy: Kent and Edgar in *King Lear*, Ford in *The Merry Wives of Windsor* and Cloten and Innogen in *Cymbeline* all do so.

Soliloquies may have more complicated expository functions too. In some, the reading aloud of a letter conveys significant information. In Lady Macbeth's first soliloquy she discovers from Macbeth's letter that he has become Thane of Cawdor, and so do we. We also hear her own response to this, so the soliloquy conveys not just necessary factual information but compelling psychological and emotional information too. We might say the same of soliloquies in which letters are read aloud by Hotspur in *Henry IV, Part 1*, Brutus in *Julius Caesar*, Malvolio in *Twelfth Night*, the Countess in *All's Well That Ends Well* and Pisanio in *Cymbeline*. In these cases, the one voice of the soliloquy speaks the voice of the letter-writer too, and this may make for sophisticated complication. 'Supposedly the voice of its sender,' says Alan Stewart in *Shakespeare's Letters*, 'the letter becomes instead a dialogue between sender and recipient.' The *letter* becomes dialogue, and so does the soliloquy. In Malvolio's case, the complication is deeper. Reading aloud the letter he believes to be Olivia's but is in fact Maria's, he is vividly *performing* his self-delusion in front of his deceivers (Maria, Belch and Aguecheek) as they eavesdrop on him, and of course performing it in front of us too. There is a sense in which all audiences are always eavesdroppers on soliloquies, and several times in this book I shall return to the impact this may have on the speaking and receiving of specific speeches.

Soliloquies may also convey complex information of a factual kind. To gauge what this might amount to, it's necessary only to consider the difficulty facing Horatio at the end of *Hamlet*. In Hamlet's dying speeches he asks Horatio to 'report me and my cause aright / To the unsatisfied' and charges him to 'tell my story'. But how can Horatio do this, since he has not heard Hamlet's (or anyone else's) soliloquies? Only by hearing them could he have fully apprehended Hamlet's abhorrence of his mother's incestuous marriage, his promise to avenge his father's death and his detestation of Claudius. The play outside the soliloquies, that is, tells only part – and that not the most significant part – of Hamlet's 'story'.

There is another kind of information occasionally conveyed by soliloquy that may be classified as opinion rather than fact. I am thinking, for instance, of Viola in *Twelfth Night* commenting on the play's clown, Feste:

> This fellow is wise enough to play the fool,
> And to do that well craves a kind of wit.
> He must observe their mood on whom he jests,
> The quality of persons and the time,
> And, like the haggard, check at every feather
> That comes before his eye. This is a practice
> As full of labour as a wise man's art;
> For folly that he shows is fit,
> But wise men, folly-fallen, quite taint their wit. (3.1.58–66)

The fact that this seems written simply to offer a finely calibrated compliment suggests that we can hear Shakespeare himself briefly speaking with Viola's voice here, in what may be a tacit compliment to Robert Armin, the comic actor who played Feste on Shakespeare's stage. But it's certainly Viola who does the speaking, since her simile for Feste's behaviour is that of the 'haggard', a wild female hawk. In its sudden register of gender, this is wholly appropriate to a soliloquy in which an Elizabethan woman assumes herself to be wisely capable of judging the performance of this difficult, sometimes even dangerous, public function by a man. But then Viola is speaking as a man too, since she is disguised as Cesario when she says this, and she is in any case being played by a boy ...

* Cinema finds soliloquies difficult to cope with but can be inventively responsive to the difficulty in ways that may influence our sense of them more generally.

Cinematic close-up and voice-over – which presents the soliloquy as a voiced interior monologue – can persuasively reinforce the notion that soliloquy is a mode of spoken thought, or, as one critic has wittily said, that the soliloquy 'turns up the volume on thought'. Cinema permits – even encourages or requires – the possibility of quiet speech into a microphone, which may give the impression of the nuanced delicacy of interior self-communion more readily than the volume necessary for the adequate projection of voice in a theatre. On the other hand, cinema almost invariably has trouble with the speaking of verse. The very long-sanctioned art of poetry and the most recently invented art of cinema find it difficult fully to accord. The spectacle of the visual may conflict with, rather than contribute to, the energies of the aural, and the chronological and sequential requirements of cinema tend to necessitate cuts to lengthy passages of blank verse, as does filmic 'cutting' itself. There is likely always to be a struggle for primacy.

Laurence Olivier, in his influential film version of *Hamlet* (1948), conducts a compelling experiment with the 'To be or not to be' soliloquy. He places it where the first quarto does, after the 'nunnery' scene. While Ophelia, played with devastating intensity by Jean Simmons, lies inconsolably stretched on a palace staircase after Hamlet (Olivier himself) has abused her, the camera veers away and, in a tracking shot and a series of dissolves, appears to move up through the battlements of Elsinore into the clouds and then to plunge down towards the sea before entering the back of Hamlet's head and pressing on even further into his cerebral cortex. The soliloquy starts up in voice-over as another shot shows us Hamlet's face. The effect, eerily emphasized by William Walton's dizzying score, is astonishingly unexpected the first time you see the film, and still astonishing on subsequent viewings. It suggests that Hamlet is contemplating suicide, as he gazes from the castle turrets down to the sea far below; he unsheathes his dagger and points it towards himself before eventually dropping it, apparently inadvertently, into the sea. On the phrase 'And lose the name of action' he turns away from the camera and walks into the mists of Elsinore.

Olivier's *mise-en-scène* literalizes Shakespeare's metaphor of the 'sea of troubles' before making it seem that we are inside Hamlet's mind while the soliloquy happens – or, as it were, while it's actually being verbally formulated. He therefore appears to be gazing into the sea of himself – or, the external world seems to have become totally coincident with his interiority, correlative to it. For at least the duration of this scene we appear not only to see with Hamlet's eyes, but to think with his brain. We have taken, as it were, a Freudian journey into the hero's unconscious, appropriately so in a film whose interpretation of the play is strongly inflected by Freudian theory. While working on the movie, Olivier had had conversations with the Freudian analyst Ernest Jones, whose work on *Hamlet* culminated in the book *Hamlet and Oedipus* (1949). In fact, in the intensity of Olivier's absorption of Freud, Hamlet's dropped knife may even represent not only his incapacity for action but his Oedipal castration – which makes it appropriate that the film's technique is influenced by American *film noir* as well as European expressionism. Probably uniquely among American movie genres, *film noir*, fascinated by disturbed states of being and often misogynistic, is edgily self-doubting, so much so that it had to wait for the French to name it.

Olivier's *Hamlet* does not employ the technique that has become almost a cliché of cinematic soliloquy – the speech direct to camera. But his *Richard III* (1955) does, influenced, he tells us in his autobiography, by his being struck by how quickly early TV viewers became accustomed to being addressed like this. (It's briefly used twice, though, in Max Reinhardt's Hollywood movie of *A Midsummer Night's Dream* [1935] when Bottom [James Cagney] speaks the final lines of his 'dream' soliloquy walking towards and directly addressing a retreating camera, and when Puck – the almost ubiquitous, magnificently cackling fifteen-year-old Mickey Rooney – directly addresses the camera to speak the epilogue.) Olivier's *Richard III* also constantly sets Richard in front of windows and casements and at the doors of rooms so that his direct-to-camera soliloquies have the air of commentaries on the action we see taking place in deep focus beyond. It's as if Richard, at once inside and outside the dramatic action – especially when he is actually seen opening the shutters on windows – is controlling, manipulating or framing it as a film director might; and manipulating the action is precisely what his soliloquies tell us he is trying to do. The constant looking in on, or gazing at, people unaware of him suggests something voyeuristic in Richard, appropriately underlining an element prominent in Shakespeare's text. In his opening soliloquy, Richard almost impudently emphasizes the cinematic technique by, at one point, extending his arm towards the camera as if beckoning us further into the throne room he stands in – and beckoning us also into his confidence.

The Ian McKellen–Richard Loncraine film version of *Richard III* (1995), which is sometimes explicitly allusive to Olivier's film, also uses the technique ingeniously to extend hazardously flattering invitations to complicity. In a tour-de-force of cinematic soliloquy, McKellen begins the opening one by playing it as a speech into a microphone at a crowded celebratory party. Then, after the camera has focused in close-up on his mouth and teeth – giving him the aspect of the demonic boar to which he is elsewhere compared – he speaks the rest of the soliloquy in a lavatory, urinating and wiping his one good hand in front of a mirror. He gazes into the mirror, still speaking, and only then (as it were) catches sight of the camera and directly addresses it, eventually beckoning us out of the lavatory – in what we might read as an allusion-in-reverse to Olivier's opening soliloquy – and ending in the open air as Clarence is taken to the Tower. This cinematic mobility adventurously emphasizes the variation of register in the soliloquy, from something approaching public proclamation – 'Now is the winter ...' – to intense self-revelation – 'But I, that am not shaped for sportive tricks ...' It also points up both the differences and the continuities between the public, party-going figure and the private malcontent of whom none of the party-goers is yet aware.

Discussing direct-to-camera soliloquy, several of the actors I spoke to while working on this book mentioned their admiration for Kevin Spacey's performance in the Netflix series *House of Cards*. Playing Frank

Underwood, a formidably malign American politician, Spacey employs direct-to-camera speeches as a notably insinuating and insidious revision of cinematic Shakespearean soliloquy technique. At one point Underwood even makes the connection explicit by quoting Mark Antony in *Julius Caesar* while also characteristically amplifying his bombast: '"Cry havoc", said he, who fought chaos with chaos,' Spacey declaims straight into the lens, "and let slip the dogs of war."' This Netflix show is based on the BBC's 1990 series, also called *House of Cards*, in which the politician, there called Francis Urquhart, was played by Ian Richardson. Andrew Davies, who adapted that series from a novel by Michael Dobbs, has acknowledged that the idea of the direct address to camera derived from Olivier's film performance of Richard III's soliloquies. Richardson and Spacey have been notable actors of Shakespeare, and both played Richard in significant productions. It's remarkable that, so late in its history and in a contemporary political context, the cinematic development of Shakespearean soliloquy retains such intense dramatic effectiveness.

There is one other way in which soliloquies can be handled by cinema, although this may seem extreme: it can omit them altogether. Orson Welles completely cuts Iago's eight soliloquies in his version of *Othello* (1952), although a few lines are salvaged in fragments of dialogue with Roderigo. This means that Iago's motivation – which he raises frequently in his soliloquies, and which has been extensively debated in the play's critical literature, as I indicate in Part IV – is left almost wholly opaque. It also makes Iago less evidently the manipulative originator of the plot, since telling us how he manipulates the plot is so large a part of what he does in his soliloquies. Instead, Welles suggests Iago's domination over characters and action by expressionist cinematography. A pre-credit sequence presents the joint funeral of Othello and Desdemona – which is not in Shakespeare, but may be assumed to follow on from the play's events – at which Iago (Micheál MacLiammóir) is imprisoned in a cage raised by pulley outside the walls of a castle to the accompaniment of an edgily insistent vocal chant by Francesco Lavagnino. The film's ensuing action, therefore, must be assumed to be flashback. The bars of Iago's cage are echoed throughout by other verticals and horizontals – pillars, columns, slats, stairs, window fixtures, ship's rigging and so on. The actors are sometimes filmed through these, sometimes shadowed by them. It's as if Iago has caged everyone, especially since the intense claustrophobia of Welles's expressionist monochrome, with its deep focus, highly contrastive *film noir* lighting (creating deep shadows) and extreme camera angles, makes even external scenes seem airlessly constricted. After Desdemona's murder, Othello (Welles himself) stands behind a portcullis, which, in another shot, towers above him in shadow in a final devastating image of entrapment. Welles has found wholly convincing cinematic images to act as equivalents for Iago's textual imagery of entrapment – 'ensnaring' Cassio with a 'web' (2.1.168–9), for instance, and making 'the net / That shall enmesh them all' (2.3.356–7) before, finally, being himself enmeshed by it too.

Welles's *Falstaff (Chimes at Midnight)* (1965), a composite of both parts of *Henry IV* and other sources, includes soliloquies, but makes them forms of dialogue, or at least of address. Hal's (Keith Baxter's) first soliloquy, opening 'I know you all', in which he makes it plain that his relationship with Falstaff and his entourage is to be only temporary, is spoken outside the tavern towards, but not directly to, the camera while Falstaff himself (Welles) stands close behind, apparently – although it's not entirely clear from his mildly puzzled expression – hearing at least part of it. When the soliloquy ends, Hal walks away from Falstaff towards the film's vast, forbidding castle and the camera holds him in an extreme long shot. This frames, brilliantly and proleptically, the inevitable divorce between the two, but is still peculiar, since if Falstaff *has* heard Hal we must wonder why he would be foolish enough to trust him subsequently. In a comparably odd way, Falstaff speaks his prose soliloquy about honour in the film directly to Hal on horseback at Shrewsbury. This seems unaccountable, since the Prince is then in the very process of virtuously exemplifying on the battlefield what Falstaff is disparaging to his face as questionable fine attitude, which would have been manifestly unallowable – treasonable, indeed – in any royal subject.

Both scenes, however, have something of the quality of tableau, and what seems to be happening is that Welles is using soliloquy as the allegorical representation of the ethically opposed worlds of the *Henry IV* plays. It's as if both characters are being emblematically frozen into the stasis of essential attitude, just as the movie throughout opposes the worlds of wood (the tavern) and stone (the castle). It may well be that Falstaff's undermining of honour in Hal's presence in this exemplary way is powerfully placed in such an anti-militaristic movie, but the stylization sits uneasily within the film's normative naturalism. It's hard not to feel, therefore, that after *Macbeth* Welles had directorial difficulty with cinematic Shakespearean soliloquy. His *Othello* brilliantly makes a strength out of this insecurity, whereas his *Falstaff*, ignoring the necessity of soliloquy's ineluctable solitude, risks absurdity. Soliloquy, while it lasts, must be for the character speaking it a form of solitary confinement. On the other hand, and quixotically, Welles sometimes frames the speeches of Henry IV himself (John Gielgud) in *Falstaff* as though they are soliloquies, although they are not, by leaving it very late into the shot or scene before we see those he is addressing; which throws into greater relief his isolation as he endures ill-health, anxiety about rebellion, guilt over the death of Richard II and sorrowful disappointment in Hal. This Shakespeare film, then, is exemplary in its demonstration that in cinema passages of Shakespearean dialogue may work well as soliloquies, but the reverse is almost never the case.

One consequence of inventively experimental techniques of voice-over, direct-to-camera and wholly cinematic substitutions for soliloquy, and the brave directorial spiritedness or insouciance that may accompany them, is that the more obvious way of managing it – by having a character simply speak while either still or in motion, followed by the camera – seems now almost fatally compromised. Once you start feeling that a soliloquizing actor, alone and speaking on screen, is doing everything possible to *avoid* the camera's lens, sometimes even irritatingly glancing or gazing almost everywhere else, then some deeply enervating inertia has set in.

* Soliloquies (obviously) make prominent use of the personal pronoun, the first person singular – 'I', the sign of the ego expressing itself – although in fact the most famous of all Shakespearean soliloquies, Hamlet's 'To be or not to be', does not use the word 'I' at all, which is one measure of its exceptionality. The number of times a character uses the word 'I' may indicate the extent of his or her self-dramatization, or, in the case of Malvolio, for instance, self-delusion. Obviously, in what follows in this book, I shall think a great deal about how soliloquists say 'I'.

* With a quite different, even contrastive, dramatic effect, the soliloquy sometimes employs the third person (the mode for which Coleridge invented the word 'illeism', from the Latin 'ille', meaning 'he'). Self-address in soliloquy is something Shakespeare would have found prominent in the Roman dramatist Seneca.

We have already seen York in *Henry VI, Part 2* address himself when he says 'Now, York, or never, steel thy thoughts ...', but possibly the most famous example of illeism in Shakespearean soliloquy is 'Richard's himself again', spoken by his son, Richard III, when he wakes from a nightmare before the battle of Bosworth. In his film version Olivier speaks the words direct to camera, on horseback just before the battle begins. In fact, however, the phrase is not Shakespeare's but Colley Cibber's in the adaptation first published in 1700, which became the version actually staged between then and 1870. This has always been a difficult soliloquy for actors, since Richard in his anguished guilt and self-chastisement seems briefly so different from himself. Olivier may have retained Cibber's half-line because he handles the speech by diminishing its fearful remorse and emphasizing its defiance. I think further about this soliloquy in Part IV.

In *The Two Gentlemen of Verona* – an early comedy with many soliloquies – Julia, in a fit of face-saving play-acting, tears to shreds the love-letter from Proteus just delivered to her by her knowing maid Lucetta. As soon as

Lucetta leaves, Julia reassembles parts of the letter and reads the words 'kind Julia' there. 'Unkind Julia!' she exclaims, in contradiction, chastising herself for mistreating the letter, 'As in revenge of thy ingratitude / I throw thy name against the bruising stones, / Trampling contemptuously on thy disdain' (1.2.110–12). Julia then reflects on the 'poor wounded name' of Proteus himself, which she also finds in the letter, and says she wants her own name to be blown into 'the raging sea'. During the soliloquy, however, her histrionic petulance melts into true desire, forcefully expressed, when she finds the two names coupled together on another fragment of the letter: 'Thus will I fold them, one upon another; / Now kiss, embrace, contend, do what you will' (1.2.128–9) – which is to fantasize, in infatuated insinuation, a kind of proxy love-making out of the letter's remnants. The 'illeism' of Julia's soliloquy stays light-hearted in its playing with the idea that the name may differ from the person who bears it, that it may fail satisfactorily to identify her. Even so, the soliloquy foreshadows the very dark side of this early comedy, in which Julia herself will eventually go in disguise, under another name – a man's name – in order to try to retrieve Proteus's by then long since faded love.

The fact that this play has so many soliloquies is one index of its early nature; it may even be the first of Shakespeare's plays. Exposition is advanced through soliloquy in a relatively naive way, as the characters tell us their thoughts, their responses to what has just happened and to the other principals. This has its charm, as we are invited into direct relationship with the soliloquists, but it means that the play lacks the more sophisticated appeal of the intricate relationship between soliloquy and dialogue that transpires when Shakespeare's work matures.

Illeism elsewhere in soliloquy suggests a more profound uncertainty about personal identity. Henry VI returns from Scotland in disguise to an England in rebellion in *Henry VI, Part 3*. Addressing himself with his own name, he acts as a prototype of those others who lose their crowns in the subsequent history plays:

> From Scotland am I stol'n, even of pure love,
> To greet mine own land with my wishful sight.
> No, Harry, Harry, 'tis no land of thine;
> Thy place is filled, thy sceptre wrung from thee,
> Thy balm washed off wherewith thou wast anointed.
> No bending knee will call thee Caesar now,
> No humble suitors press to speak for right,
> No, not a man comes for redress of thee.
> For how can I help them, and not myself? (3.1.13–21)

The pathos of the soliloquy lies partly in the way Henry addresses himself with his own diminutive – not Henry, but Harry – and partly in the way he realizes that as the monarchy, which, after all, requires that kings have certain names and not others, slips from him, even this cherished name will no longer adequately represent him. Saying 'No, Harry, Harry', Henry is also saying that he is no longer Harry. How can he be, when 'I' is 'not myself'? Ironically, though, by speaking this soliloquy, he is putting himself at risk, because he is overheard by the Keeper of the forest and, recognized as 'the quondam king', is taken prisoner. So by saying he is not himself in his soliloquy, Henry is in fact identifying himself as himself and initiating the process by which he becomes actually no longer himself – by being deposed and subsequently murdered.

Similar doubts about personal identity, now for psychosexual rather than political reasons, obtain when Angelo addresses himself at the end of Act 2 Scene 2 of *Measure for Measure*. Coldly chaste, self-disciplined and suspiciously rigorous towards those who are not, the 'precise' Angelo, as the Duke calls him, 'who scarce confesses / That his blood flows', has abruptly been overwhelmed by lust for Isabella and opens his soliloquy in bewildered, syntactically startled self-questioning: 'What's this? What's this? Is this her fault, or mine?' Forced to recognize that it's Isabella's very virtue that prompts his desire, whereas he truly never has been tempted by ordinary vice, he questions his own identity: 'What dost thou, or what art thou, Angelo' (2.3.173)? 'Angelo', the angel, believes he has been caught by a 'cunning enemy', the devil, using a 'saint', Isabella, as bait, and that this temptation will inevitably lead him into sin. The question Angelo asks himself about his own identity therefore resonates in the complex ethical arguments of the play, as it debates the relationship between chastity, mercy and the law, and as it exposes and explores distinctions between righteousness and self-righteousness in an England in which 'precisians' – Puritans – were gaining influence.

In Timon's great, shrilly misanthropic soliloquy at the opening of Act 4 Scene 3 of *Timon of Athens* ('O blessed breeding sun, draw from the earth ...'), Timon does not address himself, but refers to himself in the third person: 'His semblable, yea himself, Timon disdains.' This soliloquy, repudiating all of humanity including the speaker himself, makes it clear that by this stage in his disintegration soliloquy has become the sole means of discourse available to Timon. He has become absolute in his aloneness and has nobody but himself to speak to, even if he speaks only to establish himself as the object of his own condemnation. This is the nadir of third-person self-objectification in Shakespearean soliloquy, marking an absolute difference from the self Timon has originally possessed.

Third-person address in soliloquy may, on the other hand, fully harmonize with the self on display elsewhere in a play, as it seems to do when Thersites in *Troilus and Cressida* speaks a self-addressing prose soliloquy:

> How now, Thersites? What, lost in the labyrinth of thy fury? Shall the elephant Ajax carry it thus? He beats me, and I rail at him. O worthy satisfaction! Would it were otherwise – that I could beat him whilst he railed at me. 'Sfoot, I'll learn to conjure and raise devils but I'll see some issue of my spiteful execrations. (2.3.1–7)

Since Thersites' nature is to 'rail at' – to abuse – everyone and everything he comes across, always, this seems both characteristic and self-recognizing. Indeed, this soliloquy goes on railing as it continues. Abusing himself in the third person and identifying what he does are therefore the most obvious manifestations not only of the third- but also of the first- and only person Thersites is, locked permanently into the selfness of himself. He is perennially the enviously mean-spirited malcontent, inwardly as well as outwardly. Yet he is also capable of the leavening of spite with malicious wit, as when he tells us at the end of this venomous solitary performance 'I have said my prayers, and devil Envy say "Amen"' (2.3.19–20). This self-knowing spiritedness makes Thersites' constant railing dramatically compelling rather than wholly insufferable.

* The dramatized 'I' of soliloquies frequently addresses, apostrophizes or invokes, in the vocative, absent objects or human subjects, either identified or to be inferred. Soliloquies, that is, although spoken in solitude, are often dramatized by appearing to address something or someone else. When they do this, soliloquies may be thought a form of solitary dialogue. Occasionally, the object of apostrophe is in fact present to the soliloquist.

A very early soliloquy, Titus's in Act 3 Scene 1 of *Titus Andronicus*, offers a desperate rationale for this. His speech opens as a supplication to the Roman tribunes to spare the lives of his sons as they are taken to execution, but at a certain point the tribunes simply leave him pleading on the ground. He continues to speak, however, addressing the earth itself and then again the now departed tribunes. At this point Lucius enters, telling him that because the tribunes have gone 'you recount your sorrows to a stone'. Titus replies that this is irrelevant because the tribunes would in any case neither 'mark' nor 'pity' him:

> Therefore I tell my sorrows to the stones,
> Who, though they cannot answer my distress,
> Yet in some sort they are better than the tribunes
> For that they will not intercept my tale. (3.1.37–40)

The apostrophizing soliloquist, that is, cannot *but* speak. Even if the speaking is pointless, it's necessary, driven by an emotional imperative beyond the need to communicate. *Titus* (1999), Julie Taymor's film version, emphasizes the point by having Timon (Anthony Hopkins) speak the soliloquy while lying on flagstones as the cart carrying his sons to their deaths passes over him and disappears.

In *Shakespeare in Parts*, Simon Palfrey and Tiffany Stern discuss what they call 'midline switches' in Shakespeare – short speech units and sudden prosodic shifts in the lines of the verse, such as Romeo speaks in his final soliloquy in *Romeo and Juliet*: 'Said he not so? Or did I dream it so? / Or am I mad, hearing him talk of Juliet, / To think it was so?' (5.3.79–81). Angelo's 'What's this? What's this? Is this her fault, or mine?', quoted above, would be another example. Palfrey and Stern maintain that soliloquies are liberal with such 'switches', designed to convey the sense of dialogue. Such prosodic effects in Shakespearean verse work, therefore, as apostrophe does too, and sometimes in concert with it. In the half-line immediately following these lines of Romeo's, for instance, he apostrophizes Paris, whom he has just killed: 'O, give me thy hand, / One writ with me in our misfortune's book' (5.3.81–2).

With varying effects, but usually with tenderness and poignancy, characters apostrophize absent lovers, sometimes those who have just left the stage. In the first scene of *The Two Gentlemen of Verona* Proteus, as soon as he has the stage to himself, makes it clear how profoundly love has changed him – or so he believes – when he says, 'Thou, Julia, thou hast metamorphosed me' (1.1.66). Although his brief soliloquy here is conventional enough in its charting of the effects of love, the Ovidian concept of metamorphosis is richly appropriate to the play, not least because Proteus undergoes another profound change of mind and heart when he falls for Silvia instead (and his very name, in its adjectival form 'protean', means 'changeable').

In an exquisitely sensuous soliloquy in *Romeo and Juliet*, in which Juliet longs for the coming of the night, which will bring Romeo to her ('Gallop apace, you fiery-footed steeds ...'), her apostrophe to night ('Come, civil night') progresses to an apostrophe to the absent Romeo himself, in which the repetitions of the word 'come' and the image of his naked body make it clear that it's her blood itself that gallops in expectancy:

> Come, night, come, Romeo, come, thou day in night,
> For thou wilt lie upon the wings of night
> Whiter than new snow upon a raven's back. (3.2.17–19)

I discuss this soliloquy extensively in Part IV. Contrastively, a soliloquy by Helena in *All's Well That Ends Well* ends with the couplet 'Come night; end, day; / For with the dark, poor thief, I'll steal away' (3.2.328–9). This apostrophe concludes an address to her absent, unworthy husband Bertram who, having spurned her, has gone to war expressly to avoid her. Helena is anguished, nevertheless, that he should have risked death because of his virtually forced marriage. Self-sacrificingly, she therefore decides during this soliloquy to abandon the court so that Bertram might return there; hence her figuring herself as a thief stealing away under cover of darkness.

When Helena fears for Bertram's life, she also addresses the bullets she imagines being fired at him on the battlefield:

O you leaden messengers,
That ride upon the violent speed of fire,
Fly with false aim; move the still-piecing air
That sings with piercing; do not touch my lord. (3.2.108–11)

This apostrophe may suggest that the soliloquist – or her consciousness – is, as it were, in two places at once. Helena speaks in the Florentine court, but is imaginatively on the battlefield, terrified on behalf of her unloving but still much loved husband. Her plea to the bullets to turn from him in flight is the register of profound, almost abjectly engaged empathy. Her own torn feelings may be reflected by the terms of her address, with its near-homonym 'piecing' and 'piercing'. The 'still-piecing air' is the air that puts itself back together again after being parted by the bullets, but this entire soliloquy sings with the way Helena is herself pierced by unrequited love. The repeated 'ee' sound seems almost the onomatopoeic representation of the whistling of the bullets through the air, in a way that vividly proposes how present this battlefield is to Helena's imagination.

The effect is not pity, exactly, when Hector addresses his sword in *Troilus and Cressida* as he drags onstage an anonymous Greek warrior he has just slaughtered after yet another battle and ends in a couplet: 'Now is my day's work done. I'll take good breath. / Rest, sword; thou hast thy fill of blood and death' (5.9.3–4). We cannot feel pity for such an effective killing machine as Hector, but we do feel the completeness of his exhaustion and experience a terrible retrospective irony in these lines immediately after they are spoken when Hector himself is treacherously hacked to death by Achilles and his Myrmidons. Hector's sword has rested once and for all, but Achilles' has not, and Hector's 'good breath' has been forced to rhyme with his own dreadful 'death'.

In Act 4 Scene 3 of *Henry IV, Part 2* the mortally ill King Henry sleeps with his crown beside him on the pillow. Prince Hal, his son, opens a soliloquy wondering why he does so and then directly apostrophizes the crown itself before addressing his sleeping father:

O polish'd perturbation! golden care!
That keep'st the ports of slumber open wide
To many a watchful night! Sleep with it now:
Yet not so sound, and half so deeply sweet,
As he whose brow with homely biggen bound
Snores out the watch of night. (4.3.154–9)

Hal's exclamation uses two virtual oxymorons to evoke the crown's deeply ambivalent connotations for the one who wears it. As 'polished perturbation' and 'golden care', it's a symbol not only of power, but of the permanent anxiety that power carries with it, and this soliloquy specifically recalls Henry's own soliloquy addressing longed-for sleep at the opening of Act 3. This concludes

'Uneasy lies the head that wears a crown' and testifies to the king's envy of his subjects who, he imagines, find sleep much easier than he does. Comparably, Hal here supposes that someone wearing a 'homely biggen' – a coarse nightcap – will sleep much more soundly than a king. These soliloquies are in a kind of tandem, as the father about to leave off the crown for good, by dying, and the son about to inherit it, by royal succession, meditate on its uncertain advantages. This is notably the theme of the great soliloquy about 'ceremony' uttered by Hal, now himself crowned as king, in Act 4 Scene 1 of *Henry V*. An early statement of the theme is made in the 'molehill' soliloquy spoken by the king in *Henry VI, Part 3*, and Alex Waldmann very vividly talks us through his performance of it in Part III of this book.

Towards the end of the soliloquy in *Henry IV, Part 2*, Hal, believing his father already dead, puts the crown on his own head and makes a solemn promise to maintain it well and hand it on – even though the very gesture reminds us that his father has had it by an act of usurpation. This dutiful dedication is severely at odds with what we may think we have learnt about Hal by following his riot through the two parts of *Henry IV*, even though we know from his very first soliloquy in *Part I* that he is capable of duplicity. After speaking, he leaves the stage with the crown. Henry, however, is not yet dead, and when he wakes he cries out for the crown, speaking a soliloquy understandably suspicious of his son's motivation. The ensuing dialogue between father and son includes three lengthy speeches, two by the king framing one by the prince, in which the father rebukes his son, the son asks pardon and solemnly promises to change his ways, and they are reconciled. Explaining why he took the crown, Hal says, 'I spake unto this crown as having sense, / And thus upbraided it ...' (5.3.157–8), and tells the king (and us), in the inverted commas of reported speech, what he has said to the crown in his absence from the stage, which is essentially a condemnation of it for its deleterious effect on his father.

In this long passage of the play, then, Hal dramatizes the ambivalent significance of the crown for those who wear it by addressing it, both on stage and off. Then, by saying that he has spoken to it 'as having sense', he implicitly confesses that he has been employing the convenient fiction that apostrophe always is in soliloquy. To the extent that his soliloquy is dramatically successful, as it assuredly is, Hal is also justifying this as a technique; or, through him, Shakespeare himself is, by implication, justifying all those other instances in which his soliloquists address inanimate objects 'as having sense'. Speaking to objects would be an absurdity, even a sign of insanity, in life, but it's a dramaturgical necessity in soliloquy. That Shakespeare should place this implicit meta-commentary in one of the most highly charged emotional exchanges in his work testifies to the inexhaustibility of his theatrical confidence. He risks Hal's appearing absurd at exactly the point where the prince is abjuring the absurdity of his younger self for the responsibilities of monarchy – deeply problematic as these then prove to be in *Henry V* itself.

I have just touched on the king's great apostrophe to sleep in *Henry IV, Part 2*. It's one of many instances in Shakespearean soliloquy where abstract, rather than concrete, things are addressed, usually with ethical intent or effect. In *King John*, Faulconbridge, the Bastard, exclaims in a soliloquy's opening line 'Mad world! mad kings! mad composition!' (2.2.561), where the abstraction 'composition', meaning something like 'bribery and corruption', seems both an intensification and a critique. The 'madness' of the way the rulers of the world behave is the consequence of an inevitably mad system of political machination. Opening in vehement outrage and careering satirically on from there, this soliloquy then personifies what the Bastard regards as the vice endemic to the public affairs of England and France that form the play's plot. As he traces the 'gentleman' commodity's effect on political manners, naming 'him' no less than six times in thirty-eight lines, he utters a scathing rebuke to *Realpolitik* in a way that foreshadows the embittered satirical rages of such later Jacobean malcontents as Malevole in Marston's *The Malcontent* (1603) and Vindice in Middleton's *The Revenger's Tragedy* (1606). The soliloquy ends with the Bastard's embracing of what he has castigated as virtually a new religion: 'Since kings break faith upon commodity, / Gain, be my lord, for I will worship thee' (3.1.597–8)! The soliloquy's comprehensive political and ethical analysis issues therefore in a form of pragmatic or even cynical opportunism – although in fact the Bastard remains in many ways a 'gentleman' too, defending the chivalric ideal and unflaggingly supportive of his king. The soliloquy therefore attests to the ambivalent psychological inscrutability that makes him by far the play's most interesting character.

At the other end of the ethical scale, Posthumus in *Cymbeline* comes to deplore his maltreatment of Innogen, which he believes, wrongly, to have resulted in her death. Imprisoned and in chains, he speaks a soliloquy in which he regards his own death as the only 'sure physician' for his guilt and begs the gods to bring it about speedily. As the soliloquy proceeds, Posthumus addresses his conscience in a form of personification and then addresses the gods:

> My conscience, thou art fettered
> More than my shanks and wrists. You good gods, give me
> The penitent instrument to pick that bolt,
> Then free for ever. Is't enough I am sorry?
> So children temporal fathers do appease;
> Gods are more full of mercy. (5.4.8–13)

The manifest sincerity of his repentance provokes a masque in which Posthumus's familial ghosts appear as he sleeps, leaving him a book in which an historical prophecy is made, and Jupiter himself descends. It's as though the soliloquy's apostrophe has of itself impelled a dramatic concretization of the beneficial effects and rewards of a good conscience.

This combination of supplicatory soliloquy and externalized representation is exceptional in Shakespeare but is appropriate to the strange conjunction of personal and public morality and of psychology and stylization in the plays of his final phase.

Apostrophes to abstractions always in fact carry a suggestion of personification, and, in some soliloquies, this can be pronounced: Mark Antony's to Mischief, for instance, in Act 3 Scene 2 of *Julius Caesar*; Hamlet's to Frailty in Act 1 Scene 2 of the play; and Henry V's to Ceremony in Act 4 Scene 2. And numerous soliloquists address Fortune as if she is a goddess rather than an abstract quality.

* Soliloquies employ many elements of what the Renaissance understood by 'rhetoric'.

Macbeth's 'dagger' soliloquy opens with a rhetorical question ('Is this a dagger ...?') and a rhetorical apostrophe ('Come, let me ...') followed by a line ('I have thee not, and yet I see thee still') that may be identified as the rhetorical trope of antithesis, and I identify an instance of antimetabole in one of Macbeth's asides above. It's possible to understand Shakespeare's soliloquies from beginning to end as either the sophisticated development or the gradual erosion of a dependency on rhetorical technique. This is a large topic with many ramifications, which I consider further in my next chapter.

* Soliloquies frequently end a scene and, by doing so, assume special prominence. The soliloquist ending a scene is more than usually exposed, and also in a more than usually powerful dramaturgical position. The same holds true, possibly to an even greater extent, of soliloquies which constitute, of themselves, an entire scene. Thinking about this, though, we must remember that scene divisions are often dependent on the judgement of editors rather than clearly stipulated by quarto and Folio texts.

The concluding soliloquy may bring a summative quality to the foregoing scene and this may be emphasized if the soliloquy itself concludes with a rhyming couplet. Rhyming couplets tend to have greater climactic force, and greater memorability, than blank verse, especially when they are read, or heard, in immediate contradistinction to it. As I proceed in this book, I point out some specific effects of end-of-scene and whole-scene soliloquies.

* Some soliloquies are closely associated with death and some are spoken by the soliloquist-about-to-die. The latter include those by characters on the point of killing themselves, and the most famous soliloquy in all Shakespeare, Hamlet's 'To be or not to be', is that of an apparently potential suicide. In Part II of this book I examine further the link between soliloquies and death in the light of the way this has been theorized by some scholars and critics, and in Part IV I consider the suicidal soliloquies of both Romeo and Juliet and think also about those of Richard III and Othello which are spoken as they are about to die.

* Some soliloquies take the form of prayer, although not necessarily in any straightforward way.

The 'saintly' king in Act 3 Scene 2 of *Henry VI, Part 2* utters a prayer-soliloquy beginning 'O thou that judgest all things, stay my thoughts' in which he lets us know his suspicions about the death of Duke Humphrey. The prayer is orthodox in its Christianity, but carries a great emotional charge too, as Henry imagines himself, with grief-stricken specificity, finding a way to 'tell my love unto his dumb deaf trunk, / And with my fingers feel his hand unfeeling' (3.2.144–5). The alliteration is almost tactile in its specificity, as the dumbness and deafness register the utter deadness of this person-become-thing, now a mere 'trunk', and as the individual 'fingers' of the hand desperately reach for, but fail to find, response or reciprocity. 'Feeling' is obliged to confront its opposite, 'unfeeling', and is thereby forced into an apprehension of mortal limit, almost in a version of what Keats calls 'the feel of not to feel it'. Prayer-as-soliloquy has here become an intimate form of imaginative empathy.

In *Richard III*, Richmond soliloquizes in prayer before the battle of Bosworth in the speech beginning 'O Thou, whose captain I account myself' (3.3.108). His confidence that he has right on his side is underwritten by his voluntarily making himself a subsidiary to God in the military hierarchy, since if he, the presumptive monarch, is merely a 'captain', then God must be the general. Because his subsequent victory turns him into Henry VII, the first Tudor king and grandfather to Elizabeth I (the monarch on the throne when the play was first performed), and because this involves the death of the universally condemned Richard III, we must assume that he also has Shakespeare and his audience on his side. Even so, he seems, especially compared to Richard, an under-written and insipid character;

and his prayer-soliloquy has none of the dramatic strength of Richard's own soliloquies. Perhaps we can see ideology putting a strain on free dramatic capacity here. I shall consider further the impact of what has been called the 'Tudor Myth' on *Richard III* in Part IV.

The king's prayer before the battle of Agincourt in *Henry V*, beginning 'O God of battles, steel my soldiers' hearts' (4.1.286), is necessarily much more ambivalent in effect, since any such prayer from a leader capable of the reprisals he threatens at Harfleur ('Your naked infants spitted upon pikes') and the atrocity he orders at Agincourt ('Then every soldier kill his prisoners!') is likely to sound merely opportunistic. In this soliloquy-prayer, Henry also reminds God (and us) of 'the fault / My father made in compassing the crown' – that is, Bolingbroke's deposition of Richard II and the moral responsibility for his subsequent death – and what he is doing himself by way of prayer and chantry-building to make amends. Reminding God that 'Five hundred poor I have in yearly pay, / Who twice a day their withered hands hold up / Toward heaven to pardon blood', Henry may well be advertising an admirable, if apparently coercive, form of poor relief, but he also appears possessed of a vulgar pecuniary insistence that is mildly hectoring rather than genuinely penitential. So perhaps what we have here is a prayer-soliloquy that undermines its own humility in the very act of articulating it.

Soliloquies can also be explicitly *unsuccessful* attempts to pray. Claudius's in Act 3 Scene 3 of *Hamlet* is one such. He confesses his 'offence' and says,

> Pray can I not:
> Though inclination be as sharp as will,
> My stronger guilt defeats my strong intent
> And like a man to double business bound
> I stand in pause where I shall first begin
> And both neglect. (3.3.38–43)

Hamlet encounters Claudius while he is still trying to pray and speaks his own soliloquy ('Now might I do it') in which he decides not to kill him there and then, reasoning that if Claudius dies at prayer he will go to heaven, whereas Hamlet wishes to ensure his damnation – a desire Samuel Johnson found too horrible to contemplate, as well he might. Following Hamlet's departure, Claudius speaks again in the couplet that ends the scene: 'My thoughts fly up, my words remain below. / Words without thoughts never to heaven go' (3.3.97–8). The juxtaposition of Claudius's and Hamlet's soliloquies produces an intense metaphysical irony. Given that Claudius is still self-confessedly incapable of prayer, Hamlet could have killed him and ensured his damnation too. None of which interferes with our sense that in fact Hamlet may well have been incapable of killing Claudius anyway, and that the reason he offers for failing to do so – which seems extremely unsubtle in its theology, even for the period in which the play was written

– bears witness less to his calculation than to his lack of self-knowledge. In Grigori Kozintsev's film version (1964), Hamlet's soliloquy is omitted and Claudius's drastically abbreviated. While Claudius's (Mikhail Nazvanov's) soliloquy is spoken in voice-over, he gazes at his own reflection in a mirror. The striking cinematic image presents guiltily appalled self-confrontation rather than prayer. Later in the film, just after Claudius plans Hamlet's death with Laertes, he again catches sight of himself in a mirror, gazes briefly at his reflection and, in extreme self-disgust, hurls a carafe of wine to obscure it. The consequence of acute guilt is that he cannot stand the sight of himself; he wants his image, his self-representation, erased.

Angelo, at the beginning of Act 2 Scene 4 of *Measure for Measure*, also expresses his distracted inability to pray as a consequence of having had his life and moral code turned upside down by his sudden lust for Isabella:

> When I would pray and think, I think and pray
> To several subjects: Heaven hath my empty words,
> Whilst my invention, hearing not my tongue,
> Anchors on Isabel: Heaven in my mouth,
> As if I did but only chew his name,
> And in my heart the strong and swelling evil
> Of my conception. (2.4.1–7)

'Chew', the *OED* tells us, is used here for the first time to mean 'to keep saying or mumbling over', but it retains the intense physicality of mastication too, in a way emphasized by the proximity of the words 'tongue' and 'mouth'; and an only just submerged metaphor of pregnancy informs Angelo's concluding lines. The soliloquy therefore induces a queasy sense of the way the spirituality of prayer and the concentration it demands have been replaced by the disordered physical and sexual obsession now suffusing Angelo's consciousness. The imagery of the passage inhabits the same discursive world as the play's plot, in which sex and pregnancy are strongly motivating elements.

Soliloquies may also be negative prayers – forms of blasphemy, curse or imprecation. Probably the most extreme is Timon's savage cursing of Athens, which forms the whole of Act 4 Scene 1 of *Timon of Athens*. Opening with his apostrophe to the city's protective wall to 'dive in the earth / And fence not Athens' (4.1.2–3), the soliloquy ends with his quasi-blasphemous appeal to the gods to universalize his detestation of the Athenians: 'And grant as Timon grows his hate may grow / To the whole race of mankind, high and low! / Amen' (4.1.39–41). The blasphemy is clinched by the way Timon ends his prayer to the pagan gods with the word most usually associated with orthodox Christian prayer. 'Amen', in this context, given a line to itself, means not so much 'So be it' as 'May it be everything abominable that it currently is not' and carries, therefore, a ferociously negative charge.

The fact that some soliloquies in Shakespeare have an association with prayer may derive ultimately from one of the pre-theatrical sources proposed for them, and I discuss prayer as an origin of soliloquy in my next chapter.

* There is a relationship between soliloquy and the ever recurrent 'aside' in Shakespeare's plays, in which the presumed 'fourth wall' of stage space is breached by an actor speaking directly to an audience. Thinking about this is complicated, however, by the fact that virtually no asides are marked as such in the quartos and Folio texts of Shakespeare, however manifestly they are intended; they are left to the discretion of the actor. Shakespeare would not have called them 'asides', although the word 'aside' is used as part of an adverbial phrase in plays of the period. (Shakespeare's shortest soliloquy, the three-word line, 'My mother dead!', spoken by the hero of *King John*, is of course shorter than most asides; but the hero is alone on stage, albeit very briefly, when he says it, and this qualifies it as a soliloquy. In Part III of this book, Alex Waldmann talks very interestingly about performing it. The longest soliloquy in Shakespeare is Richard of Gloucester's in *Henry VI, Part 3*, which has seventy-one lines.)

The exceptionally lengthy fifteen-line aside of Macbeth's that I discussed above – to which attention is called by the others on stage, as I have said – is virtually a soliloquy, but a soliloquy, as it were, under observation. In *Macbeth*, as it happens, asides are particularly prominent. Usually in Shakespeare's plays they are less lengthy and sometimes very short indeed. However, appearing to be brief interior monologues spoken aloud as if characters cannot contain themselves, they are sometimes, as Macbeth's is, highly significant in terms of characterization and plot. Here are some representative cases.

In Act 3 Scene 1 of *Richard III*, speaking to Prince Edward, the nephew whose murder he will eventually arrange, Richard dissembles in speech and then, in an aside, provocatively comments on his dissembling in lines that both tell us what he is up to and offer an extremely arresting analogy: 'Thus, like the formal Vice, Iniquity, / I moralize two meanings in one word' (3.1.82–3) – 'formal' means 'unmistakable' or 'precise'. Richard's comparison of himself to 'the formal Vice' of medieval morality plays displays, or even parades, a kind of diseased self-knowledge, while also more or less inviting an Elizabethan audience to measure and judge him against a type they will either know or know about. I say more about the Vice and morality plays in Part II.

In an aside early in *The Merchant of Venice* Shylock tells us of his obsessive detestation of Antonio, letting us know that 'If I can catch him once upon the hip, / I will feed fat the ancient grudge I bear him' (1.3.42–3). This foreshadows Shylock's demand for a pound of Antonio's flesh, which initiates the main action of the play. The aside is particularly noteworthy because Shylock has no soliloquies. It therefore encourages speculation about what a soliloquy of Shylock's might be like, giving us a tiny window into his interiority. 'Feed fat', for instance, with its relished alliteration, seems inordinate as 'feed' alone would not, and Shylock's demand of Antonio is indeed inordinate – as is, arguably, the penalty eventually exacted for it. And 'ancient' makes the 'grudge' seem tribal or cultural rather than merely personal; in the very next line Shylock makes it plain that his hatred of Antonio responds to Antonio's own hatred of 'our sacred nation'. This brief aside is therefore instinct with the energies of both Jewish feeling and anti-Semitic prejudice that propel the plot.

It's probably Claudius in *Hamlet* who speaks the most significant aside in all Shakespeare. Responding to something Polonius says about the frequency of hypocrisy in human affairs, he comments, aside, on the truth of the observation and says:

> How smart a lash that speech doth give my conscience!
> The harlot's cheek beautied with plastering art
> Is not more ugly to the thing that helps it
> Than is my deed to my most painted word.
> O heavy burden! (3.1.49–53)

This lets us know for the first time that Claudius suffers guilt – although it does not specify exactly what he feels guilty about – in a way that seems at least partly to confirm what the Ghost has told Hamlet. This is revelatory information for an audience. It puts us in a different position from Hamlet himself in relation both to the Ghost and to Claudius, since Hamlet fears that the Ghost may be an evil spirit come to lead him by deception to damnation. The aside also lets us know the extent of Claudius's self-loathing, not only because he tells us how guilty he feels but because he, a king, humiliatingly compares himself to a harlot. Social and moral status are obviously involved in this, but the gender relation when this royal male likens himself to a female prostitute is especially self-lacerating. Claudius's aside is preparatory in these ways to his soliloquy in Act 3 Scene 3, which I have discussed above, and so indicates how closely related to soliloquy aside may be.

Asides also construct a relationship between actor, character and audience, which supplies a context for, and background to, that complex inter-relationship as it obtains in soliloquies proper. In some plays or performances, asides may also become more obvious engagements with an audience, in which the speaker has manifest designs upon us. In this respect, asides may be considered the persistence of forms of audience address in medieval theatre – which gives Richard III's comparison of himself to the Vice a further, meta-textual, significance, since the medieval Vice stood at once both inside and outside the dramatic action. This is especially so when asides are spoken by the great manipulative Machiavels in Shakespeare – notably Richard, Duke of Gloucester, in *Henry VI Part 3*, and then the same character when he becomes Richard III, Iago in *Othello* and Edmund in *King Lear*. In these cases, aside forms a kind of rhetorical complement to politically motivated soliloquy. As such, its closest contemporary mode is probably the villain's remarks to the audience in pantomime. The possibility of this association for an audience of serious theatre may disconcert some actors, but Alan Cumming in an interview for the Globe Theatre's *Muse of Fire* series says that 'In Shakespeare's time they absolutely engaged with the audience; it was like a panto ... I think Shakespeare should be more like a panto.' (This extensive and excellent series of interviews with Shakespearean actors, directors and critics may be found at https://globeplayer.tv/museoffire.)

In the way asides include the audience, they form a continuous reminder that the play *is* a play. They have an inherently meta-theatrical quality that disrupts any smooth continuum of theatrical illusion, and, in this, they also constitute a necessary context for soliloquy. Alan Cumming likes it that when he played Hamlet at London's intimate Donmar Warehouse in 1993 he could look at every individual member of the audience at some point, allowing him to consider his soliloquies 'a little discussion' with them. The architecture of the present Globe Theatre on London's South Bank imitates that of Shakespeare's original Globe in so far as this is ascertainable – which is not actually very far, some people think, including the very sceptical Ian McKellen in his *Muse of Fire* interview. However, that theatrical space does give actors more than usual access to the audience in the pit, the 'groundlings' of Shakespeare's time, who stand or mill about there during performances, and it also gives members of the audience more than usual access to one another. Actors at the contemporary Globe, taking advantage of these opportunities, will sometimes emphasize the meta-theatrical nature of aside by addressing an audience member directly, for instance, or by taking someone's hand confidentially, or by appearing to flirt with someone in the crowd. Whether this happened also in Shakespeare's Globe itself we cannot know for a fact, but Cumming believes that it must have.

Asides also act as a complement to those many textual emphases in Shakespeare's plays on their own nature as theatre, with their frequent use, actual or implied, of the play-within-a-play structure. In her seminal study *Shakespeare and the Idea of the Play* (1962), Anne Righter defines the relationship between actor and audience in Elizabethan theatre as 'a near-perfect accomplishment, a brilliant but perilous equilibrium'. She touches only briefly on soliloquies, but her judgement, and especially the sense of risk contained in the word 'perilous', is worth bearing in mind when we think about both soliloquies and asides.

We need to consider one further thing about aside relevant to soliloquy. The *OED* tells us that the word 'aside' was first used in the sense in which I am using it here – and therefore first became a noun – in the early eighteenth century and defines it, a little tautologically, as 'words spoken aside or in an undertone, so as to be inaudible to some person present; words spoken by an actor, which the other performers on the stage are supposed not to hear'. 'Supposed not to hear' is accurate, but sometimes asides are in fact overheard, or half-heard, or the person who utters them fears they could be.

In *The Two Gentlemen of Verona* the clown Speed comments, in an aside spoken in doggerel verse, on an elaborate ploy of Silvia's to get Valentine to write a love letter to her, and Valentine asks him 'How now, sir? What, are you reasoning with yourself?' (2.1.131–2). *Henry VI, Part 1* contains a 'dialogue' between Suffolk and Margaret in which Suffolk speaks entirely, the stage direction says, 'to himself', debating whether, and how, he might woo her, and Margaret similarly speaks 'to herself', eventually saying of Suffolk's speeches 'He talks at random: sure the man is mad' (5.2.106). In *The Comedy of Errors* Dromio of Syracuse speaks an aside fearing that he has entered a land of 'goblins, elves and sprites', and Luciana asks 'Why prat'st thou to thyself and answer'st not' (2.2.192)? In these cases, asides appear to lay themselves open to the accidents of overhearing.

Conversely, York in *Henry VI, Part 2* keeps Buckingham waiting for an answer while he speaks an aside about his anger at what has just been said to him, and then apologizes for keeping him waiting – 'Buckingham, I prithee pardon me / That I have given no answer all this while' (5.1.32–3) – ascribing his motivation to his 'deep melancholy'. The actor playing Buckingham must engage in stage business of some kind while York speaks his aside. York's drawing attention to the fact that he has been speaking is as disruptive of conventional assumptions about asides as is the sense that they may well, on occasion, be overheard.

These are all instances, then, which boldly expose the convention to some manifest objections, including the most obvious one, voiced by Margaret, that people talking to themselves are ordinarily assumed to be mad. Since the aside is, as I have suggested, so closely related to the soliloquy, these are also cases which tell us something about soliloquies proper too, and, as I explain in Part II, whether soliloquy is to be regarded as speech that may be overheard has been a problematic and contentious issue in its critical history.

* Soliloquies, if they are of any length, will vary considerably in tone and register and may well include a certain 'choric' element.

In Macbeth's 'dagger' soliloquy the choric mode seems to develop in these lines:

> Now o'er the one half-world
> Nature seems dead, and wicked dreams abuse
> The curtained sleep; Witchcraft celebrates
> Pale Hecate's offerings; and withered Murder,
> Alarumed by his sentinel, the wolf,
> Whose howl's his watch, thus with his stealthy pace,
> With Tarquin's ravishing strides, towards his design
> Moves like a ghost. (2.1.20–27)

It's possible to understand this part of the soliloquy – which seems almost inset into the personal speech, as though it should be printed in italics – as the individual hero's abstraction of himself from the particularities of his immediate situation with the effect of setting it within or against a larger cosmic scene. The abstraction then creates an atmosphere appropriate to the horror the hero is about to set in motion. It's as if Macbeth, grown larger than himself, possesses an almost superhuman capacity, privy as he now appears to be to the processes of Witchcraft, Hecate and Murder, and having arcane knowledge of the dreams of others. In this way, he briefly plays chorus to his own action.

Other major characters in some plays also occasionally act with quasi-choral authority, as though standing at least to one side of the action: the wittily contemptuous hero himself in the opening soliloquy of *Richard III*, for instance. In fact, we may trace in this soliloquy a marked advance in Shakespearean soliloquy over previous Elizabethan dramatic soliloquy. Richard's 'Now is the winter of our discontent ...' acts as a kind of prologue to the play, but one spoken, exceptionally, by its title character. Letting us know that he intends to play the villain since he cannot play the lover (even though in fact he goes on in the very next scene to do exactly that), Richard becomes self-consciously Machiavellian. The soliloquizing hero as his own Machiavel may be read as a sophisticating variation of the opening of Marlowe's *The Jew of Malta*, where the character Machiavel speaks a prologue followed in the first scene by the hero Barabas's first soliloquy. By explicitly including the Machiavellian element in the opening soliloquy of his central character itself, Shakespeare is both advancing on Marlowe and fulfilling the promise of Richard of Gloucester's soliloquy in *Henry VI, Part 3* in which, as we saw above, he tells us he can 'set the murderous Machiavel to school'.

The intrusion into individual soliloquy of a choric element may owe something to Shakespeare's use, in the writing of some soliloquies, of the choruses in Seneca's plays; those in which both Henry V and Henry VI envy the presumed simple life of common men are influenced in this way. I return to both choral soliloquies and the Senecan and Marlovian influence on

Shakespearean soliloquy in Part II, and I closely examine Richard's opening soliloquy in Part IV.

* The soliloquists in Shakespeare's plays are usually their most significant characters, but occasionally characters of minor importance or anonymous characters speak single soliloquies. Their relative rareness can make them especially effective.

An anonymous English soldier emerges at the end of Act 2 Scene 1 of *Henry VI, Part 1* to tell us, in a four-line soliloquy, that merely by shouting Talbot's name he can terrify French soldiers into running naked from the battlefield. By doing so, he dramatizes, with a newly democratizing ferocity, the vast power wielded by the aristocracy over common soldiers.

The anonymous Scrivener in *Richard III*, whose soliloquy gets a scene to itself, appears 'with a paper in his hand' and comments on the cynically murderous scheming represented by this proclamation against Hastings. He complains that he has had to write out the reasons for Hastings' death *before* his accusation, arrest and trial and then extrapolates a moral in a concluding couplet whose quasi-choric prophecy shadows the rest of the play:

> Who is so gross
> That cannot see this palpable device?
> Yet who so bold but says he sees it not?
> Bad is the world, and all will come to nought
> When such ill dealing must be seen in thought. (3.6.10–14)

The irony of this is first historical, in that the Scrivener's written record will be all that posterity – history itself, *we* – will learn about Hastings's death; but it's also individual, because the Scrivener tells us not only that he is obliged to go along with the deception but that, taking pride in his work, he is glad to have managed it well. The fact that the soliloquy is fourteen lines long and ends in a rhyming couplet gives it the appearance of at least a quasi-sonnet, which may even suggest that this Scrivener is himself a kind of written text, totally subsumed by function. This man who tells us what he is obliged to write, and comes before us only *as* a writer, must express himself in a form that advertises its own writtenness. Given that the sonnet is a courtly form, it's yet a further irony that its appearance in the mouth of a commoner passes a scathing judgement on current courtly manners.

In *Romeo and Juliet* Capulet imperiously demands that a servant 'trudge about / Through fair Verona' (1.2.33–4) to find those named on a list whom he has invited to his feast. When Capulet and Paris leave the stage, the anonymous servant explodes into a short prose soliloquy complaining that he can hardly do what has been required of him since he cannot read. This is funny of course, but the soliloquist is also revealing himself as doubly subjected: by Capulet's bullying and by his own deficient education. Despite the latter, his soliloquy parodies a passage of John Lyly. So Shakespeare is also, for those recognizing the allusion, raising a smile at the idea of an illiterate servant apparently remembering the elaborately mannered and periphrastic Epistle Dedicatory of Lyly's *Euphues*. Is this a perverse compliment to the character, though, or an invitation to condescension?

The Porter in *Macbeth* has a wonderful prose soliloquy in which, after Duncan's murder, the whole tone of the play is briefly transformed. Even so, by figuring himself as the 'porter of hell gate' – like a devil porter in the old mystery plays – he reminds us that the Macbeths have just condemned themselves to an actual hell.

The Boy in *Henry V* speaks a prose soliloquy in which his youth is emphasized, condemning the thievery of Bardolph, Nym and Pistol and concluding 'I must leave them and seek some better service; their villainy goes against my weak stomach, and therefore I must cast it up' (3.2.51–3). The ethical weight of this soliloquy makes it even more bitterly piercing to learn only a few scenes later that the French have cruelly killed all the boys taken prisoner. The 'better service' the Boy intends to seek has been found only in the grave, and his soliloquy and what follows it underline the extreme ambivalence of this play's treatment of war.

These voices of the unnamed, which display, variously, shrewdness of observation, the inventive will to survival, the strength of humour, the outrage of insulted feeling and the virtue of ethical intelligence, suddenly summon to the stage the vast clamour of human energy that we often sense almost within earshot of what is in fact spoken in Shakespearean theatre and that every so often unignorably presses its way in.

* Occasionally, to extremely powerful or subtle effect, an individual soliloquy may be choreographed as one element in the staging of double or even multiple soliloquies.

The soliloquies of Henry IV and Prince Hal and those of Claudius and Hamlet that I discuss above are major cases in point. In Act 2 Scene 5 of *Henry VI, Part 3*, the ironically interlacing soliloquies of the king, the son who has killed his father and the father who has killed his son, which dramatize in an almost operatic trio the actuality of civil war, supply another. Alex Waldmann describes in Part III his ineluctable emotional reaction as an actor playing the king.

The overlapping, mutually observed soliloquies of Berowne, the King, Longaville and Dumaine in Act 4 Scene 3 of *Love's Labour's Lost*, in which they read their sonnets, also display an almost musical dramaturgy. In that elaborate, even baroque, dance of performed sonnet and soliloquy, Shakespeare himself performs a drama of irony, discrepancy and dissimulation of a kind that pushes the soliloquy ingeniously and resourcefully into new permutations. In his film version (2000) Kenneth Branagh appositely turns the play into a pastiche 1930s Hollywood movie; the interplay of soliloquies in this scene is presented as the over-hearing of separate songs of the period by Gershwin, Porter and Berlin instead of Shakespeare's original sonnets.

* We tend to think of soliloquies as written primarily in blank verse (which may, as we have seen, end in a couplet, or more than one couplet). But great soliloquies are also written in prose; and they occur in verse forms other than blank verse too.

When we read Shakespeare's blank-verse soliloquies, we are reading examples of his metrical art at its finest – at its most subtle, complex and experimentally flexible, as it conveys the intricacies and individualizing inflections of speech and thought themselves. The prose soliloquies have their own, different intensities and strengths, and I have already looked at a few. All kinds of character speak prose in Shakespeare, from the 'highest' to the 'lowest' in the social order, but those from the higher bracket speak usually only in verse in their soliloquies. Their interiority and self-perception are inherently constituted in what are always to some degree elevating iambics, as if this is, as it were, virtually the DNA of their imaginative generation. The paradigmatic case is Prince Hal stepping forward to speak at the end of Act 1 Scene 2 of *Henry IV, Part 1* the soliloquy beginning 'I know you all ...' and modulating as he does so from prose into verse; I consider this closely in Part II.

Exceptions do occur though, as when Hotspur's 'out of this nettle, danger, we pluck this flower, safety' soliloquy at the beginning of Act 2 Scene 3 of the same play is initiated by the reading aloud of a prose letter from which he continues to quote as his prose soliloquy progresses. Lady Macbeth, on the other hand, at the opening of Act 1 Scene 5 of *Macbeth*, finishes reading her husband's prose letter aloud before speaking the verse soliloquy that takes off from it.

In Part II, I also think about the Clown's (Lancelet Giobbe's) prose soliloquy in *The Merchant of Venice*. That he speaks a soliloquy at all is made the more remarkable by the fact that none of the play's main characters do, as I have already said; so the use of prose probably calls rather more than customary attention to itself here, in a soliloquy wholly congruent – from below, as it were – with the play's major preoccupations.

In addition to Thersites, whom we have already looked at, other outstanding prose soliloquists in Shakespeare include Malvolio in *Twelfth Night* and Benedick in *Much Ado About Nothing*. In one of his soliloquies Benedick even accounts for the fact that he speaks only in prose when he tells us that, more hopelessly 'turned over and over ... in love' than the great poetic lovers Leander and Troilus, he cannot express his love in rhyme, as they can: 'I was not born', he says, 'under a rhyming planet nor can I woo in festival terms' (5.2.39–40). He is born to speak prose, therefore, as I suggested above, Hal and others are genetically constituted to soliloquize in verse; indeed, Benedick is a brilliant master of prose repartee. His self-knowledge in the midst of the havoc induced by love has endearing humour and pathos, especially since lack of self-knowledge has characterized him previously; so he is not in the least diminished by such a genesis. Confident that he loves even more than Leander and Troilus do, although he cannot express his love in verse, he knows that his virtue lies in the loving, not the versifying. Shakespeare's great prose soliloquists speak great prose because prose is what they are; they are derived from it and, articulating it, bring it to new perfection. The fact that your nature and your being, the essence of your self-conception, expresses itself in prose does not make you *prosaic*. Of no Shakespearean characters is this truer than of Bottom in *A Midsummer Night's Dream* – especially in the magnificently confused soliloquy he speaks when he wakes from what he regards as his 'dream' – and, pre-eminently, Falstaff in *Henry IV, Parts 1* and *2*.

Falstaff has eleven soliloquies over the course of the two parts of *Henry IV* – more than anyone else in Shakespeare, although some are quite brief. It's striking, however, how little insight these give into any interiority in him, or, rather, how they testify that with him interiority is almost wholly co-extensive with exteriority. There are perhaps only three occasions when we learn anything about him in soliloquy that we would not otherwise know. In one, he appears to say that his love for Hal is so great that he feels almost drugged by it, but the object of the remark is ambiguous and he may in fact be referring to Poins. In another, ending a hymn to the benefits of alcohol, he says 'If I had a thousand sons, the first human principle I would teach them should be to forswear thin potations and to addict themselves to sack' (*Part 1*, 4.2.120–3). This is enlightening about Falstaff's 'principles' and his unconventional notions of effective paternity, but it may also hint at regret for his apparent childlessness – and this possibly sheds further light on his love for Hal, which has often been read as quasi-paternal. And in his final soliloquy, while he is still in Justice Shallow's company, he foresees keeping Hal amused with stories about Shallow. This is psychologically accurate, and touching, about how we do think, even as we undergo them, about sharing our experiences with those we love, as if they will not be fully present to us until we do. It's obviously significant that even the vaguest intimations of an inner life in Falstaff all at least touch on his love for the Prince. When he plans to laugh with Hal about Shallow, therefore, it pierces us to the heart because we realize by then the reception he is in fact going to get from the one he so deeply loves when he returns to London.

Otherwise in his soliloquies Falstaff behaves when alone, speaking to himself, essentially he does when in dialogue and in company. In one soliloquy, he tells us that he has 'misused the King's press damnably' – that is, that he has abused his commission in the army to make money for himself by recruiting inept soldiers. Despite the word 'damnably', however, he does not appear to intend self-rebuke and ends the soliloquy in dismissive unconcern. In another, as we have seen, he cynically ponders the concept of 'honour'; although what he says contributes to the nuanced scrutiny of the politics of militarism offered by the *Henry IV* plays, in which the word 'honour' frequently recurs, his contribution would be more effective if it seemed less manifestly self-interested and if his own actions less amply demonstrated his adherence to the equivocal principles of what he calls his 'catechism' of maxims. And several times his soliloquies do what he frequently does in his dialogue too: they engage in a rhetoric of disparagement. This is true of the one which considers Justice Shallow, which also reveals what a prose soliloquy in Falstaff's mouth might do to compensate for the lack of interiority.

Falstaff is about to leave Shallow's farm in Gloucestershire and ponders his return when he will 'fetch off' (swindle) those he has just encountered there:

> As I return I will fetch off these justices. I do see the bottom of Justice Shallow. Lord, Lord, how subject we old men are to this vice of lying! This same starved justice hath done nothing but prate to me of the wildness of his youth and the feats he hath done about Turnbull Street, and every third word a lie, duer paid to the hearer than the Turk's tribute. I do remember him at Clement's Inn like a man made after supper of a cheese paring. When 'a was naked he was for all the world like a forked radish with a head fantastically carved upon it with a knife. 'A was so forlorn that his dimensions to any thick sight were invincible. 'A was the very genius of famine, yet lecherous as a monkey, and the whores called him mandrake. 'A came ever in the rearward of the fashion, and sung those tunes to the overscutched housewives that he heard the car-men whistle, and sware they were his fancies or his goodnights. And now is this Vice's dagger become a squire and talks as familiarly of John a'Gaunt as if he had been sworn brother to him; and I'll be sworn 'a ne'er saw him but once in the tilt-yard, and then he burst his head for crowding among the marshal's men. I saw it and told John a'Gaunt he beat his own name, for you might have thrust him and all his apparel into an eel-skin. The

case of a treble hautboy was a mansion for him, a court; and now has he land and beefs. Well, I'll be acquainted with him if I return, and 't shall go hard, but I'll make him a philosopher's two stones to me. If the young dace be bait for the old pike, I see no reason in the law of nature but I may snap at him. Let time shape, and there an end. (*Part 2*, 3.2.300–31)

Prose is relished here, as metaphor, opinion, extravagant simile, report and memory almost crowd one another out in the rich inventiveness of Falstaff's belittling of Shallow. His soliloquy willingly tells us of his plan in a way consistent with his boasting elsewhere, but the almost reckless exuberance of its language also reveals things Falstaff would be less happy to have us know. Perhaps we do even see 'the bottom' of Sir John Falstaff here. Although we may also find Shallow ridiculous, we may still decide that Falstaff's relentless depreciation of Shallow's leanness is a form of compensatory displacement, given his own immense girth, which others (Hal especially) frequently rebuke. And we will find his chastising of Shallow for the 'vice of lying' astonishing hypocrisy, since we can have little confidence that the sardonic community of the phrase 'we old men' is intended to include the speaker himself, although we have every reason to believe it should. The soliloquy also seems informed by envy. Shallow remembers Falstaff from his days in Clement's Inn, where 'Jack Falstaff, now Sir John' was just a boy and page to the Duke of Norfolk. Shallow has since made good in a way Falstaff clearly has not. Falstaff's impulse to con him out of money may well derive, then, from envy of the wealth made plain by that 'land' and those 'beefs' and from envy too of Shallow's title ('Justice'), which the actor playing Falstaff might well articulate with witheringly emphatic sarcasm, and of his social standing ('squire'). Falstaff manages to itemize, in this congested linguistic space, a great deal of what constitutes Shallow's enviable social and financial authority, and security, in his environment.

Revealing more to us than Falstaff thinks, his soliloquies, which become more frequent as the plays proceed, therefore become sites of adverse judgement. There is little to admire in the self they display, and Falstaff in the earlier part of *Henry IV*, whom some have always seen as a figure of 'madcap' misrule, diminishes subsequently when the liar, con-man and corruptly cynical recruitment officer gradually steps further forward.

This prose soliloquy also draws on a range of temporally specific information of a kind verse soliloquies are unlikely to encompass. This lends piquancy and liveliness to Shakespeare's prose but it also makes it difficult, and we need footnotes. In its similes, metaphors and linguistic figures, this passage of just over 300 words alludes to the period's urban topography, xenophobia, root-carving, animal lore, plant mythology, fashion, transport conventions, practices of prostitution, friendship vows, courtly tournaments, uses of eels, kinds of musical instrument, alchemical lore and cultural memories of medieval theatre. Falstaff is composed of a riot of discrete contemporary particulars; his prose seems gathered from the very air he, or his author, breathes. Shakespeare's genius is to have marshalled into just viable coherence what seems on the very point of atomization – so that Falstaff, lacking much in the way of interiority, appears instead to burst out everywhere in soliloquy as a kind of centrifugal linguistic event, an occasionally shaming display of semiotic belly. He is carnivalesque, like the also big-bellied Sancho Panza in Cervantes' *Don Quixote*, but *dangerously* so, since he has no conception whatever that the permissions he takes need ever be subject to limit. Not recognizing this is a major ethical blemish, and it receives its terrible punishment; but the lack of limitation in his prose, which supplies us with such intense satisfaction, seems itself to constitute a kind of counterweight, raising aesthetics almost to the power of an ethic. The prose of Falstaff's soliloquies may be the site of adverse judgement, but it's irresistible. Condemning himself out of his own mouth, he is also mouthing himself *almost* into a kind of forgiveness.

The soliloquies not written in blank verse or prose are fascinating but exceptional, and fascinating in some ways because they are exceptional. Soliloquies spoken by, among others, Costard, Romeo, Friar Laurence, the Helena of *A Midsummer Night's Dream*, Hermia, Pandarus, the Duke in *Measure for Measure*, the Helena of *All's Well That Ends Well* and Edgar are exclusively in couplets. *Macbeth* includes a soliloquy by the hero that is just a single couplet. It ends the scene in which Macbeth arranges Banquo's murder and addresses his absent intended victim: 'It is concluded: Banquo, thy soul's flight / If it find heaven, must find it out tonight' (3.1.143–4). The first and second soliloquies by the Chorus in *Romeo and Juliet* are sonnets, befitting the play's frequent alignment with and inclusion of sonnet form, notably the dialogue-in-sonnet of the lovers when they first meet in Act 1 Scene 5. The epilogue spoken by the Chorus of *Henry V* is also a sonnet. And Orlando speaks an attenuated sonnet-soliloquy (or a *dizain*) in *As You Like It*. Olivia, Viola and Sebastian in *Twelfth Night* all speak soliloquies in quatrains rhyming AABB. Pandarus in *Troilus and Cressida* speaks a soliloquy in a combination of prose and couplets, and the Duke in *Measure for Measure* voices one in octosyllabic couplets. Apemantus in *Timon of Athens* soliloquizes in a strange combination of verse and prose, which may well indicate that this soliloquy was written by Thomas Middleton rather than Shakespeare. Gower's final two choral soliloquies in *Pericles* differ from his earlier octosyllabic couplet soliloquies first with pentameter couplets and then with pentameters with alternating rhymes.

* Soliloquies offer their speakers the opportunity for self-reflection, as I say above; but they may also on occasion be self-reflexive. That's to say, the soliloquist may, in one way or another, show some awareness of himself or herself as a dramatic character.

Such soliloquies also take their place among the numerous references in the plays to the theatre itself: as medium, metaphor and, sometimes – when the play houses a play, a masquerade or a masque within itself – as a prominent element of the dramatic action, as happens, for instance, in *A Midsummer Night's Dream*, *Henry IV Part 1*, *Hamlet* and *The Tempest*.

Macbeth utters what is probably Shakespeare's most famous theatrical self-reference when he turns theatre into universal metaphor:

> Life's but a walking shadow, a poor player
> That struts and frets his hour upon the stage
> And then is heard no more. (5.5.22–4)

When Macbeth speaks these lines he is not, strictly speaking, uttering a soliloquy because Seyton, who has brought him the news of his wife's death, which prompts them, remains on stage while he speaks. Even so, Macbeth is by this point so turned inward upon himself as to make virtually all he says soliloquy, and his words are certainly not addressed to Seyton – although, given the pronunciation of the word 'Seyton', they may actually, and appropriately, be addressed to 'Satan'. Speaking them, Macbeth is also thinking at least as much of his own now inevitable death as he is of his wife's.

The soliloquy takes a self-reflexive turn too when Richard II begins one in the play's final act. Surprisingly, given the extent of his self-dramatization, this is Richard's sole soliloquy, but it's also one of the longest in Shakespeare, longer than any of Hamlet's:

> I have been studying how I may compare
> This prison where I live unto the world;
> And, for because the world is populous
> And here is not a creature but myself,
> I cannot do it. Yet I'll hammer it out. (5.5.1–5)

We already know from the dialogue of Exton and the servant that Richard is about to be murdered, and within sixty lines or so of completing this soliloquy he is dead. So his evocation of the workings of the vividly living imagination has great ironic power in retrospect. By studying to compare, Richard is dramatizing himself as a kind of poet, even a kind of 'metaphysical' poet (like John Donne), since his attempted comparison is so apparently inordinate. Throughout the play Richard has been an actor and, almost, the theatrical director of his own downfall; and later in this soliloquy he exhibits self-knowledge when he says, 'Thus play I in one person many people, / And none contented.' In its opening lines, though, just before he is brought to what he himself calls 'nothing', he sees himself not as an actor but as a writer, and an insistent, indefatigable one – so much so that the final line above, 'I cannot do it. Yet I'll hammer it out', seems almost a foreshadowing of the last words of Samuel Beckett's *The Unnamable* – 'I can't go on, I'll go on', that often cited twentieth-century statement of writerly remorselessness. Perhaps it's possible to see just behind the uncompromising urgency of Richard's words the implacable relentlessness of the writer William Shakespeare himself.

In quite a different register, Falstaff almost explodes theatrical illusion when he stabs the already dead Hotspur in *Henry IV, Part 1* so that he can boast about killing him and then very knowingly says, in a prose soliloquy direct to an audience, 'Nothing confutes me but eyes, and nobody sees me' (5.4.125–6), whereas the eyes of an audience are full upon him and every member of it is therefore able to confute him. The soliloquy has already toyed with meta-theatricality because Falstaff has played dead to save his skin (provoking a soliloquy from Hal) and then says he fears that the dead Hotspur next to him on stage will 'counterfeit too and rise', which is what the actor playing ('counterfeiting') Hotspur will in fact do as soon as the following scene ends. It's hardly a step away from this to the similarly subversive moment in Beckett's *Endgame* when Clov turns his telescope on the auditorium and says 'I see ... a multitude ... in transports ... of joy.' Shakespeare, like Beckett, understood the comic and subversive energies involved when the conventions of theatre are disrupted or flouted. And not only comic, of course – since by seeing Falstaff at this shocking and shaming moment we are judging him too, just as our laughter at Clov is checked by our knowledge of the desperate circumstances in which he finds himself. At such moments, Shakespeare may seem almost already aware not only of Beckett but of Bertolt Brecht's *Verfremdungseffekt* or 'alienation effect'; Brecht's work is frequently allusive to or influenced by Shakespeare. 'Brecht and Beckett', says Peter Brook in *The Empty Space*, his brilliant short book about the theatre, 'are both contained in Shakespeare'.

* Some soliloquies – probably at least the opening few lines of Macbeth's 'dagger' soliloquy and of the one that opens *Richard III*, and certainly some of Hamlet's – are exceptionally well known and will probably have been memorized by at least some members of most audiences. This makes them particularly difficult for actors to perform.

This was so as early as the eighteenth century. When Georg Christoph Lichtenberg saw David Garrick play Hamlet at the Theatre Royal, Drury Lane in 1775, he said of the 'To be or not to be' soliloquy that 'a large part of the audience not only knows it by heart as well as they do the Lord's Prayer, but listens to it, so to speak, as if it were a Lord's Prayer ... with a sense of solemnity and awe'. Alan Rickman, in his *Muse of Fire* interview, says that 'as soon as you start' a famous soliloquy 'a very weird hush happens in the house', and Anthony Sher in *Year of the King*, written while he was playing Richard III in Stratford in 1984, tells us that when he speaks the phrase 'Now is the winter …' he has 'the horrifying sense that if I pause at all here they will all join in and finish the line in chorus'. The director John Barton, who co-founded the Royal Shakespeare Company with Peter Hall in 1960, says in his book *Playing Shakespeare* that this is 'the hardest problem of all' for the actor of a Shakespearean soliloquy.

Coping with the fame of certain soliloquies is compounded for the actor by the need to handle also the fame of certain performances of them, and this is itself rendered even more intense by the permanence given to some performances by cinema. Anthony Sher talks about his early anxiety about one previous performance of Richard III in particular: 'Has Olivier done the part definitively? Surely not. Surely the greatness of the play is lessened if such a feat is possible? Surely contemporaries thought the same about Irving, Kean, even Branagh? The trouble is, Olivier put it on film.' He did so, however, in a way open to vigorous parody, an opening Peter Sellers royally took when he spoke the lyrics of The Beatles' 'A Hard Day's Night' in the TV show *The Music of Lennon and McCartney* (1965) as if performing a soliloquy by Olivier's Richard. Slumped (and humped) and dressed all in black, Sellers speaks direct to camera as, in closer and closer close-up, his intimacy becomes suggestive, drawing out to the point of absurdity what is only an implication in the Olivier manner. (You can view this at www.youtube.com/watch?v=zLEMncv140s.)

It's not unknown for actors performing soliloquies to hear members of the audience reciting along with them, not necessarily even *sotto voce*. Barton talks about the 'excessive reverence' that might impel such behaviour, but it might equally be the product of excessive self-regard. 'I've been in productions where they've had their books out,' said Noma Dumezweni in conversation with me, 'but *reciting*, that must be the nadir of horror.' Thinking about actors' methods of coping may be instructive about the nature of soliloquy, and in Part IV of this book some actors let us know how they manage.

An extreme method of trying to make the over-familiar strange again occurred when Jonathan Slinger, playing Hamlet for the RSC in 2013, came on stage singing Ken Dodd's inanely cheery song 'Happiness' ('the greatest gift that I possess') just before speaking the 'To be or not to be' soliloquy; Slinger talks about the rationale for this in Part III. The need to cope must also have been at least one of the motives for Benedict Cumberbatch's much-commented-upon speaking of this soliloquy at the very beginning of the play in the previews to the Barbican production in London in 2015 – although it was moved closer to its textual place in the run itself.

In fact, many other productions too have displaced this most famous of all soliloquies. Kenneth Branagh's screen version (1996) situates Hamlet (Branagh himself) in front of a two-way mirror behind which Claudius and

Polonius are watching. As he speaks, he moves menacingly forward, and on the phrase 'with a bare bodkin' draws his dagger from its sheath and brandishes it at the mirror. The voyeurs recoil in fear, and the moment foreshadows Hamlet's killing of Polonius behind the arras in his mother's bedroom. Here a soliloquy is spoken while the speaker is literally alone in a specific space but in fact intruded on by others viewing and listening in. This has its meta-textual implication too, since, voyeuristically listening in like this, Claudius and Polonius are doing what we, in the audience, always do when we watch and hear Shakespearean soliloquy. In the extremely violent scene with Ophelia (Kate Winslet) that follows, Hamlet rams her face against the mirror, and, in a reverse-angle shot, we see her cheek pressed against the glass, as we must assume the voyeurs themselves see it. Is theatre a form of violation, a kind of aggression?

Coping with over-familiarity is also one reason why directors of *Hamlet* may occasionally choose to use the first quarto rather than the canonic text. In that version, the too famous soliloquy disconcertingly begins 'To be or not to be I there's the point, / To Die, to sleep, is that all? I, all ...' It's almost as if the class dunce has failed to memorize accurately but is doing his best, nevertheless, under pressure, when called upon. But the first quarto version does in fact have attractions of its own. And it's just true that this soliloquy has become especially hard to *hear* in any production whatever, since most people in any audience are so very obviously *hearing it again*.

Michael Almereyda appears to take on exactly this difficulty in his screen version (2000) set in contemporary New York City. Like most Shakespeare movies, this one cuts a great deal of the play's dialogue, but, quite exceptionally, retains something at least of all Hamlet's soliloquies. We hear the 'To be or not to be' soliloquy, or something like it, not once but three times in the film: first, when a kind of TV psycho-therapist sanctimoniously spouts specious nonsense about what it means 'to be' ('it means to inter-be'); next, when Hamlet (Ethan Hawke) puts a gun to his head in footage apparently on his own computer screen and speaks the soliloquy's opening line; and finally when, first in voice-over and then in person, he speaks a great deal of the soliloquy in a video shop, walking down an aisle whose sections are labelled, again and again, 'ACTION' – the movie genre, that is, available on these shelves. This *mise-en-scène* insists that, even in the world of virtual reality in which this Hamlet spends so much of his time, everything is prompting him to 'act', to do the Ghost's bidding and exact revenge. What he in fact does is merely to stock up on 'action' movies. Watching them is a displacement activity while he remains inactive and 'acts' only in the sense of playing the fool – although this Hamlet does make his own video which becomes this movie's version of the play designed to 'catch the conscience of the king'. Almereyda's conceit *does* paradoxically renovate the almost impossible speech, even while the repetitions reveal how deeply both director and actor have internalized the near-impossibility of such a thing.

If coping with a well-educated, perhaps self-admiring, audience is 'the hardest problem' for the actor of a soliloquy, it's by no means the only one. The feats of memory called upon can be staggering: Richard of Gloucester has a soliloquy of seventy-one lines in *Henry VI, Part 3* and Richard II's is sixty-six lines long. Hamlet speaks seven soliloquies, totalling two hundred and fifteen lines.

Some actors have commented too on the fact that occasionally in performance the full force and brilliance of the words they are speaking in soliloquy will hit them properly for the first time, no matter how often they may have previously rehearsed or spoken the lines. This phenomenon is unlikely ever to have occurred to any member of an audience, I think, but it's not hard to see how disconcerting it might be for an actor.

During a long run, actors must also cope with repeating the most famous soliloquies many times, night after night. Some find this tedious – Richard Burton famously did – but others, such as Ben Kingsley, are wholly sanguine about it. In his *Muse of Fire* interview, he says that 'repetition's not a chore – it's another chance'. In Part III of this book the actors I interviewed have their say on this.

* Sometimes we may value a particular soliloquy not only or even primarily for its psychological and dramatic interest but simply because it contains an intensely memorable line or two. In this respect, the soliloquy may be judged to behave at least as much like a lyric poem as it does like the usual kinds of theatrical utterance.

An example occurs in a short soliloquy by Proteus in *The Two Gentlemen of Verona*, in which he reflects on his love for Julia, fearing that his father's discovery of it will put an end to it:

> O, how this spring of love resembleth
> The uncertain glory of an April day,
> Which now shows all the beauty of the sun,
> And by and by a cloud takes all away. (1.3.84–7)

These lines, which, isolated like this, may be read as a quatrain rhyming on its second and fourth lines, read ironically in retrospect, after Proteus has himself put an end to his love by falling for his best friend's love instead. So the lines do have their psychological and dramatic point. The metaphor that makes love a spring awakening is conventional, but Shakespeare superbly raises it above convention in the intensely memorable even if entirely simple phrase 'The uncertain glory of an April day'. It's possible that this line was in James Joyce's mind when he had Leopold Bloom in the 'Hades' episode of *Ulysses* remark that 'the sky is as uncertain as a child's bottom', bringing Shakespeare down to earth on a June day in a Dublin cemetery. It's certain that it was in T. S. Eliot's when he revised it to quite different effect in his sequence 'Ash-Wednesday' with the phrase 'The infirm glory of the positive hour', inclining meteorology towards metaphysics.

A further instance is Troilus's brief soliloquy on sexual anticipation as he waits for Pandarus to bring Cressida to him in *Troilus and Cressida*, which opens, 'I am giddy; expectation whirls me round' (3.2.16–27). The sexual ache, which is as much a matter of a rather specialized form of anxiety as it is of desire, is captured with mounting intensity as the soliloquy proceeds. The lines 'Th' imaginary relish is so sweet / That it enchants my sense' (3.2.17–18) make it clear why Keats was so devoted to this play. His long poem 'The Eve of St Agnes' includes memorable stanzas on sexual anticipation, uses the word 'enchantment' and conveys implied sexual merging as a 'solution sweet'. The opening of 'Ode to a Nightingale' – 'My heart aches and a drowsy numbness pains / My sense' – may also echo Troilus here.

That Shakespearean soliloquies may be considered almost stand-alone lyric poems is sometimes ascribed to the influence of Romantic interpretations, and these have certainly had huge impact on their literary and critical reception, as I explain in Part II, but I think there is also something inherent in some of them that prompts this kind of reaction. It's as though, while the soliloquist remains in character, something larger than his or her own immediate concerns at the moment of utterance breaks the surface of speech and gets itself expressed in a supremely memorable perfection of language.

* There are some instances in Shakespearean theatre of monologues by characters speaking alone on stage that should probably not be classified as soliloquies.

The Herald in Act 2 Scene 2 of *Othello*, alone on stage, gets a scene to himself to proclaim Othello's licensing of a 'liberty of feasting' to celebrate both the defeat of the Turkish fleet and his own marriage. The feasting is responsible for Cassio's drunkenness and its appalling consequences. So the proclamation, which can be played as if addressed to us as audience, has a clear dramatic point, but this is entirely a matter of plot and not of thought or attitude. The Herald is a cipher rather than a character, so this is scarcely to be accounted a soliloquy.

Lance's superb comic monologues (in prose) with – and about – his dog Crab in *The Two Gentlemen of Verona* seem anecdotal, self-contained and addressed to the audience in a way that both recalls the direct audience address of medieval mystery and morality plays and anticipates contemporary stand-up comedy. Playing the crowd, and getting the dog to play the crowd too – by raising or wagging its tail at an appropriate point, for instance – Lance invites and cajoles an audience and solicits response: 'Look you ...'; 'Nay, I'll show you the manner of it ...'; 'You shall judge ...' These monologues may have been adaptations of routines by the comic actor Will Kemp, a member of Shakespeare's theatre company, who would have played Lance. Unlike soliloquy, they seem wholly directed outward rather than inwardly attentive.

Wolfgang Clemen, however, considers the monologue in Act 2 Scene 3 ('Nay, 'twill be this hour ere I have done weeping') a soliloquy because it's organically integrated into the play's structure, if not its plot, by offering an ironic perspective on the main action of the lovers. What Lance regards as the heartless behaviour of his dog is, Clemen thinks, an oblique comment on Proteus's behaviour to Julia. Inheriting the Italian *commedia del arte* tradition of the sly servant accompanied by an animal, the speech is 'a milestone in the development of Shakespeare's dramatic art'. It's certainly a great speech, and I have seen it performed hilariously, but I am not sure that many readers or audiences would pick up the ironizing analogy Clemen proposes. My own view is that the speech is better considered a comic monologue than a soliloquy proper, and therefore an addition to the range of Shakespearean dramatic forms. Lance has a true soliloquy later in the play when he lets us know that he loves a woman he will not name – although he still has dogs in mind, telling us that 'She hath more qualities than a water-spaniel, which is much in a bare Christian' (3.1.267–8). We can regard this as structurally integrated, if structural integration is what we seek, because it parallels similar declarations of love earlier by Valentine and Proteus, and later Proteus has a soliloquy in which he says of his self-demeaning attitude to Silvia that 'spaniel-like, the more she spurns my love / The more it grows and fawneth on her still' (4.2.14–15).

* There are some soliloquies in Shakespeare that should be thought of rather as 'soliloquies'. That is, they are written for particular play-within-a-play situations and are therefore wholly or partly pastiche, parody or burlesque. As such, however, they may be revealing about Shakespeare's understanding of the nature of soliloquy.

In Part II I look at the parody soliloquies in the mechanicals' play in *A Midsummer Night's Dream*. In the play Hamlet calls *The Mousetrap* Lucianus speaks a brief soliloquy in couplets before pouring poison in the sleeping king's ear. It's a very Senecan monologue, of a deliberately old-fashioned kind, and it includes a reference to Hecate – as does Macbeth's 'dagger' soliloquy, in a play written six years after *Hamlet*, as we saw above. Thinking about the mechanicals' play in Part II, I offer a view of Shakespeare's 'ironic' imagination. We may have another example here, where a souped-up Senecan rhetoric written as a form of imitation in one play eventually becomes subdued to a more genuinely startling, even terrifying, psychological effect in another.

* Soliloquies often include hints or virtual instructions as to how they should be played; they offer indications of gesture, expression or even stage direction.

For instance, among a random selection from the soliloquies I quote earlier in this section, the actor playing Macbeth is instructed by the 'Is this a dagger ...?' soliloquy to attempt to clutch a non-existent dagger and then to draw an actual dagger from its scabbard; the actor playing Richard of Gloucester in the 'I'll drown more sailors' soliloquy is probably instructed to make some attempt to mime the 'plucking down' of a dagger; and Iachimo in the 'She hath been reading late' passage is plainly instructed to move towards the trunk when he says 'To th' trunk again'.

These may seem obvious elements of soliloquy, and this may even seem a trivial point, but noticing such things emphasizes how soliloquies are intensely theatrical in their conception, purpose and effect – although, as we shall see in Part II, they have often been read as literary rather than dramatic occurrences. Soliloquies in Shakespeare are always keyed to event – 'event' in the sense of action, but also in Hamlet's sense of 'outcome'. Their rhetoric has consequence, both for the immediacy of stage action and for the further direction of plot – as well as, of course, for our sense of character, psychology and emotion.

PART II

Soliloquies in theory

1. Now I am alone

When Rosencrantz, Guildenstern, Polonius and the Players leave him in Act 2 Scene 2 of *Hamlet*, the hero conveys intense relief in what is, in effect, a self-addressed stage direction. 'Now I am alone', he says, and launches into his second, self-castigating soliloquy, 'O what a rogue and peasant slave am I!' Speaking while alone on stage, in the solitude of self-confrontation, is typically taken as the sure signal of soliloquy, and editorial stage directions usually use Hamlet's word 'alone' to define the soliloquist's situation. The editors of the Arden 3 *Richard III*, for instance, open the play with the stage direction '*Enter* RICHARD, Duke of Gloucester, *alone*' before printing the text of one of the most famous of all Shakespearean soliloquies – and the only one that actually opens one of his plays – 'Now is the winter of our discontent ...' The word used in the Folio and quarto editions of the play, however, is '*solus*', the Latin for 'alone'. Combined with 'loqui', the Latin deponent infinitive for the verb 'to speak', this forms the word *soliloquium*, which gives us the English 'soliloquy'. Shakespeare relishes the word 'solus' in *Henry V* when the fractious Nym says to Pistol 'Will you shog off? I would have you *solus*.' Pistol, misunderstanding, returns the word as a curse: '*Solus*, egregious dog? O viper vile! / The *solus* in thy most marvailous face, / The *solus* in thy teeth, and in thy throat ...' (2.1.45–8). Although Shakespeare knew the word *solus*, however, he did not know that what he was writing for Hamlet and Richard III and for so many other characters in his plays were 'soliloquies'.

The word is first recorded by the *OED* in 1613 in the third edition of the lexicographer Robert Cawdrey's *A Table Alphabet*, although in fact it has recently been traced further back. Usually regarded as the first English dictionary, the *Alphabet* defines soliloquy as 'private talke'. The word *soliloquium* was first used by Augustine in his *Liber Soliloquiorum* (*Book of Soliloquies*) in the fourth century AD, which was freely translated into Old English under Alfred in the ninth century. In Augustine, however, the word means not 'speaking alone', but entering into a particular kind of dialogue – between the soul and God, for instance, or between different faculties of the mind itself, such as the reason and will. The word *soliloquium* in medieval England, therefore, had specifically religious connotations and was associated with prayer and private meditation. This usage of the English 'soliloquy' persists as far as the eighteenth century – witness a title published in 1738, *Devout Exercises of the Heart in Meditation and Soliloquy*. The connection between prayer and Shakespearean soliloquy has been considered significant, and I discuss it further below; and, as I pointed out in Part I, some soliloquies are the dramatic representations of prayers.

By the time of the Restoration, however, the word had also come to have its fully modern theatrical sense. In 1693, in the 'Epistle Dedicatory' to his play *The Double Dealer*, William Congreve tells us what we are to understand by it: 'When a Man in Soliloquy reasons with himself ... we ought not to imagine that this Man either talks to us, or to himself; he is only thinking, and thinking such Matter as were inexcusable Folly in him to speak.' Congreve's definition was formulated only many years after Shakespeare wrote his soliloquies, by a dramatist writing very different kinds of plays from Shakespeare's own. Together with the crucial fact that Shakespeare would not have thought of such speeches in his own plays as 'soliloquies', this should alert us to the possibility that he may have meant something very different by them. As we shall see, whether Shakespearean soliloquy is to be regarded as 'only thinking' has been a contentious issue in the history of its understanding and reception. Even so, the subsequent literary influence of Shakespearean soliloquy has tended strongly to reinforce Congreve's concept of the soliloquy as the representation of thought.

This is especially true of the effect of Hamlet's soliloquies, which became for Romantics and Modernists alike the epitome of interiority and self-consciousness, a model for the way the self can become wholly absorbing. Probably the most notable example is the voluble, intensely self-analytical and procrastinating Samuel Taylor Coleridge saying in 1827 that 'I have a smack of Hamlet myself, if I may say so', but other autobiographical essays and letters of the Romantic period demonstrate comparable self-identification. The essential privacy of individual experience in Romantic literature – whose acme in Wordsworth John Keats identified as the 'egotistical sublime' – led these writers to privilege the private reading of Shakespeare over public performance. This may be regarded as the ultimate consequence of eighteenth-century editorial practice as it developed with the poet Alexander Pope, who suppressed the plays' theatricality in favour of their literary qualities. Although he did systematically add act and scene divisions, Pope signposted in the margins what he called the plays' 'most shining passages', many of which occurred in soliloquies. He also compiled indexes to 'Thoughts, or Sentiments' and accompanied his text with a 'Table of the most considerable [speeches] in *Shakespear*'. The editorial tendency was to place emphasis on descriptive and narrative passages that might act as the equivalent of stand-alone poems or set pieces. William Dodd's anthology *The Beauties of Shakespeare: Regularly Selected from Each Play* (1752) further popularized the tendency, presenting Shakespeare less as a dramatist than as a kind of guide to human nature.

The Romantic preference for the private reading of Shakespeare over seeing plays in performance is clear in Charles Lamb's famous contention that *King Lear* is unperformable. In his essay 'On the Tragedies of Shakespeare, considered with reference to their fitness for stage representation' (1811), he also says that he is 'utterly unable to appreciate that celebrated soliloquy in *Hamlet*, beginning "To be or not to be", or to tell whether it be good, bad, or indifferent, it has been so handled and pawed about by declamatory boys and men, and torn so inhumanly from its living place and principle of continuity in the play, till it is become to me a perfect dead member'. Since for the Romantics the imagination was the most significant aesthetic factor in both the writing and reading of poetry, Shakespeare's characters, and notably his tragic heroes and heroines, were to be more adequately encountered on the page than the stage, to be better absorbed from a text than from the performance of an actor in a theatre. Soliloquies may well seem more the representation of thought when silently read than when heard in an actor's voice. The Romantic prejudice persists into the later nineteenth century and beyond: A. C. Bradley in *Shakespearean Tragedy* (1904) treats the plays almost as if they are Victorian novels, and says explicitly that the force of certain passages 'can be felt only by a reader'.

Soliloquy, then, came to seem far less (or even not at all) a rhetorical construction of personality and far more the representation of an inviolable interiority. Read in this way – as interiority, as the representation of thought and as the instrument of imaginative empathy – the Shakespearean soliloquy feeds into the revolutionary forms of Romantic literature themselves. It has an impact on Romantic odes, notably those of John Keats, including 'Ode to a Nightingale', on Coleridge's 'conversation poems', such as 'Frost at Midnight' and 'This Lime-Tree Bower My Prison' and on the Wordsworthian and Byronic subjective adaptations or subversions of epic, including *The Prelude* (which remained unpublished, however, in Wordsworth's lifetime) and *Childe Harold's Pilgrimage*, those epics of the self, of the 'egotistical sublime' in process and action.

The Shakespearean soliloquy may even have been influential on Jane Austen's development of experimental techniques for the depiction of consciousness. Moving the novel further towards psychological maturity, she wrote in forms of what has been called 'free indirect speech', in which third-person narrator and the character's individual perceiving consciousness appear to merge. At one point in *Emma* (1815) the word 'soliloquy' is used to describe the heroine's empathetic imagining of the unease of her close friend Mrs Weston: '"My dear, dear, anxious friend," – said she, in mental soliloquy' (Book II, ch. V). In *Mansfield Park* (1814), a novel that imaginatively represents a debate between the conflicting ethics of the novel and of drama, Fanny Price's reflections after receiving a vitally significant letter from Edmund, the man she loves, are defined as 'soliloquies' (Book III, ch. xii), and in the same novel Henry Crawford, after reading *Henry VIII* aloud, says that 'Shakespeare one gets acquainted with without knowing how', to which Edmund replies 'we all talk Shakespeare' (Book III, ch. iii). In *Sense and Sensibility* (1811) we hear that three of the main characters have been reading *Hamlet* aloud together and in *Persuasion*

(1818) characters discuss *Childe Harold's Pilgrimage*. Austen's use of the word 'soliloquy' with its significant qualifier 'mental' in *Emma* suggests that she is transposing or appropriating it from its by then customary usage in relation to theatrical performance, but it may also imply that soliloquies spoken aloud on the Regency stage were well understood as the representation of thought too.

Subsequently, nineteenth-century poets – prominently Tennyson and Browning – invented the dramatic monologue, the most significant form introduced into the poetry of the period, largely in response to Shakespearean soliloquy. Designed to objectify, by dramatizing, the lyric impulse at a moment when, for various reasons, verse drama itself had become virtually impossible for poets, dramatic monologue is a form in which a named character speaks at some length in a way that defines his or her personality or disposition. The reader may respond with some sympathy, but this will usually be tempered, sometimes very severely indeed, by adverse judgement, as we come to realize that we are listening, in some cases, to speakers identifying in themselves, without their realizing it, forms of pathology or criminality. The speaker in dramatic monologue also addresses an implied interlocutor, characterized in some way but usually unnamed. So the Shakespearean soliloquies that most interested these poets were those with a strong implied dialogic element, such as Hamlet's 'O, what a rogue and peasant slave am I' in which he asks 'Who calls me villain? Breaks my pate across?' almost as if expecting a reply. Browning's 'Caliban upon Setebos' explicitly acknowledges the debt by deriving its characterful speaker and his situation from *The Tempest*, in a dramatic monologue concerned with 'natural theology' in the years immediately succeeding the publication of Darwin's *Origin of Species*.

Dramatic monologues such as these were highly significant in the formation of Anglo-American modernism, since both T. S. Eliot and Ezra Pound adapted them to their own purposes in their early work. Eliot was also deeply influenced by late nineteenth-century French symbolism, including the work of Stéphane Mallarmé and Jules Laforgue, in which Hamlet is a significant figure. Combining elements of that with the dramatic monologue, he invented the dramatic *interior* monologue of poems such as 'The Love Song of J. Alfred Prufrock' (1915), in which the Shakespearean connection is implied when its hero, forlornly ruminating, makes a self-undermining comparison – one that slyly introduces, in the two words which end its opening line, a reference to the most famous of all soliloquies:

> No! I am not Prince Hamlet, nor was meant to be,
> Am an attendant lord, one that will do
> To start a progress, swell a scene or two ...

Advising us in the passage initiated by these lines, despite the disclaimer, that something of Hamlet's soliloquizing inheres in these early twentieth-century lines of internal reverie too, Prufrock moves Hamlet's incapacity for action to a wholly new depth of languid inertia. Subsequently, *The Waste Land* (1922) may be read as a series of interlocking dramatic monologues or soliloquies, and it's also densely allusive to Shakespeare. Partly in response, W. H. Auden, in his poetic sequence *The Sea and the Mirror* (1944), has Eliot as well as Shakespeare in mind when he designs it as a set of soliloquies spoken by various characters in *The Tempest*.

The Shakespearean soliloquy had a strong impact too on modernist fiction. James Joyce developed certain French narrative models into the hugely influential technique of the 'stream of consciousness' in *Ulysses* (1922), but *Hamlet*, and especially its hero's soliloquies, is also a prominent element of that invention. *Ulysses* frequently alludes to the play, and one of its three major protagonists, Stephen Dedalus, is, like Hamlet, dressed in mourning throughout the long day on which *Ulysses* is set and wears what he calls a 'Hamlet hat'. More importantly, he is also revealed in his interior monologues, or in the stream of his consciousness, as having, like Coleridge, a smack of Hamlet about him too, in his relentlessly intellectual self-debate; one of the novel's episodes, that known as 'Scylla and Charybdis', represents a discussion of Shakespeare in the National Library of Ireland in Dublin in which *Hamlet* is especially prominent.

With the rise of theatrical naturalism in the nineteenth century in such writers as Ibsen and Chekhov, the stylization of soliloquy was no longer a feasible dramatic option; but when it to some extent returns in theatre, it does so in a self-aware and ironic way in work influenced by both Eliot and Joyce. In Samuel Beckett's *Endgame* (1957), the self-reflexive Hamm (whose name must derive in part from the name 'Hamlet') is sardonic but also elegiac about soliloquy, aware that he is about to use a long-outmoded theatrical convention:

> *Hamm:* Did anyone ever have pity on me?
> *Clov:* What? (*Pause.*) Is it me you're referring to?
> *Hamm (angrily):* An aside, ape! Did you never hear an aside before? (*Pause.*) I'm warming up for my last soliloquy.

This is also witty about the convention of theatrical aside, which Hamm's question 'Did you never hear an aside before?' exposes *as* mere convention. The question is sublimely redundant. *Obviously*, he never heard an aside before, because he is a character in a play, not a member of its audience, and although everyone in the theatre can, of course, hear an aside it's assumed that only the audience does. (Even so, there are, as we saw in Part I, moments in Shakespeare when characters almost overhear asides.)

Comparably, *Krapp's Last Tape* (1958) is newly inventive and exploratory with soliloquy, restoring it to a novel form of theatrical life. Alone on stage, the play's hero and sole character listens, on a reel-to-reel tape recorder, to a soliloquy – a spoken diary entry – recorded thirty years earlier, on his 39th birthday. He then records a new soliloquy commenting on the old one. By adapting to original dramatic purpose what was at the time a relatively recent (and is now a long defunct) technological innovation, Beckett discovers new possibilities of gravity and pathos in soliloquy by making it a retrospective possibility. Listening to his earlier self, Krapp's 'I' becomes, briefly, 'he', in a version of the Shakespearean 'illeism' I discussed in Part I, and Krapp irritably fast-forwards the tape when he finds his younger self sententious or declamatory, in a mode long sanctioned by theatrical soliloquy. There are ways in which it can be useful to think of Shakespearean soliloquists as 'overhearing' themselves when they speak, but they cannot literally *hear* themselves, as Beckett's Krapp can, dramatizing the sad intermittences of personality and desire.

The fact that the heritage of Shakespearean soliloquy, developed from Romantic readings of it, should be so strongly literary, rather than purely theatrical, may seem less remarkable if we credit the argument advanced in Lukas Erne's book *Shakespeare as Literary Dramatist*: that Shakespeare wrote at least his histories and tragedies for the published page as well as for the stage, in a culture changing during his lifetime from a predominantly oral to a prominently literary one. This is, Erne thinks, the reason why plays such as *Romeo and Juliet*, *Henry V* and *Hamlet* exist in radically different shorter and longer versions, the former playable within what *Romeo and Juliet* calls 'the two hours' traffic of our stage' and the latter intended for a readership in the study rather than an audience in the theatre. Erne suggests that the versions addressed to readers offer greater complexity and ambiguity of characterization and encourage more attention to style and nuance. Shakespeare is to be considered, he argues, an author of published drama from 1598 on, when his name appeared on the title pages of his printed plays and when Francis Meres, in *Palladis Tamia*, classified him almost at the top of an English literary canon. Although by no means everyone has been persuaded by Erne's argument, the fact that certain Shakespearean soliloquies have been absorbed so deeply into some major subsequent literature may suggest that later writers of non-dramatic texts have at least intuitively sensed some purely literary as well as dramatic possibility in them, and have benefited from the intuition.

Given such cases of literary and theatrical inheritance – and many others could be adduced too – it's impossible to divorce any consideration of Shakespearean soliloquy from the history of its reception.

*

When a Shakespearean soliloquist says 'Now I am alone', or when Shakespeare himself or an editor says that Richard III enters 'solus', the assertion is not unproblematic. It can sometimes seem that almost anyone at any time in Shakespeare is likely to behave essentially as if he or she is alone, speaking in front of others as though withdrawn into private reflection, moving from dialogue into monologue and sometimes becoming increasingly distracted from the situation at hand while the monologue transgresses all obvious limits.

At the beginning of Act 3 Scene 1 of *Measure for Measure*, the Duke counsels Claudio, under sentence of death, to adopt a fortifying attitude to mortality, advising him to 'Be absolute for death' and to 'reason' with life. Then, just a couple of lines into his speech, he continues to address an implicitly personified 'life' for forty further lines, in exactly the way a soliloquist would. Later in the scene, Claudio himself responds to Isabella's comparable counselling with a fifteen-line speech beginning 'Ay, but to die, and go we know not where' in which he expresses his terrified inability to take any such advice. His devastating meditation on the actualities of death becomes increasingly self-absorbed, in the way a soliloquy would, rather than dialogically directed – which is, of course, given Claudio's plight, psychologically entirely credible. That these are two of the most famous speeches in Shakespeare emphasizes their memorably soliloquy-like nature. They follow closely on Isabella's own soliloquy at the end of the previous scene, beginning 'To whom should I complain?', making it seem that this whole passage of *Measure for Measure* presents characters insulated in introspection rather than inter-related in conversational exchange.

The same might be said of the dialogues between Lear and the Fool in *King Lear*, where 'dialogue' is in effect a form of joint monologue, as they talk at cross-purposes and as Lear's self-absorption makes manifest his derangement, just as the actual soliloquies spoken by the hero in *Timon of Athens* do. In *Shakespeare Our Contemporary* Jan Kott thinks of Lear and the Fool as playing out an existential *folie-à-deux* like that of Vladimir and Estragon in Beckett's *Waiting for Godot* or Hamm and Clov in *Endgame*; Beckett may well have had Lear and the Fool in mind in the composition of both plays. Lear has no true soliloquies in the play, but when he speaks as though he is soliloquizing he creates a space for the ignored Fool to become, in effect, a kind of chorus, commenting on him. Their dialogue therefore consists not so much of speeches between them as of the acerbic verbal friction between two recognizable types of Shakespearean soliloquist, the madman and the chorus, who just happen to have coincided for once. Grigori Kozintsev's film version (1971) draws out some of these implications when he makes Lear's dialogue seem soliloquy – by isolating him inside a carriage as he speaks while the Fool is tethered to its axle, for instance, and when Lear's 'O, reason not the need!' speech, addressed in the text to Goneril and Regan, becomes an actual cinematic soliloquy, addressed only to the skies. When Beckett's odd couples speak more *at* than *to* each other, then, as if soliloquizing in front of each other, Lear and the Fool seem to be within earshot.

A large percentage of what Richard II says sounds like soliloquy, although, as I said in Part I, he has in fact only one soliloquy in the entire play, spoken just before his death. In one scene alone, Act 3 Scene 2, after his return from Ireland, he has several speeches nominally addressed to

Aumerle that would be mistaken for soliloquies if published out of context. The one beginning 'Needs must I like it well' apostrophizes the English earth at extravagant length, and the one opening 'No matter where. Of comfort no man speak!' is a brilliantly self-pitying meditation on 'the hollow crown / That rounds the mortal temples of a king' (3.2.160–1). These speeches are magnificent, but magnificently narcissistic too, and to soliloquize in front of others is to dramatize one's own self-dramatization.

In *The Merchant of Venice* Shylock has speeches that also sound like soliloquies, not because he is self-dramatizing, but because his self-involvement seems to reflect and distil his alienation, as a Jew, from the Christian world he so perilously inhabits. His consciousness is sealed into an envelope of isolation by his identity, his religion and the despised (but, to this society, wholly necessary) trade of moneylending in which he engages.

And who is Mercutio (whom Shakespeare invented out of a few sentences in his source) speaking to in the astonishing Queen Mab speech in *Romeo and Juliet* (1.4.53–94), with its great fireworks display of rhetorical figures? He begins by addressing Romeo in response to his teasingly paradoxical and punning, but also ominous, declaration that lovers 'lie' in bed asleep 'while they do dream things true', telling him that Queen Mab is 'the fairies' midwife' who controls peoples' dreams. But then the vividness of his evocation of the fairy queen and her magical night-time transformations seems to transport him from all immediate company into a self-entranced reverie, as though he is himself dreaming while awake. Romeo can stop him, forty-three lines later, only by interrupting him while still in full flow. 'Peace, peace, Mercutio, peace, / Thou talk'st of nothing' (1.4.95–6), he says, identifying him by name for the first time and suddenly replacing the macho banter of their earlier dialogue with yearning tenderness. While Romeo's desperate repetitions suggest his anxiety about Mercutio's loquacious rapture, the word 'nothing' is probably a *double entendre* (for 'vagina') provoked by the characteristically suggestive culmination of Mercutio's speech. Using the word, Romeo seems himself to have been briefly caught up into Mercutio's trance.

In Franco Zeffirelli's screen version (1968), John McEnery's neurotically febrile Mercutio appears to become almost demented as he speaks, as if propelled out of himself by his own wayward words, his voice echoing around an Italian piazza. When he stops speaking he embraces and then casts a long, lingering look at Romeo (Leonard Whiting), who returns it. This implies that Mercutio's uncontainable or hysterical loquacity is the product of homoerotic interest in his friend – an interpretation influential on subsequent theatrical productions and on Baz Luhrmann's film *William Shakespeare's Romeo + Juliet* (1996) in which the speech becomes a wild, drug-induced tirade by a Mercutio (Harold Perrineau) wearing flimsily spectacular drag. He must be coaxed down from his frenzied and increasingly fraught state by a pleading Romeo (Leonardo DiCaprio) grown pale with apprehension. Appropriately, Mercutio's rhetorical fireworks are complemented in the movie by an actual display of fireworks, with its inevitably orgasmic connotations, on 'Verona Beach', the setting of this hallucinatory episode – a kind of Venice Beach, California, blowing its mind.

These are all notable cases of characters speaking as if alone in soliloquy while they are in fact in company. A further, truly impressive one does not, like these, emerge from any exacerbated or elated state of being, but just from routine social business. In Act 1 Scene 2 of *All's Well That Ends Well*, Bertram is introduced to the King of France, who had been an intimate friend of his late father. Noting that Bertram now looks just like him – although he proves to be nothing whatever like him in character – the king begins a magnanimous eulogy, which is also an elegy. Only briefly interrupted by Bertram, this lasts over forty lines, during which the king seems almost wholly abstracted into reverie and retrospect. The speech is Shakespeare's most comprehensively sympathetic testimony to the realities of aging, the melancholy effects of even consolatory memory and the enrichment of reliable affection between male friends.

That it seems, in its unpredictable surge of emotional surplus, exactly like a soliloquy, although it is not, is attested by tributes paid to it by the poets Ted Hughes and John Berryman. Hughes reads it as possessing almost a form of self-consciousness, as if 'the play itself is thinking ... searching among all possible images for new images of itself, and trying them on', and Berryman calls it 'this protracted marvel of ungovernable re-creation and mourning, richer ... than Dante's of Brunetto'. This is extraordinarily high praise, since the passage of Dante that Berryman has in mind is the fifteenth canto of the *Inferno* in which the poet meets his old teacher Brunetto Latini in hell. It's a passage whose poignancy has inspired many subsequent poets to acts of translation or emulation. Berryman's observation also suggests how a single Shakespearean speech – coming almost, it seems, out of nowhere – may occasionally appear a total revelation of character, motive or circumstance, in the manner of the speeches in Dante's *Commedia*. Hughes's almost vitalist view that at such times a Shakespearean play may seem itself to be thinking is also worth bearing in mind when considering soliloquies, and Berryman's word 'ungovernable' is exactly right for one effect produced by some soliloquies – that the characters speaking them are barely in control of their utterance, or become surprised by where their words are taking them.

Although the King of France in *All's Well* is not a soliloquist speaking alone on stage, then, he is still undoubtedly speaking something like a soliloquy. This makes it plain that Shakespearean soliloquy is the adaptation and greater concentration of some forms of psychological and linguistic manner already operative in Shakespeare's dialogue. Soliloquies emerge naturally out of Shakespearean characterization, out of the understanding that to be human is inevitably to be locked into one's own consciousness, or that communication itself is fraught with the risk that anyone might slip at any moment from public discourse into private reverie – might become, as Macbeth does in front of Banquo, who points it out, as we have seen, 'rapt' in rumination.

In the film *Withnail & I* (1987), written and directed by Bruce Robinson (who in his youth played Benvolio in the Zeffirelli *Romeo and Juliet*), two 'resting' actors realize in their own lives a version of an abiding Shakespearean preoccupation – that of male friendship, with, in this case, undercurrents of competitive envy and repressed homoerotic attraction. 'Playing the Dane' is a motif in the film, and it sometimes employs the cinematic soliloquy convention of voice-over to represent the thoughts of the unnamed 'I' character (Paul McGann). In the movie's final scene, the alcoholic Withnail (Richard E. Grant) – alone, drunk and weeping in the rain – voices, in front of a pen of not manifestly appreciative London Zoo wolves, Hamlet's 'What a piece of work is a man' speech. In the play, this is delivered in dialogue with Rosencrantz and Guildenstern, whom Hamlet recognizes as false friends. Its use as an entirely credible soliloquy makes for a wonderfully appropriate, universalizing, ironic and melancholy ending to Robinson's movie. Michael Almereyda's screen version of *Hamlet* (2000), probably in homage to *Withnail and I*, opens with the hero (Ethan Hawke) also treating 'What a piece of work is a man' as a soliloquy: he watches himself speaking it on a computer screen in front of images of war. The speech's original lurch from Renaissance–humanist exaltation to cynical deflation now becomes dejectedly satirical postmodern *anomie*.

*

For a soliloquist to say 'Now I am alone' is problematic in another, more obvious, way because the speaker – the actor who speaks – is of course not alone at all, but in a theatre in front of an audience. Apparently speaking to him or herself, the soliloquist is overheard by many. What exactly, or even approximately, this transaction involves has been the subject of a great deal of debate, and at different times in its history the Shakespearean soliloquy has been very differently understood, played and staged. It's remarkable how little common agreement there is about what soliloquy is, or what it represents. I offer here an account of its origins and some of its occasions and effects, without at all claiming that it can be reduced to a set of usable or workable conventions.

So: where did Shakespearean soliloquy come from? What is Shakespeare likely to have had in mind when he wrote speeches for characters to deliver while alone, or believing themselves to be alone, on stage?

2. Origins

i. Medieval

The very structure of the Elizabethan playhouse was adapted from the religious staging of medieval mystery plays. The roof above the performers was known as 'the heavens' and the area under the stage, at least in a stage direction in Thomas Heywood's *The Silver Age*, as 'hell'. Although that term was not uniformly or invariably used to designate any one part of the playhouse's structure, the platform stage was symbolically understood as the earth itself, positioned between heaven and hell. It's worth bearing this in mind when references to 'heaven' and 'hell' occur in Shakespeare's plays. When Macbeth speaks the final line and a half of the 'dagger' soliloquy on which I commented in Part I, for instance – 'it is a knell / That summons thee to heaven, or to hell' – the Elizabethan actor may have gestured towards the roof or canopy above him and the under-stage below or the 'discovery space' behind (a famous stage direction in Marlowe's *Doctor Faustus* indicates that 'hell is discovered', which presumably required the drawing back of the curtain in front of that space). The metaphysical significance of Macbeth's soliloquy would therefore have been dramatized as a theatrical event too and the early modern world in which earth, heaven and hell were ontological categories was mapped on to the theatrical space itself. 'Mapping' is the appropriate metaphor because, at least for the duration of the play, the world had become, in the universalizing name for the most famous of the spaces in which Shakespeare's plays were performed, the theatre called the 'Globe' – the place which the Chorus in *Henry V* calls, in a soliloquy, 'this wooden O'.

It's hardly surprising, then, that Shakespeare's plays occasionally reveal an inheritance from the native English drama which preceded Elizabethan theatre – from, that is, both mystery and morality plays. These characteristically employ soliloquies by allegorical characters such as Mercy, Mankind, Everyman, Age and Conscience, and by God and the Devil. The soliloquies are directed to and intended to involve the audience, because the plays are a means of theological or moral instruction, guidance in the means of salvation. The dramatic struggle of opposites – between allegorical figures of good and evil – draws on a tradition of *psychomachia*, of representations of 'the conflict of the soul' initiated by a Latin poem of that title by the fourth-century Christian author Prudentius. In the late medieval morality play *Mankind*, for instance, the title character introduces himself, in soliloquy, like this:

My name is Mankind. I have my composition
Of a body and of a soul, of condition contrary.
Betwix them twain is a great division;
He that should be subject, now he hath the victory.

The play's plot subsequently charts the course of the battle – the plot *is* the psychomachia. This explicitly didactic, morally corrective and exemplary form of theatre has a close connection with the sacrament of Penance, in which individuals confess their sins and are absolved of them by a priest. The audience is addressed as if it's another character in the drama and is conceived of either as humankind in general, as it might be by a priest in a sermon, or as if in a specific situation, when it's summoned into the dramatic action – to witness an execution, for instance, or to hear a proclamation.

Although nurtured by the orthodoxies of Catholicism and reflective of its sacramental system, the mystery and morality plays survived the Reformation long enough to become part of the cultural memory of Elizabethan audiences. In the drama performed at the time Shakespeare began to write, we encounter some clear legacies from medieval psychomachia. In Christopher Marlowe's *Doctor Faustus*, first performed in 1594, the Good and Evil Angels struggling over Faustus's soul are a direct inheritance from allegorical characterizations. In some of Shakespeare's soliloquies, a comparable conflict or psychomachia is internalized and sophisticatedly transformed into the expression of perturbed emotion and psychology. Such 'confessional' soliloquies as those of Angelo in *Measure for Measure* and Claudius in *Hamlet*, for instance, which I discussed in Part I, may be regarded in this way. So too, in comic vein, may the soliloquy of the Clown Lancelet Giobbe (as Arden 3 names the character customarily known as Gobbo) at the opening of Act 2 Scene 2 of *The Merchant of Venice*. Trying to decide whether to desert his current master Shylock, he reports a debate between his 'conscience' and 'the fiend': '"Budge," says the fiend. "Budge not," says my conscience.' Eventually deciding that 'my conscience is but a kind of hard conscience', he takes the 'more friendly counsel' of the fiend and ends the soliloquy by telling the (presumed) fiend that he is doing so. The complicated joke is that in anything other than comic soliloquy, to adopt the course proposed by a fiend would lead to the soliloquist's damnation, as it does in Marlowe's *Doctor Faustus*; but the Clown, by going against his conscience to quit the Jewish Shylock, *may*, given the theology and prejudice of the time, be putting himself closer to Christian salvation. The 'condition contrary' of psychomachia becomes altogether less clear cut, therefore, engaging closely with the ethical issues raised extensively in the play.

Characteristically, the soliloquies of medieval plays also employ a conflicting imagery of light and darkness. This may well lie behind Macbeth's 'dagger' soliloquy, in which the traditional Christian theological contrast between heaven and hell is paralleled by another, more subliminal, contrast between light, with an associated imagery of seeing, vision, sight and eyes, and darkness, with an associated imagery of dead nature, wicked dreams and curtained sleep. (The personifications of Witchcraft and Murder also recall the allegorical characterizations of the medieval plays.) This mode of contrast, and indeed Macbeth's plight in the soliloquy, in which he spurs himself into doing evil even while expressing a strong consciousness of good, may derive ultimately from psychomachia. In fact, the hallucinatory dagger itself might be either a dreadful warning from the forces of light or – more likely – a dire temptation from those of darkness. So this soliloquy of Shakespeare's, which is astoundingly original and inventive in the way it conveys mental anguish and the anxiety of decision-making, inherits, even while radically transforming, a very traditional dramatic mode.

Even though Marlowe's good and bad angels are clearly imported from medieval theatre, he never alludes explicitly to this theatre, but Shakespeare does – which may imply that his knowledge of it, perhaps derived from his Stratford upbringing, was more intimate. In *King Lear*, Edmund speaks a soliloquy ('This is the excellent foppery of the world') just before Edgar enters. On seeing him, Edmund says 'Pat he comes, like the catastrophe of the old comedy. My cue is villainous melancholy, with a sigh like Tom o' Bedlam' (1.2.134-6). The 'catastrophe' is the contrived dénouement of the medieval plays. It's revealing that the 'old comedy' is recalled in a soliloquy, because Edmund's manner of address, taking the audience into his confidence and then conveying his plan to them, operates very much as the confiding soliloquies of medieval plays do. By proceeding to dupe Edgar in the way he subsequently does, Edmund is also initiating an action of his own, which he intends to bring to a preconceived 'catastrophe'. The conclusion of *King Lear*, however, includes Edmund's own catastrophic unmasking and death.

'My cue is villainous melancholy', says Edmund, and soliloquies by other characters in Shakespeare may be considered 'cued' in this way too – notably those of Richard III and Iago. Whereas Marlowe's Barabas in *The Jew of Malta*, first performed in 1592, inherits characteristics from the medieval figure of the Vice only tacitly, Richard III, in an aside, explains, as we saw in Part I, how he has just been wittily disingenuous and finds in the old drama an analogy for the subtlety of his wordplay: 'Thus, like the formal Vice, Iniquity, / I moralize two meanings in one word' (3.1.82–3). The Vice figure in morality plays – sometimes called Haphazard, Iniquity or Ambidexter – would indeed, like Richard here, display mischievously or sinisterly persuasive linguistic duplicity. The Vice also characteristically boasts about this ability and invites the audience to applaud it. Richard's comparison is appropriate in this way too because in the play's opening soliloquy he inherits this vainglory when, telling us that he is 'determined to prove a villain / And hate the idle pleasure of these days' (1.1.30–1), he also immodestly reveals the 'plots' he has laid against Clarence and the king, which turn out to be those that form part of the plot of *Richard III* too.

Comparably, in the deviously barbed play-acting of Act 2 Scene 4 of *Henry IV, Part 1*, Prince Hal, playing the role of the king, his father, reprimands Falstaff, playing the Prince himself, for consorting with 'that reverend Vice, that grey Iniquity, that father Ruffian, that Vanity in years' (2.4.441–2) – with, that is, Falstaff himself, identified in the guise of personified, quasi-medieval allegorizations. As we saw in Part I, Falstaff is the most notable prose soliloquist in Shakespeare, and, although he is not vicious in the way Richard III is, something of the medieval Vice nevertheless clearly inheres in Shakespeare's conception of him – or, at least, in Hal's – and he is frequently boastful. Although the Vice could be thrillingly attractive to an audience, he was emphatically not merely a figure of fun: in *Twelfth Night* Feste tells us in a song, identifying the prop by which the medieval character was known, that the Vice was one 'Who, with dagger of lath, in his rage and his wrath, / Cries "Aha!" to the devil' (4.2.125–6). The Vice, that is, was an intimate of Satan's, and Falstaff in fact speaks with dangerous levity to Hal in *Henry IV, Part 1* about beating him out of his kingdom 'with a dagger of lath' (2.4.131), underlining the connection.

The introductory, concluding and linking speeches of medieval religious plays probably influenced Shakespeare's use of soliloquies as prologues and epilogues – Rosalind's in *As You Like It*, for instance, Puck's in *A Midsummer Night's Dream* and Prospero's in *The Tempest*. Such allegorical soliloquists as Time in *The Winter's Tale* and Rumour in *Henry V* – which also has its soliloquizing Chorus – may be comparably indebted. The stage direction for the entry of Rumour actually describes the figure as 'painted full of tongues', which would have made the allegory visually immediate, as a medieval instructive religious illustration would. The choric figure in *Pericles* is a representation of the medieval poet John Gower, and he opens the play with a soliloquy in octosyllabic couplets, the form in which the actual Gower wrote his long poem *Confessio Amantis*. In the light of the inheritance I have suggested here, this may be a tribute not only to this early English poet himself, but to the entire dramatic tradition of which Shakespeare was such an inventive beneficiary.

ii. Classical into Renaissance

Both Greek and Latin drama make use of soliloquies. Shakespeare knew little or no Greek, but in his grammar school in Stratford he would have absorbed an education in the Latin language and some of its classic texts. These would have been analysed by the methods of the conventional Renaissance schema classified and illustrated in Elizabethan rhetorical manuals based on classical models. A wide variety of rhetorical tropes or figures would have been identified and then imitated in compositional exercises. The rhetorical categories were sometimes applied pedantically in a way that made them subject to ridicule in the period itself: Holofernes in *Love's Labour's Lost* is a satire on the figure of the Elizabethan schoolmaster, and Berowne in that play disparages 'Taffeta phrases, silken terms precise, / Three-piled hyperboles, spruce affectation, / Figures pedantical' (5.2.406–8). Even so, knowledge of 'the arts of language' was the very ground of Shakespeare's own adventures in English and in what Worcester in *Henry IV, Part 1* calls 'a world of figures' (1.3.208).

When Shakespearean soliloquists debate with themselves, they may well, therefore, be using rhetorical tropes. Hamlet's 'To be or not to be' soliloquy can be classified as an example of aporia, a doubting or deliberating with oneself, and Falstaff's soliloquy about honour in *Henry IV, Part 1* ('Yea, but how if honour prick me off when I come on? How then?') is an instance of antipophora, a reasoning with oneself. It goes without saying that we do not need to know this arcane terminology to read or understand Shakespeare's soliloquies. Nor do we need to know any of the terms for the numerous rhetorical figures they contain. However, it does make a difference to know that Shakespeare would have understood that these figures had all been minutely classified by type and that he could probably have identified many of them. He would therefore have been aware while writing – at least if he had paused to think about it – that he was deploying them, but, of course, he may well not have had to think about it at all, so deeply would he have internalized the classificatory systems, just as we have internalized grammatical and syntactical systems and structures.

The classical texts studied as part of the training in rhetoric included the plays of the Roman writers of 'New Comedy', Plautus and Terence, and of the tragedian Seneca. Two plays by Plautus, the *Menaechmi* and the *Amphitruo*, supply the plot of one of Shakespeare's earliest plays, *The Comedy of Errors*, and traces of both Plautine and Terentian influence have been discovered in a wide range of others too – and not only comedies – from *Twelfth Night* and *Much Ado About Nothing* to *Pericles* and *The Tempest*. In both classical dramatists, plots often turn on the overhearing of soliloquies by eavesdroppers, as they do sometimes in Shakespeare: in *Love's Labour's Lost*, for instance, in *Much Ado About Nothing*, and, extremely resourcefully, in *Twelfth Night*. In that play, when Toby Belch, Maria and Sir Andrew Aguecheek overhear Malvolio's self-deluding soliloquy as he reads what he believes to be Olivia's letter to him, the consequences threaten to entirely destroy the play's hitherto comic spirit. We may laugh at the deflation of Malvolio's pomposity and self-conceit, but laughter turns sour when we witness the wholly disproportionate suffering that ensues. The fact that some Shakespearean soliloquies are overheard is significant, since it means that soliloquies are, like asides, in some cases at least the representation of speaking aloud to oneself, and not of interior thought, of thinking. I return to the topics of speaking aloud and representing thought below.

The tragedies of Seneca reached a wide audience through popular sets of vernacular translations: John Studley's piecemeal versions in an edition of 1566 and Thomas Newton's *Seneca: his tenne tragedies* in 1581. Many Elizabethan revenge-dramatists were influenced by such Senecan plays as *Medea*, *Thyestes* and *Troades*, and the very term 'tragedy' as generic description came into English in 1559 with Jasper Heywood's version of the latter. Speeches, including soliloquies, in Elizabethan theatre consequently inherited an element of Senecan rhetorical grandiloquence or bombast, of what Ben Jonson, translating Horace's *Ars Poetica*, calls 'bombard-phrase, and foot-and-half-foot words'. We hear it in Thomas Kyd's *The Spanish Tragedy*, in Christopher Marlowe's *Tamburlaine* and in Shakespeare's own three *Henry VI* plays written in the early 1590s, possibly as an ambitious response to *Tamburlaine*. (As I write, however, the just published *New Oxford Shakespeare* ascribes these plays, as we have seen, to the joint authorship of Shakespeare and Marlowe.) As early as 1589, in fact, Thomas Nashe was condemning Elizabethan tragedies that indulged in alliterative Senecan rant, making slyly specific reference to the *Ur-Hamlet* of the 1580s as if he is merely making a verbal slip: 'English Seneca read by candlelight yields many good sentences, as "Blood is a beggar" and so forth, and if you entreat him fair in a frosty morning he will afford you whole *Hamlet*s, I should say handfuls, of tragical speeches.'

While it's true that Senecan monologues tend to be bravura, even excessive, rhetorical performances, it's important to remember that the Elizabethans probably did not realize that these extremely bloodthirsty plays were almost certainly never staged but read aloud in company. In addition, because Seneca's plays are constructed almost entirely out of monologues and so little is in fact enacted in them, Senecan tragedy fiercely concentrates event and action into memorable speech. At least in the excellent modern English versions by Emily Wilson, these speeches or soliloquies still seem intensely compelling in their evocations of the desperate or deranged states of mind of murderers and avengers such as Phaedra, Medea and Hercules. The vehemence of their language seems their only way of retaining, against all the odds, some form of identity when everything else in their lives and social or domestic worlds is under threat. It's as though they are speaking, or shouting, themselves into continued existence as they shape themselves to the newly appalling necessities their lives contain. So it's really not difficult to see how Shakespeare and other Elizabethan dramatists would have found these speeches intoxicating and have practised to emulate them in their own, contemporary English, drama.

Kyd's *The Spanish Tragedy* is explicit about its indebtedness when the hero, Hieronimo, reads from a copy of Seneca's *Agamemnon*, but this is the play, nevertheless, in which we hear the true note of the Elizabethan blank-verse soliloquy breaking free of Senecan rhetoric for the first time, most notably in some of Hieronimo's own soliloquies. We know that Shakespeare was deeply compelled by *The Spanish Tragedy* because of its influence on both *Titus Andronicus* and *Hamlet*. That he was also compelled by its soliloquies is plain from the way Richard III's opening speech – which begins 'Now is the winter of our discontent / Made glorious summer by this sun of York' – alludes to, by reversing, some of the lines of the monologue with which *The Spanish Tragedy* opens. Speaking a Senecan prologue as an alliterative ghost from beyond the grave, Andrea says there that 'in the harvest of my summer joys / Death's winter nipped the blossoms of my bliss' (1.1.12–13).

It's at the beginning of Act 2 Scene 5 of the play, when the terrified, apprehensive Hieronimo speaks his first soliloquy as he is about to discover the hanged body of his son – the moment that turns him from a decent human being into a maddened Senecan avenger – that we can take the first soundings of something subtler than bombast:

> What outcries pluck me from my naked bed,
> And chill my throbbing heart with trembling fear,
> Which never danger yet could daunt before?
> Who calls Hieronimo? Speak, here I am.
> I did not slumber, therefore 'twas no dream,
> No, no, it was some woman cried for help,
> And here within this garden did she cry,
> And in this garden must I rescue her. (2.5.1–8)

These relatively muted lines have some of the characteristic effects of soliloquy as it is developed further by Marlowe and Shakespeare. They have the syntax or rhetoric of question and exclamation, which are directed to the self as well as to the audience, and in this case the questions are not merely rhetorical, as it turns out, since Hieronimo is on the very point of discovering what has in fact caused the outcries that plucked him from his bed: the murder of his son. They also have the rhetoric of apostrophe, of address to an absent person or thing ('Who calls Hieronimo? Speak, here I am'), which becomes so much an intimate part of the Shakespearean soliloquist's ability to give the appearance of entering into a dialogue with him or herself. The impression of self-debate is furthered by the self-doubt in the repeated negative, 'No, no ...'. Any performer of this soliloquy is almost bound to shake his head when saying that. So, we might say, Kyd has scripted some stage directions, some notes to actors, into the very terms of the soliloquy itself, and Shakespeare subsequently advances and sophisticates this technique, as I noted in Part I.

The other repetition in this brief passage, 'within this garden / in this garden', emphasizes Hieronimo's rectitude and resolution. This is his garden and he is responsible for what happens in it – and the iambic rhythm hits the word 'in' with force in the final line above, as it picks up and further accentuates the second syllable of 'within' in the previous line. Although terrified of what he might find, Hieronimo is therefore obliged to act on behalf of someone he (wrongly) believes to be suffering. We read this in his character in the soliloquy, but we read something else there too when he immodestly tells us of the boldness of his heart 'Which never danger yet could daunt before', where the alliteration emphasizes the boast. A strong sense of his own valour, together with an implacable determination and perseverance, is exactly the combination that eventually drives Hieronimo mad and produces the play's plot. So, you might say, the whole of *The Spanish Tragedy* is contained in miniature in these lines from its first soliloquy, which also contains in germ the potential for a long tradition of blank-verse soliloquy. This makes it entirely appropriate that when T. S. Eliot ends *The Waste Land* he cites the play and remembers its soliloquist in the line 'Why then Ile fit you. Hieronymo's mad againe', since that poem, as I have said, is one of the places where the Shakespearean soliloquy most fruitfully fetches up in its sustained afterlife.

In *Titus Andronicus* Shakespeare writes a deeply Senecan play, and both *Richard III* and *Macbeth*, which have long been regarded in critical tradition as comparable, have strongly Senecan elements. The opening soliloquy in *Richard III* resembles a Senecan prologue in that it seems relatively detached from the rest of the play, provides background information and predicts the future course of action, and Lady Macbeth's horrifying 'unsex me here' soliloquy owes a debt to Seneca's *Medea*. In *Hamlet*, Polonius recommends the visiting players to the Prince by telling him that in their repertoire 'Seneca cannot be too heavy nor Plautus too light' (2.2.336–7). 'Heavy' is Polonius's characterization of the Senecan rhetoric, and Hamlet does indeed appear to relish the bombast of Aeneas's speech about Priam's slaughter, which he recites for the Players, a speech he says he 'chiefly loved', 'The rugged Pyrrhus, he whose sable arms ...' (2.2.383). This seems to be not uncomplicatedly a parody but more a form of fustian, an outmoded manner that would have been recognized as such by Shakespeare's first audiences. It's in this same scene that Hamlet himself speaks the soliloquy 'O, what a rogue and peasant slave am I!', which is indebted to a monologue in Seneca's *Thyestes*; and the 'To be or not to be' soliloquy itself appears to draw on a chorus from the *Troades*. Both speeches, however, are far from bombastic.

Elsewhere in *Hamlet*, though, the bloodthirsty soliloquy beginning ''Tis now the very witching time of night' is a much less subtle rehearsal of some Senecan tropes. It's a performance of Senecan vehemence with, you might say, a vengeance, and is almost literally 'bloodthirsty' because Hamlet says during it 'Now could I drink hot blood' (3.2.380), becoming momentarily the very epitome of a Senecan avenger. The critic William Empson thinks, or so he says, that Hamlet's predicament is that he is stuck in 'an absurd old play' he does not want to be in, but he must have been forgetting this soliloquy, because here, for a moment, the hero in fact seems wholly attuned to his revenge-tragedy plot. The soliloquy is an adaptation of the rhetorical exercise known as chronographia, the formal description of the time of day; it also employs what has been characterized as 'a rhetoric of insatiability' inherent in Seneca. The speaker, that is, cannot get enough of whatever it is he or she needs or desires – blood, sex, death, damage, pain for others, power, revenge. It's hard therefore to attach the soliloquy to any idea we may form from his other soliloquies about the nature of Hamlet's interiority.

So Shakespeare's indebtedness to Seneca is complicated and penetrates very deeply. It means that sometimes what seem Shakespeare's most distinctive exercises in interiority have a rhetorically constructed element. Speeches that appear convincingly to give us access to individual human minds in motion, to the spontaneous articulation of singular personality, may be partly dependent on exterior sources and on a range of rhetorical tropes. Shakespeare's genius lies in the efficacy of his employment of the tropes in their newly immediate dramatic moments and in his transformative abilities with them, as he adapts them to his own powers of characterization. *Hamlet* underwrites his ambivalence about Seneca in its recognition of both the continued appeal of rhetorical declamation *and* the need to adapt it further or move beyond it towards greater psychological and emotional complexity. This recognition is an essential motivating impulse behind the development of Shakespearean soliloquy.

In 'Shakespeare and the Stoicism of Seneca' (1927), T. S. Eliot makes a further significant point about the influence. Distinguishing Shakespeare from the other dramatists of his time, he proposes that what he particularly takes from Seneca is 'the attitude of self-dramatization assumed by some of [his] heroes at moments of tragic intensity'. Although his own example from *Othello* has proved contentious, the observation itself is insightful and repays consideration. How might a tragic hero in a drama appear *self*-dramatizing, and what might the consequences be for our sense of both tragic character and Shakespearean tragedy itself? Does self-dramatization, if it happens, necessarily diminish tragic intensity, effect and consequence?

*

In recent years, scholarly work on rhetoric and cognition – on, that is, the faculty of knowing, or the work of consciousness and perception – has fascinatingly proposed that rhetoric as it's expressed in the Elizabethan manuals may configure thoughts themselves as well as the means of communicating them. In *Shakespeare, Rhetoric and Cognition*, Raphael Lyne suggests that rhetorical tropes may 'find and trace the patterns of thought, rather than preceding the patterns of speech'. If metaphor and other rhetorical tropes are the forms in which thought itself works, this alone may indicate why the rhetorical figures of Shakespeare's language, notably in his soliloquies, seem so accurately to convey the impression of thinking – why they give us what Lyne memorably calls the sense of 'thought-in-action'.

iii. Marlowe

Christopher Marlowe wrote the first major blank-verse plays of the English Renaissance, most notably the two parts of *Tamburlaine the Great*, *Doctor Faustus*, *The Jew of Malta* and *Edward II*. *The Jew of Malta* has affinities with Shakespeare's *The Merchant of Venice* and *Edward II* with his *Richard II*. Critics frequently present Marlowe as Shakespeare's great precursor or rival, the poet and playwright with whom he had to engage before he could realize his own poetic and dramatic possibilities – before, in fact, he could fully become himself – although we must remember that Shakespeare's early work, the earliest comedies and the first tetralogy of history plays, was produced before Marlowe's death in 1593. (As we have seen, however, the *New Oxford Shakespeare* of 2016 and 2017 proposes Marlowe as co-author of the *Henry VI* plays.) Marlowe is the only one of his contemporaries to whom Shakespeare overtly alludes, and there are numerous other implicit citations and engagements too. Among many such, Juliet's 'Gallop apace, you fiery-footed steeds' soliloquy in *Romeo and Juliet* probably derives in part from Marlowe's great unfinished poem *Hero and Leander*, and in Part I of this book I suggested that a soliloquy by Iachimo in *Cymbeline* has Faustus's final soliloquy well within earshot.

Jonathan Bate has a brilliant chapter on the relationship in *The Genius of Shakespeare*, but Harold Bloom, notably in both the second edition of *The Anxiety of Influence* and in *Shakespeare and the Invention of the Human*, has been the most inveterate pursuer of the inter-connections, although in fact he appears to miss the *Cymbeline* one. The relationship becomes probably the most rigorous case history in Bloom's charting of the poetic and psychological 'anxiety' denominated by his famous book. For this critic, some recognition of Marlowe is likely to crop up almost anywhere in Shakespeare, from the beginning to virtually the very end of his work. Marlowe seems, as it were, watermarked into the early Shakespearean text, from the rants in *Henry VI* indebted to those of Barabas in *The Jew of Malta*, through the similarly indebted speeches of Richard III and Faulconbridge the Bastard in *King John*. Faulconbridge, Bloom thinks, initiates what we understand as true 'Shakespearean character': he is individual in his language, heroic as well as comic and in possession of a psychic interior, richly rendered in superb soliloquies. With the sequence of *Love's Labour's Lost*, *Richard II* and *Romeo and Juliet*, Shakespeare then overcomes the initial Marlovian influence. The explicit allusion to *Hero and Leander* in Act 3 Scene 5 of *As You Like It* and, even more, Touchstone's comparison of himself in that play to Ovid among the Goths in a passage that famously appears to allude to the circumstances of Marlowe's death ('it strikes a man more dead than a great reckoning in a little room', 3.3.12–13) represents a final 'exorcism' of Marlowe's presence. Falstaff and Iago – both great soliloquists – then become dramatized enactments of that victory. Edmund in *King Lear* is to be regarded as a representation of Marlowe himself, now become merely 'a shadow strongly controlled by Shakespeare'. And at almost the end of Shakespeare's writing life, *The Tempest* is still to be read in a Marlovian light – as a response to *Doctor Faustus*, with Prospero acting as a kind of anti-Faust figure.

This is a thrilling critical narrative of inheritance, dependency, development, survival and triumph, although you may not agree with every move it makes. I think myself that soliloquies in *Henry VI, Part 3* – Henry's 'molehill' speech at the beginning of Act 2 Scene 5 ('This battle fares like to the morning's war'), in some respects, and Richard of Gloucester's at the end of Act 3 Scene 2 ('Ay, Edward will use women honourably'), in many – are in advance of anything in Marlowe and tonally quite distinct from him. But Bloom's account does disclose how crucially important to Shakespeare's self-invention as a writer Marlowe was, and soliloquies are centrally significant in that process. *Tamburlaine*, *Faustus*, *The Jew of Malta* and *Edward II* all open with soliloquies, and Gaveston's in *Edward II*, as he reads Edward's letter inviting him to England after his father's death, is a remarkable opening soliloquy by any standards. Its homoerotically charged reference to the Ovidian material of *Hero and Leander* appears to make the lines a form of intimate authorial self-reference too, as Gaveston apostrophizes the absent Edward:

> Sweet prince, I come; these, these thy amorous lines
> Might have enforced me to have swum from France
> And like Leander gasped upon the sand,
> So thou wouldst smile and take me in thy arms. (1.1.6–9)

It's not only the fact that Gaveston's form of address coincides with Horatio's final adieu to Hamlet ('Goodnight, sweet Prince') that seems to make these lines a foreshadowing of Shakespeare. It's also that Marlowe manages the new dramatic instrument of blank verse so well, with delicate caesurae, enjambment, subtle repetitions (including the internal rhyme of 'come' and 'swum'), expressive sibilance and the modulation into a literary simile both astonishing and astonishingly apt: astonishing in its hyperbole, but also because the embrace of Hero and Leander is heterosexual; astonishingly apt, because it makes it plain that the love between Gaveston and Edward is sexual too. Marlowe's 'mighty line', as Ben Jonson called it in a poem in memory of Shakespeare, here becomes something quite other than itself – it becomes, in fact, the very register of vulnerable desire.

Other soliloquies in Marlowe are comparably remarkable. Tamburlaine speaks many in which the blank-verse line is given its head, but he too, in a lengthy lament for his wife Zenocrate in Part I ('Ah, fair Zenocrate, divine Zenocrate!'), becomes different from himself in soliloquy. This relentlessly single-minded, megalomaniacal destroyer and conqueror appears suddenly double-minded, revealing tender reverence for his wife in a conceit in which he finds her more beautiful than the 'immortal flowers of poesy'. No one would suppose Tamburlaine to have even known of the existence of poesy without his telling us so like this, alone on stage with his grief still raw. So the soliloquy gives greater subtlety, even if quite briefly, to the relentless straightforwardness of his character. Above all, Faustus's initially self-addressed final soliloquy in *Doctor Faustus* as he is about to be taken to Hell ('Ah, Faustus, / Now hast thou but one bare hour to live, / And then thou must be damned perpetually') magnificently traces a devastating emotional arc from recognition through fantasized avoidance and imploration to final despair and imprecation. The exacerbation of the soliloquy's exclamatory rhythms and increasingly desperate apostrophes to the sun, the earth, the stars, God himself, the 'adders and serpents' of the hell that gapes before him, and then to the devils Lucifer and Mephistopheles who await him there, make this the very epitome of a consciousness first refusing inescapable necessity and finally losing all control in ultimate panic. Terrifying enough in a secular age, this must have been almost inconceivably more so for an Elizabethan audience that shared its apparent metaphysical beliefs. In all these cases we hear, for the first time on the English stage, the sound of individual minds expressing their most profound – and volatile – emotions and, at least to some extent, conducting debates with themselves and growing before our eyes into something they have not yet been.

In one of Barabas's soliloquies in *The Jew of Malta* we can trace the kind of development that must have most deeply influenced Shakespeare. When Act 2 Scene 1 opens, Barabas has been dreadfully mistreated by the Christians of Malta, and is attempting, with a stratagem planned with his daughter Abigail, to recover some of the property recently seized from him by the state. He laments his lot, referring to himself in the third person:

> Thus like the sad presaging raven, that tolls
> The sick man's passport in her hollow beak,
> And in the shadow of the silent night
> Doth shake contagion from her sable wings,
> Vexed and tormented runs poor Barabas
> With fatal curses towards these Christians.
> The incertain pleasures of swift-footed time
> Have ta'en their flight and left me in despair,
> And of my former riches rests no more
> But bare remembrance – like a soldier's scar,
> That has no further comfort for his maim. (2.1.1–11)

Barabas is partly derived, I have said, from the Vice figure in medieval morality plays. In *The Jew of Malta* he also becomes the malevolent Machiavellian instigator of a particularly hideous means of exacting revenge on the burghers of Malta. His soliloquies sometimes degenerate into mere rant, as do Tamburlaine's. But not this one – and this one gives us access to something that confuses our feelings about him, to considerable dramatic profit.

The opening lines have a mournful iambic tread appropriate to Barabas's striking image of the ill-omened raven that was thought by the Elizabethans to predict the coming of death. Their hushed solemnity is aided by the soft sibilants of 'sad', 'presaging', 'sick', 'passport', 'shadow', 'silent', 'shake' and 'sable'. This delicately responsive versification measures out the gravity of Barabas's simile as he muses on his mistreatment, seeing himself as an ill-omened creature of darkness and fatal contamination. This prompts us to ponder the justice of his case and to reflect, as the play proceeds, that he has been made what he is – a malignly ingenious inventor of frightful stratagems of revenge – by the anti-Semitic injustice of his treatment and the pain of his enforced loss. There is self-pity in Barabas, but it's made to seem wholly understandable by the appropriateness of this comparison to the raven and by that other with which this excerpt from the soliloquy ends, in which the desolating memory of his former wealth is likened to 'a soldier's scar, / That has no further comfort for his maim.' The sudden vividness of the simile is made especially striking by the way the penultimate line disrupts the regular iambic movement of the verse with a strong caesura. It's as though Barabas is pondering exactly the comparison that will best express his plight, as though he is working out what to think (or to say) next. The sibilance of 'soldier's scar' echoes that of the opening lines, as if itself a kind of remembrance – an effect underlined by the passage's comparable chiming of end-rhyme, internal rhyme and off-rhyme: 'despair', 'former', 'more', 'bare', 'scar'. And the syntactical period running from 'The incertain pleasures' to 'maim' is perfectly constructed so that the climactic word is released by the sentence to take the full force of the final stressed iambic foot.

Marlowe's phrase for fleeting temporality, 'The incertain pleasures of swift-footed time', which forms a full iambic line, may have contributed to Shakespeare's also full-line phrase for changeable weather in *The Two Gentlemen of Verona*, 'The uncertain glory of an April day', which I glanced at in Part I. Barabas's soliloquy of a maimed consciousness turned in upon itself to articulate a wound with such resonance seems so immediately precursory to some Shakespearean soliloquies as to make us almost wish to consider these lines 'Shakespearean'. But this would be to corrupt proper acknowledgement into spurious compliment. In more than one sense, Christopher Marlowe is very much his own man, but William Shakespeare is, in some significant senses, Christopher Marlowe's man too.

iv. Montaigne

Michel de Montaigne, the sixteenth-century French aristocrat who invented the personal essay, has been proposed as an influence on Shakespearean soliloquy. In his book *1599*, James Shapiro wants to explain what he regards as Shakespeare's major breakthrough in the writing of soliloquies in that year, between the composition of *Julius Caesar* and of *Hamlet* only six months later. The first two volumes of Montaigne's work were published in France in 1580, but he began to be known in England only in the late 1590s, and was published in a superb English translation by John Florio in 1603. Shakespeare undoubtedly knew his Montaigne. Gonzalo's utopian 'commonwealth' speech in *The Tempest* draws heavily on Florio's translation of the essay 'Of the Cannibals', and Stephen Greenblatt, in his introduction to *Shakespeare's Montaigne: The Florio Translation of the Essays*, maintains – although perhaps not wholly persuasively – that Shakespeare also uses passages from 'Of the Affection of Fathers to Their Children' to construct the forged letter Edmund passes off, with dire consequences, as his brother Edgar's in *King Lear*. In addition, Edmund, pretending to be concerned about Edgar, claims that the letter may have been written 'but as an essay or taste of my virtue' (1.2.45), and Greenblatt detects in the word 'essay' a playfully knowing allusion to Montaigne.

In James Shapiro's view, Shakespeare may well have encountered Montaigne early in his career, since he had good enough French to read him in the original. However, he thinks, it was only at the end of the century, when a deeply sceptical temper and a new interest in ways of expressing subjectivity obtained, that Montaigne became particularly pertinent for him. The consequence was a sudden maturation of his soliloquies. This is not manifest, however, in any appropriation of language or philosophy, thinks Shapiro. Rather, Montaigne's essays offered a model for the presentation of 'a mind at work', with their assertions, contradictions, variations in self-confidence and pacing, and so on.

It's certainly relevant to the Shakespearean soliloquy that Montaigne's experimentally original essays concern the writer in a state of what we might call permanent impermanence. In 'Of Repenting', he says, in Florio's version, 'I describe not the essence but the passage; not a passage from age to age ... but from day to day, from minute to minute. My history must be fitted to the present. I may soone change.' The great phrase 'not the essence but the passage' seems wonderfully, if fortuitously, appropriate to the fluctuating self on display in Shakespearean soliloquy. Nevertheless, Shapiro's account of the influence seems to me to underestimate the extent to which Shakespeare had already managed to make his soliloquies evocations of subjectivity in transit, and maturely so, before *Hamlet*. Brutus's 'It must be by his death' speech in *Julius Caesar* is not as inwardly searing and complex as some of Hamlet's soliloquies, but it still models a mind not only at work but very busily at work to make itself different from itself, a mind in the process of hypocritical self-persuasion; that soliloquy, which I consider further below, performs a remarkable feat of psychological ingenuity. If Shakespeare read Montaigne in French, then it's possible that Montaigne could have influenced the soliloquies of *Julius Caesar* too, but I do not myself consider the influence on the soliloquies to have been proven, even if it is suggestive.

3. Soliloquy and self

In early modern English, the word 'self' had the sense of the Latin *ipse*, meaning, the *OED* says, 'to indicate emphatically that the reference is to the person or thing mentioned and not, or not merely, to some other', and usually glossed 'selfsame'. So in *Antony and Cleopatra* Dercetus tells Caesar that the wound that killed Antony has been inflicted by 'that self hand / Which writ his honour in the acts it did' (5.1.21–2), and in *King Lear* Regan flatters her father by insisting that she is made of 'that self mettle as my sister' (1.1.69). When Shakespeare's characters speak reflexively of 'self', they do so as if identifying a physically specific element of their being, or a location for it, as Cressida does when, self-reproachfully, she tells Troilus 'I have a kind of self resides with you, / But an unkind self that itself will leave / To be another's fool' (*Troilus and Cressida*, 3.2.143–5).

The distinctively modern sense of 'self' is defined by the *OED* – apparently assuming all selves to be male selves – as 'that which in a person is really and intrinsically *he* (in contradistinction to what is adventitious); the ego (often identified with the soul or mind as opposed to the body); a permanent subject of successive and varying states of consciousness'. It dates only from the late seventeenth century, first occurring in a poem by Thomas Traherne written around 1674 (but not published then). In its modern sense, the *OED*'s word 'ego' was not available to Shakespeare either: the dictionary ascribes its first usage in the sense of 'the conscious thinking subject, as opposed to the *non-ego* or object' to 1789. Nor were the words 'personality', in its sense of 'a person considered as the possessor of individual characteristics or qualities', which the *OED* ascribes to 1678, or 'individual', in the modern sense of 'distinguished in nature or attributes from others; having a striking or unusual character; distinctive', whose first usage is ascribed to Sir Thomas Browne's *Pseudodoxia Epidemica* in 1646.

Even so, it's the sense of inwardness, of private interiority, in Shakespeare's soliloquies that has made them seem the very proofs and models of self-consciousness, the location of a definitively modern subjectivity, the ground of the very *idea* of the self. This is especially true of Hamlet's soliloquies as he struggles with the complexities of the ethical and metaphysical issues inflicted upon him by his extraordinarily difficult predicament. In liberal humanist thinking, the modern individual is born with the secularizing impulse of the Renaissance, and the soliloquy – the individual's intimate mode of self-address – is the most powerful register of that individualizing interiority. So, for Harold Bloom – a humanist, even if one who considers himself 'a Jewish gnostic' – Shakespeare 'invents the human': his theatre inaugurates the concept of human personality and consciousness. We see it displayed in his major characters, Bloom thinks, especially in Falstaff and Hamlet. These characters develop by reconceiving themselves in both action and speech, and the reconception is sometimes achieved by 'overhearing' themselves (although this seems to me much more true of Hamlet than of Falstaff). Although Lutheran Protestantism was advancing the concept of the inner self earlier, nothing prepared for the Shakespearean genius that brought it fully into being. It's also axiomatic for Bloom that the Shakespearean self, although we witness it in the process of development, is essentially 'given'.

So his statement of the humanist position is, at one point in *Shakespeare: The Invention of the Human*, explicitly made as a challenge to, or contradiction of, other possible positions when he says that the model for Shakespeare's concept of the self is 'not self-fashioning but self-revision'. The term 'self-fashioning' is particularly associated with the critical school of new historicism because Stephen Greenblatt, an influential initiator of that school, entitled a collection of his essays *Renaissance Self-Fashioning: From More to Shakespeare*. The 'fashioning' or 'constructing' of a self is a preoccupying matter for that American critical procedure, or set of procedures and practices. Various kinds of Marxist-derived or Marxist-oriented and poststructuralist criticism, influenced by Jacques Lacan and Michel Foucault's ideas about the voiding of self and the social mobility of power relations, have had notable things to say about Renaissance soliloquy. For this kind of critique, the self is far from 'given'; it's inherently disunited and discontinuous. The Shakespearean soliloquy consequently becomes the site of a deconstructive enquiry into the integrity of the liberal humanist subject itself and the nature of individuality.

Raymond Williams, whose broadly Marxist work was influential on the school of cultural materialism, which is often understood as a British equivalent of new historicism, explores the soliloquy in his long essay 'On Dramatic Dialogue and Monologue (particularly in Shakespeare)' in his book *Writing in Society*. Soliloquies often share linguistic forms with common prayer, he says there, and hence no clear distinction between 'public' and 'private' spheres is, of any necessity, maintained within them. Soliloquies, often from a position of personal crisis, engage with a common condition, and those of *Hamlet* ought properly to be considered in tandem with a range of other types of discourse in the play, in which speaking subjects are also dispersed from stable identity and relationship. Williams distinguishes, however, between the 'generic–objective' soliloquy, which uses the word 'we' rather than 'I', and the 'reflexive–subjective' one, arguing that the soliloquy is not 'inner speech' in any exclusive sense but becomes so with the development of capitalism, which prioritizes individualism over commonality.

Comparably, but from a poststructuralist position, Catherine Belsey, in *The Subject of Tragedy: Identity and Difference in Renaissance Drama*, understands the internalization of previously external modes of conflict in the Renaissance soliloquy – that of the good and bad angel, for instance – as always liable to fracture. The repressed externalization can return in a way that will disintegrate the unified subjectivity the soliloquy seems almost designed to maintain. The consequence for Hamlet, for instance, is that he can never be fully present to himself, or to the audience, in his own speeches. For Belsey, this existential non-presence alone constitutes his interiority or essence; his 'essence' is, as it were, in fact permanently evaporating into his existence at any dramatic moment. By implication, it's this, rather than any depth of psychologically credible characterization discoverable 'within' him, that continues to make him so fascinating – or so unreadable.

Critiquing the very nature of such accounts of Renaissance secularization and individuation, Brian Cummings in *Mortal Thoughts: Religion, Secularity and Identity in Shakespeare and Early Modern Culture* in effect proposes a radical re-structuring of the terms of the debate itself. The problem with viewing soliloquy as an agent of capitalism or a function of secularization, he thinks, is that this is to conceive of it, wrongly, as cognitive rather than performative, as if it were a rendition of pure mind. The soliloquy is not transparent introspection, but rhetorical composition, and we should place more attention on the role of the implied listener. Cummings proposes therefore that we remove the idea of secularization from the history of soliloquy and return to the original conception of soliloquy as prayer, where the listener was God. So Hamlet does not 'speak his mind'. Rather, he 'confronts us with a fragmentary repository of alternative selves, and searches within for the limits of being' as he addresses 'an implied presence beyond the self'. Doing this is for the actor playing Hamlet 'to empty himself from the stage into the presence of death', as someone at prayer might do in addressing God. We saw in Part I that some soliloquies are prominently preoccupied with death; for Cummings, this 'emptying' would presumably be the ultimate reason why this is so. His quasi-theological way of understanding Shakespearean soliloquy is recent in the history of its reception. It may well mark a newly influential critical turn, even if it's not clear that the banishment of the secular idea from the consideration of soliloquy will happen any time soon.

These, then, are some of the modern contexts – theological, philosophical, political and literary – in which Shakespearean soliloquy has been understood by modernity. I would add only that when critics write at their most engaged and insightful about the great Shakespearean soliloquies, it's remarkable how alike people from different, even conflicting, schools of thought tend to sound. Discussing Hamlet's 'To be or not to be' speech, for instance, one critic says that it's 'the center of Hamlet, at once everything and nothing, a fullness and an emptiness playing off against each other ... [it] can be called his death-speech-in-advance, the prolepsis of his transcendence'. This sounds both deconstructive and quasi-theological, but it's neither Catherine Belsey nor Brian Cummings – it's the professed humanist Harold Bloom.

4. Staging soliloquy

In *Shakespeare and the History of Soliloquies*, James Hirsh provides the most substantial account of the soliloquy in recent critical writing, and Brian Cummings commends him for his view of soliloquy as performative, not cognitive. Cummings also, however, finds Hirsh 'aggressively doctrinaire'. This is because, maintaining that there are three types of soliloquy in Western theatrical history – audience-addressed speech, self-addressed speech and interior monologue – Hirsh believes that self-addressed speech alone was the convention of Elizabethan theatre and the one to which Shakespeare adhered. Soliloquies of this kind represent 'a character in the process of *talking* himself into a course of action or a frame of mind', and the Elizabethan period was the only one in which soliloquy was understood in this way. So, to perform Shakespearean soliloquy as it has subsequently been performed in theatrical history – as if it's the representation of thinking, or as if it's meant as direct address to an audience – is an anachronistic misunderstanding that derives from the fact that Elizabethan self-address came to seem, after the late seventeenth century, embarrassingly unrealistic.

Hirsh supplies a great deal of evidence to support his view and offers some stimulating readings of individual soliloquies in consequence. He is particularly thought-provoking on the regularity with which soliloquies are overheard in Shakespeare, or are in danger of being so – obviously, in order to be overheard, a soliloquy must represent speaking out loud to oneself rather than the interior process of thought. I have already glanced at overheard soliloquies, and Hirsh cites more. There is Juliet's in Act 2 Scene 2 of *Romeo and Juliet*, the 'balcony scene' in which she apostrophizes Romeo, assuming him to be absent; in fact, very much present, he overhears her and responds (I consider the implications of this further in Part IV). There is Hal's in Act 5 Scene 4 of *Henry IV, Part 1*, which Falstaff overhears since he is the still very much living 'corpse' being addressed. And Thersites in Act 5 Scene 2 of *Troilus and Cressida* overhears Cressida's brief soliloquy on the 'fault' in women and comments scurrilously in a soliloquy of his own on what she has just said. Hirsh also cites some dialogue that appears to confirm his argument. The Steward in *All's Well That Ends Well* tells the Countess that he has overheard Helena talking to herself: 'Madam, I was very late more near her than I think she wish'd me; alone she was, and did communicate to herself her own words to her own ears; she thought, I dare vow for her, they touch'd not any stranger sense' (1.3.104–8) – 'any stranger sense' means 'anyone else's hearing'.

Clearly, at least some characters in Shakespeare must be presumed to speak aloud to themselves in soliloquy, and about the weightiest matters. The Steward has overheard Helena expressing her love for Bertram, the Countess's son, and bitterly regretting the fact that their incommensurate social status is likely to keep them apart. Helena's unreciprocated love for Bertram is the motor of the play's plot, so this act of overhearing, although it happens offstage, is highly significant. As we saw in Part I, the dangers of overhearing can be even greater than they are for Helena here: Henry VI's death is the consequence of his being overheard by the keepers of the wood in *Henry VI, Part 3*. Probably the most notable instance of an overheard soliloquy in all Shakespeare, though, is Enobarbus's address to the moon as he dies, apparently of extreme melancholic grief, in *Antony and Cleopatra* (4.9.15–26). Castigating himself for his desertion of Antony, he ends by crying his name out twice in grieving exclamation, and is overheard by soldiers of the night watch. Thinking him asleep or in a faint, they then discover, and reveal to the audience, his death.

Despite such supporting evidence, Hirsh's view is indeed inflexible. Even if we allow that a single Elizabethan convention did operate in relation to soliloquy, we might still think that some soliloquies distinguish themselves from others by the extent of their apparent inwardness, interiority, intensity and so on, and must have seemed then, as they do now, much less like talking to oneself and much more like internal reflection. The word 'thought' figures in some soliloquies, suggesting that if any such Elizabethan convention did operate, then Shakespeare was intent on extending, elaborating or destabilizing it, as he did with other dramatic conventions too. Richard III ends the play's opening soliloquy when he sees the subject of part of his speech, Clarence, approaching, by saying 'Dive, thoughts, down to my soul; here Clarence comes' (1.1.41). This appears to suggest that what he has been doing in the previous forty lines is indeed thinking, although he seems to an audience to have been speaking, and the actor playing him has of course been speaking. In *Richard II*, Richard's sole soliloquy fixes on the act of thinking itself as he hammers out the conceit of comparing his prison to the world, almost as though he is a poet in meditative composition. In the soliloquy's opening thirty lines, the words 'thought' and 'thoughts' are repeated eight times, and when Richard brilliantly conceives of his labour as almost an act of copulation between his brain and his soul he says that the product will be 'A generation of still-breeding thoughts' (5.5.8). His metaphor may well seem a usable definition of the generative process of cognition audible in soliloquies other than this one too.

Styles of theatrical performance change radically over the years, as any performance history, and especially its illustrations or photographs, amply demonstrates, and as any theatre-goer who has lived long enough will have proved upon his or her own pulses. Conventions cannot stand still in theatre, and types of theatrical space and modes of staging will all make a difference. The soliloquy is what it has become over time, and it may inherit, develop or even contradict whatever it may have been, or may have been thought to have been, at its origin. What performers of soliloquy mainly do nowadays in the theatre is to communicate with the audience, either breaking the fourth wall of the traditional proscenium-arch stage or taking advantage of the greater intimacy possible on the contemporary platform and thrust stages. This is clear from many of the interviews in the Globe Theatre's *Muse of Fire* series and from my own interviews with actors in Part III of this book. Contemporary actors neither talk to themselves nor pretend that the audience is not present. Indeed, some actors regard the audience for a soliloquy as a kind of partner in debate. Sometimes they directly involve the audience in physical action, as when Jonathan Slinger playing Hamlet in Stratford in 2013 threw a skull to someone in the front row. Such gestures of engagement, often controversial, imply a very different idea of soliloquy from the withdrawal into apparently private reflection or determined declamation that was characteristic in performance from the eighteenth century until, probably, the 1960s. Witness Alec Guinness, for instance, in a statement made in 1988 quoted in Mary Z. Maher's *Modern Hamlets and Their Soliloquies*: 'Both in Guthrie's modern dress production [of *Hamlet*] at the Old Vic in 1938 and again in my own disastrous production in 1951 the soliloquies were delivered in the conventional way – as introspective speeches, as if the character was thinking aloud to himself and not ... explaining his situation to an audience, as is sometimes now the case.'

The 'conventional way' as Guinness identifies it here has a long theatrical pedigree. This may be illustrated by several accounts of famous actors performing Hamlet's soliloquies over a lengthy period of theatrical history, from the late eighteenth to the mid-twentieth century:

> Thus he comes on to the stage sunk in contemplation, his chin resting on his right hand, and his right elbow on his left, and gazes solemnly downwards. And then, removing his right hand from his chin, but ... still supporting it with his left hand, he speaks the words 'To be or not to be', &c, softly, though, on account of the absolute silence ... they are audible everywhere. (David Garrick at the Theatre Royal, Drury Lane, in 1775, described by Georg Christoph Lichtenberg)

> It was too strong and pointed. There was often a severity, approaching to virulence, in the common observations and answers. There is nothing of this in Hamlet. He is, as it were, wrapped up in the cloud of his reflections, and only *thinks aloud*. (Edmund Kean at the Theatre Royal, Drury Lane, 14 March 1814, described by William Hazlitt)

> Mr. Irving's intention is not to make points, but to give a consistent reading of a Hamlet who 'thinks aloud'. For one instant he falls 'a-cursing like a very drab, a scullion'; but only to relapse into a deeper

> despair, into more profound thought. He is not acting, he is not splitting the ears of the groundlings, he is an artist concealing his art: he is talking to himself; he is thinking aloud. (Henry Irving at the Lyceum Theatre, November 1874, described by Clement Scott)

> Mr. Gielgud ... delivers the 'Rogue and peasant slave' soliloquy grandly, rendering it like the first movement of some tremendous concerto and so that the 'To be or not to be' speech, which follows almost immediately, has the tenderness of a Mozartian slow movement. (John Gielgud at the New Theatre, 18 November 1934, described by James Agate)

If, as Alec Guinness says, by 1988 an actor 'sometimes' abandoned such methods in favour of doing it as if 'explaining his situation to an audience', this has now become almost universally the style – so much so that many actors talk about playing soliloquy as if the character's thinking might be affected, or his or her mind changed, by audience response. Mary Z. Maher suggests that David Warner's performance of Hamlet in Stratford in 1965 was greatly influential on this altered manner. Warner was interrupted in the 'O, what a rogue and peasant slave am I' soliloquy one night at the question 'Am I a coward?' when a member of the audience shouted out 'Yes!' Continuing with the soliloquy's further questions, 'Who calls me villain, breaks my pate across, / Plucks off my beard and blows it in my face, / Tweaks me by the nose, gives me the lie I' th' throat / As deep as to the lung? Who does me this?', Warner was answered by the unexpected interlocutor's identification of himself. Warner went on, now as if in dialogue with that person, 'Hah, 'swounds, I should take it; for it cannot be / But I am pigeon-liver'd ...' Far from being disconcerted, Maher says, Warner considers this one of the greatest nights of his acting career. Speaking these lines to an audience seemed exactly the right thing to do and wholly supported by the text in a way that made Shakespeare's dramaturgy newly awe-inspiring to the actor.

One further account, then, of an actor playing Hamlet:

> This is a Hamlet desperately in need of counsel, help, experience, and he actually seeks it from the audience in his soliloquies. This is probably the greatest triumph of the production: using the Elizabethan convention with total literalness, Hamlet communes not with himself but with you. For the first time in my experience, the rhetoric, spoken as it was intended to be, comes brilliantly to life. (David Warner at the Royal Shakespeare Theatre, Stratford-upon-Avon, on 27 August 1965, described by Ronald Bryden)

'The Elizabethan convention'? Not as understood by James Hirsh – but, certainly, as interpreted by a brilliant and influential modern performer of an Elizabethan play.

*

We need to consider briefly, then, some major elements of staging and performance history that have affected the speaking of soliloquies.

Our knowledge of the design and structure of the Elizabethan playhouse is dependent on scant archaeological evidence and on only one actual sketch of a theatre interior (the Swan), which may be only the copy of a copy, so anything said about it is highly speculative. In addition, we have good reason to believe that theatre designs were not standardized, and some of Shakespeare's later work was performed in the candle-lit indoor theatre of Blackfriars from late 1609 or early 1610, as well as in the open yard of the Globe theatre. Even so, it seems clear that the design made use of a platform stage permitting the play's spectators to impinge on the actors from almost all sides. This fundamentally differed from the proscenium-arch stages introduced with the Restoration, although these did originally retain an open forestage extending about twenty feet into the auditorium. However, the fore-stage was reduced over time, and the English theatre, from the post-Restoration period until very recently, was dominated by a proscenium arch, with its notional 'fourth wall' through which spectators view the action, with painted scenery and stage furniture creating an illusionary 'picture stage' behind the arch.

We do not know, then, exactly what the features of Shakespeare's original Globe and Blackfriars theatres were, but the presumed simulacra in Shakespeare's Globe theatre and the Sam Wanamaker Playhouse on the South Bank in London, and the recreation of the Blackfriars theatre by the American Shakespeare Center in Staunton, Virginia, give us some idea of the kinds of inter-relationship between performers and audience that may have obtained in them. These may vary from easy rapport through embarrassment to menace, depending on the performer's intention and the audience's constitution. The contemporary Globe, sometimes boisterously or even belligerently interactive, also suggests what some of the other conditions of Shakespeare's theatre may have been like. We can gauge the effect of daylight rather than theatrical lighting; the tendency of those the Elizabethans called the groundlings – the people standing in the spaces immediately in front of the stage in the yard – to wander about during performances; the distraction of things external to the theatre that can be heard within it and sometimes intrude (pigeons, for instance); the marked tendency of the audience, who are more than usually able to do so, to look at one another as well as at the on-stage activity, which makes the theatrical space differently social or erotic; and the invitation to actors sometimes to play one part of the audience off against another – to underline a point about varying social or financial circumstance, for instance. Such factors now affect and may also have then affected the performance of solitary soliloquy. The proscenium-arch stage, on the other hand, almost of itself induces a certain inwardness and withdrawal on the part of the actor speaking soliloquy, who must look out to an audience not easily seen in the darkness.

This kind of stage was not the only change introduced into English theatrical performance with the Restoration. Women acted for the first time, and a middle-class theatre audience became newly prominent. These transformations occurred at the same time as the development in the general culture of neo-classical taste. A newly decorous London theatre grew wary of what now seemed vulgarities in Shakespeare's plays and required the staging of adaptations rather than original texts. Sometimes these modifications of theatrical class and taste affected the actual texts of soliloquies, as when, in the 1660s, William Davenant altered what he regarded as the vulgarity of the line 'To grunt and sweat under a weary life' in Hamlet's 'To be or not to be' soliloquy to 'To groan and sweat under a weary life' and felt that it was more appropriate that the native hew of resolution 'Shews sick and pale with thought' than that it be 'sicklied o'er with the pale cast of thought'. These may seem relatively minor adjustments, but they indicate the kinds of refinement considered necessary in post-Restoration theatre, which were inimical to vital elements of Shakespearean drama. Full-scale adaptations of Shakespearean plays, sometimes retitled, survived on the English stage from the 1660s until the late eighteenth century, and such 'refinements' obviously affected ways of playing soliloquy. Which is not to say that adaptation did not occasionally have some merits. As we have seen in Part I, Colley Cibber's 'Richard's himself again' persisted as a suggestive and usable revision of Richard III's final soliloquy until the advent of cinematic Shakespeare itself, when Laurence Olivier used it, along with other Cibber variations, in his 1955 screen version, which acknowledges Cibber in its opening credits.

The performance of soliloquies, at least as metamorphic an art as anything else in theatre, has been manifestly and profoundly affected by many subsequent changes in theatrical space, casting, styles of acting and the generally obtaining, temporally specific conceptions of 'Shakespeare'. David Garrick's eighteenth-century theatre of spectacle gave way to Edmund Kean's Romantic performances, which were, Coleridge said, 'like reading Shakespeare by flashes of lightning'. This is both compliment and derogation. Compliment, because it suggests the intense illumination Kean could bring to his Shakespearean roles; derogation, because it implies a certain element of melodrama in the conception and realization, and the lack of a governing interpretative principle or concept. The implication may be that such a thing would be better provided by a Coleridge than a Kean, by the critic in his study rather than the actor on his stage. Coleridge very influentially discussed Shakespeare's plays as 'dramatic poems' whose 'proper place' was 'in the heart and in the closet'; the critic's task was to find and illuminate their 'organic unity'.

Great actors in the Romantic period and subsequently, including Garrick, Kean, Sarah Siddons and Sarah Bernhardt, were renowned for evenings of theatrical entertainment in which Shakespeare's plays were reshaped to flatter the company's leading actors and for virtuoso concert performances that included recitations of Shakespearean soliloquies entirely detached from their plays. In the nineteenth century, great actor-managers such as John Philip Kemble and Henry Irving were renowned for their performances of soliloquies, especially the tragic soliloquies. A strong element of declamation often obtained in these, and performances were conceived of as a set of 'points' to be recognized and applauded (literally, one by one) by an audience. This is what William Hazlitt and Clement Scott mean by 'pointed' and 'points' in their respective descriptions of Kean and Irving above. 'Points' were elements of stage business and highly stylized attitudes or facial expressions to denote specific emotional states.

Mark Twain satirizes this in an episode of *The Adventures of Huckleberry Finn* (1884), in which conmen known as the Duke and the King claim to be 'David Garrick the Younger' and 'Edmund Kean the Elder' when they stage a pastiche Elizabethan or Jacobean tragedy. An 'Immortal Soliloquy' is spoken in an absurd parody of Romantic theatrical 'pointing' or posturing. It's a meaningless amalgam of garbled lines from *Hamlet* and *Macbeth*, although it does show an awareness of how a Shakespearean soliloquy might proceed in rhythm and period (and of how significant the word 'do' is in *Macbeth*). The Duke and the King realize that all a 'Shakespearean' soliloquy needs to do to impress an audience is to *sound* impressive, entirely irrespective of content, because such an audience is self-flatteringly ready to be duped. The speech goes on like this for twenty-five lines:

> To be, or not to be; that is the bare bodkin
> That makes calamity of so long life;
> For who would fardels bear, till Birnam Wood do come to Dunsinane,
> But that the fear of something after death
> Murders the innocent sleep,
> Great nature's second course,
> And makes us rather sling the arrows of outrageous fortune
> Than fly to others that we know not of.

The reform of Shakespearean production in the first decades of the twentieth century prominently included the outlawing of stage practices such as pointing. The early years of the century also witnessed a neo-Elizabethan movement in the theatre in which some fore-stages were restored – by, for instance, covering over the orchestra pit – and a new simplicity of staging was established in the productions of, among others, William Poel and his follower Harley Granville-Barker, who also wrote extensively and influentially about the staging of the plays. This new theatre coincided with, and was heavily influenced by, both abstraction and the rediscovery of the 'primitive' in other art forms. Consequently, the performance of soliloquies took on a new inwardness and intensity, decisively retreating from previous styles of declamation. In the 1930s the brilliantly intense musicality of the performances of John Gielgud made his Hamlet, Richard II, Romeo and Macbeth seem almost the definitive index of 'Shakespearean style'. Gielgud himself, however, recognized the virtues of quite another way of doing things when he gave opportunities in his own productions to Laurence Olivier, whose kinds of theatrical iconoclasm – he was rough where Gielgud was smooth, and rapid where Gielgud was mellifluous – then became, in turn, the dominant style. Olivier's way of speaking classic soliloquies in his self-directed films of *Henry V* (1944), *Hamlet* (1948) and *Richard III* (1955) became so much the immediately recognizable (and idiosyncratic) norm as to have made them also the butt of comedic parody, as we saw in Part I.

Following on from the neo-Elizabethan movement of the early years of the twentieth century, many notable contemporary kinds of Shakespearean performance take advantage of theatrical spaces that may in some ways be considered a 'return' to what we understand of Elizabethan and Jacobean ones. As we have seen, the Globe, the Wanamaker and the Virginia Blackfriars attempt an imitation of Elizabethan playhouses, in so far as their designs are recoverable, and the redesigned main stage at the Royal Shakespeare Theatre now also has, like the Swan Theatre next to it, a platform stage. The prevalence of such stages in contemporary theatre does tend to make the proscenium-arch spaces seem outmoded – as anyone moving from a production at the new Everyman in Liverpool to one at the old Playhouse will be aware – although actors and directors attempt to accommodate new styles to the old spaces, if not always very successfully. The proscenium-arch stage also suffers because cinema offers the illusion of variable space on a fixed-position screen so comprehensively as to make the 'stage picture' illusionism of the proscenium almost bound to pale by comparison.

The contemporary platform stages are also most commonly devoted nowadays to some version of what is known as *directors' theatre*, from the German *Regietheater*. Post-war English theatrical Shakespeare has, that is, been dominated by the directorial style not of those who are also themselves actors, like the old actor-managers, but of directors with strong academic affiliations. Such figures as Peter Hall, Peter Brook, John Barton, Terry Hands, Sam Mendes, Adrian Noble, Trevor Nunn, Declan Donnellan, Nicholas Hytner and Dominic Dromgoole have been prominent – and they are all also, it will be noticed, men. Many read English at Cambridge (and John Barton was a don there), and their productions tend to reveal a marked engagement with contemporary critical readings of the plays, as if designed to contribute knowledgeably to, or decisively modify, a critical-academic tradition as well as to offer a theatrical experience. Obviously, such productions will only successfully do the former when they successfully do the latter first, and there is no such thing as a viable production of Shakespeare that pleases only a tiny handful of its audience. Even so, the consequence of such theatre is that, almost certainly, such productions will have more to say to those already knowledgeable about a play and aware of the critical debate regarding it.

Despite challenges, both theatrical and academic, to directors' theatre – Kenneth Branagh, for instance, seems currently to be emulating and updating the role of the actor-manager – this is still very much the dominant mode. The predominance of men has, however, been mitigated considerably in recent times by influential productions by many women directors, including Buzz Goodbody, Deborah Warner, Ariane Mnouchkine, Jude Kelly, Maria Aberg, Sarah Frankcom and Phyllida Lloyd. More recently, too, the practice of gender-blind and colour-blind casting and the end of the assumption that Shakespeare must be spoken in Standard English have also had significant impact on the way soliloquies are considered and performed. Comparable impact has been made too by the London Donmar Warehouse productions in 2012 and 2014 of *Julius Caesar* and *Henry IV*, both also staged in the United States. These hugely male-dominated plays were performed by all-female casts, and Dame Harriet Walter talks in Part III of this book about performing the soliloquies of Brutus and Henry IV.

Thinking about the impact of directors' theatre on Shakespearean soliloquy, we might pause over one indicative case. John Barton's production of *Richard II* at the Royal Shakespeare Theatre in 1973 was directed very much in accordance with the principles outlined here, and Barton has himself straightforwardly maintained that the director's task is analogous to that of the literary critic. What he found 'implicit' in *Richard II*, and what made this production a strikingly unorthodox account of the play, was the view that Bolingbroke, as well as Richard himself, is subject to and anxious about the inevitability of historical process. The usurper and the usurped, equivalent in subjection, are mirror-images of each other. The roles of Richard and Bolingbroke were therefore played in turn, on alternate nights, by the actors Ian Richardson and Richard Pasco – which meant that to get the full effect of the interpretation you had to see the play twice. The process of mirroring seemed to Barton unfortunately incomplete in Shakespeare's text, however, because, unlike Richard, who speaks one of the greatest of all Shakespeare's soliloquies, Bolingbroke has no soliloquy at all. Barton therefore adapted from *Henry IV, Part 2* lines for a Bolingbroke soliloquy designed to show his weary resignation to the process of history, culminating in the famous generalization made by the king Bolingbroke becomes in that play – 'Uneasy lies the head that wears a crown' (3.1.31).

The bestowing by a director of a soliloquy on a character for whom Shakespeare has so strikingly failed to provide one may seem presumptuous, and reviewers have sometimes been hostile to what they regard as the idiosyncrasy or self-advertising novelty of individual interpretations. Although such theatre may at times seem closer to adaptation than to interpretation, Shakespeare can take and absorb a great deal while still being, in sometimes vividly, experimentally and excitingly new ways,

Shakespeare. It might even be said that what enables Shakespeare to go on *being* Shakespeare is the fact that knowledge of his work is – in the theatre, in the cinema and in the critic's study – not a teleological process. It does not move towards, anticipate or desire an end. Rather, we read the text and the text reads us at a point of always renewed intersection between creative and receptive or critical minds in close conversation. It's at that intersection that the work is constantly brought into being. We might think of Shakespeare becoming Shakespeare, then, by *overhearing* himself, like one of his own soliloquists, as his words move surprisingly and unpredictably through time.

5. Some kinds of soliloquy

i. Choral soliloquy

In Act 3 Scene 2 of *Hamlet*, the hero arranges for a play to be performed before the court with the aim of compelling the king to reveal his guilt. During a short break in the action, Hamlet responds to a query from Claudius by offering some information about it. He identifies it as *The Mousetrap*, although we have previously heard it called *The Murder of Gonzago*; he comments on the appropriateness of his title, in a way that must seem opaque to everyone except Hamlet himself; he says that it draws on an actual event; and he discloses the names of its characters. He possibly increases suspense by revealing that the plot will turn out to involve villainy, and he insists – with heavy irony – that such wrongdoing as the play might dramatize need have no effect on the clean consciences of this audience. Then he ends by introducing the character Lucianus as he appears on stage about to poison the Player King, Gonzago. Ophelia, who has also been listening, responds 'You are as good as a chorus, my lord' (3.2.237), by which she presumably means that he has just behaved like the choral soliloquists of Elizabethan drama. Her observation may have the irony of a mildly flirtatious put-down, since 'as good as' may in fact mean 'as bad as', and Hamlet is, after all, presumptuously interrupting the show with information that might well seem surplus to any audience's requirements.

Shakespeare uses choral soliloquies, an inheritance from classical and medieval theatre, sparingly but effectively and sometimes complexly, notably in the history plays and the final plays, and Ophelia rightly identifies in Hamlet's brief speech some of their attributes. There is no doubt that choral soliloquies are to be directly addressed to the audience – which is why those who consider soliloquy as exclusively self-addressed speech or as the representation of thought would exclude them from the definition of soliloquy. I suggested in Part I that some lines of Macbeth's 'dagger' soliloquy and some soliloquies by Richard III and the Bastard in *King John* seem to take on an almost choric function, and there are other speeches in Shakespeare that are not choruses proper but act in comparably choral ways. The dying John of Gaunt's great speech in *Richard II* is an outstanding case. As it opens, Gaunt even seems to set himself explicitly in the choric role of commentator when he says 'Methinks I am a prophet new inspired' (2.1.31) and continues, in quasi-prophetic (or quasi-choric) manner, to foretell Richard's downfall. In fact, Richard himself has, in the very opening words of the play, virtually prepared for Gaunt's assumption of such a role by addressing him, intending no compliment, as 'Old John of Gaunt, time-honoured Lancaster', as though he derives from a world alien to that of contemporary politics. Gaunt's speech is nominally addressed to York, but when it expands to become a sort of 'state of England' address – 'This royal throne of kings, this sceptred isle ...' – with its great, repetitively rhetorical single period swelling and dying over twenty-fine blank-verse lines, it has become something scarcely to be credibly articulated by the tongue of a single character. Rising to his occasion, this individual has swollen into representative historical status – he has become choric.

Other characters may occasionally assume a choric function, then, but the true chorus is a soliloquist and requires the stage to himself. Or *her*self: although the usual assumption has been that the chorus is male, gender is not always specified, and the role is often nowadays taken by a woman. The choral soliloquy proper has a large part to play in Shakespeare's varied sense of the dramatic possibilities of soliloquy and is sometimes distinguished by being spoken in a different verse form from the usual blank verse of the plays.

The chorus may be a named character such as the medieval poet Gower in *Pericles*, who fills in the play's episodic plot by acting as a kind of anchor to its shifting marine topography. He speaks usually, as we have already seen, in octosyllabic couplets, which recall actual medieval verse, and the archaism is appropriate to a play whose plot derives from ancient sources.

The chorus may be a personified abstraction relevant to the play's themes. 'Time' in *The Winter's Tale* is one such, separating the first half, or first movement, of the play from the second with a soliloquy in Act 4 Scene 1 accounting for the sixteen-year-gap between the two and introducing the new character Florizel and the now 16-year-old Perdita, whom we last met as a new-born baby. Presumably to reflect the time-lapse, Time speaks in sixteen rhyming pentameter couplets, although this is an imitative formal symmetry almost certainly to be noticed, if at all, on the page but not in the theatre. Comparably, the abstraction called Rumour in the 'induction' soliloquy in *Henry IV, Part 2* sets the actual terrors of the civil war portrayed in the rest of the play in a kind of mythological context, which makes it seem that human affairs are subject to forces beyond all individual control and swayed at least as much by falsehood as by truth. In *Troilus and Cressida*, the prologue is spoken by the 'Speaker of the Prologue, in armour', as befits the martial material of the following play, and, in fact, this Speaker ends his soliloquy with a couplet wittily (and immoderately) establishing a metaphorical relationship between the fighting of a battle and the performing of a play when he advises the audience to 'Like or find fault; do as your pleasures are; / Now good or bad, 'tis but the chance of war'.

In both *Romeo and Juliet* and *Henry V*, the chorus is named simply, in accordance with function, 'Chorus'. In the latter, the role is more complex than usual. Although the Chorus mainly underwrites monarchical values, his soliloquies are sometimes at odds with the play's action. The choric introduction to Act 4, for instance, presents 'The royal captain of this ruined band' walking around the camp before Agincourt 'With cheerful semblance and sweet majesty' to encourage his men: 'A largess universal, like the sun, / His liberal eye doth give to everyone, / Thawing cold fear ...' (4.1.43–5). In fact, though, what we see in the scene immediately following is something quite different: Henry is in disguise and, far from encouraging his men or manifesting 'sweet majesty', appears to be looking for signs of loyalty – or disloyalty – in them. 'He seems', in fact, says Tony Tanner, 'to be seeking the reassurance he should be offering.' So the relationship between choral commentary and action opens an interpretative gap for reader or audience, and that gap is one measure of this play's enquiry into the politics of militarism and monarchy. Comparably, the Chorus's final soliloquy arrests triumphalist emotion even as it's being expressed. Just after Henry has welcomed the French Kate as his Queen, thus uniting the kingdoms, the play's plot is complete, but the Chorus steps forward to speak an epilogue reminding us of the inescapable historical fact that during the reign of the product of this union, Henry VI, everything his father gained in France was lost (and, although of course the Chorus does not say this, Shakespeare's first tetralogy had already dramatized this). The discrepancy between what the Chorus tells us therefore and what the play shows us compels greater subtleties of response and judgement.

Both Olivier's and Kenneth Branagh's (1989) film versions of *Henry V* retain the Chorus. In the latter, Derek Jacobi plays the role in modern dress. At the beginning of the movie, he strikes a match on a totally dark screen, and then switches on the lights of what we discover to be a deserted film studio while he speaks the 'O for a muse of fire' soliloquy. Walking through the studio, with its cameras, arc-lights, microphone booms and other apparatus as he speaks, he finally throws open its doors on to the first scene of the action, which is played throughout in Elizabethan dress. The Chorus therefore stands literally on the threshold between the mechanisms of illusion and the illusion itself – except that the player of this Chorus is himself part of the cinematic illusion, followed as he must have been by an unseen camera and microphone boom. And, in fact, the doors Jacobi throws open are already the vast wooden ones of some Elizabethan castle keep rather than those of a contemporary film studio, and the opening of doors subsequently becomes a sustained motif in the film. Jacobi reappears several times, still in modern dress, to speak parts of the other choral soliloquies from locations within the action itself, as though he is following it about – like a movie camera, perhaps. At Agincourt, for instance, he appears to be in a state of sweaty distress. This is interruptive and a bit tiresome, but it leads neatly to the movie's final shot when Jacobi speaks his last choral soliloquy while shutting one final door on the action, bringing it full circle and obscuring our access to it. It's as though he is sealing off for ever the optimistic tone of the conclusion of the play's action as he reminds us of the defeat soon to come in English history.

Epilogues and valedictory and soliciting applause are types of chorus too. Some are written for actors who remain in their roles and others for actors who step out, or at least slightly to one side, of them, but variations may occur in actual performance, and cinema has been inventive in this regard. In the text, Puck at the end of *A Midsummer Night's Dream* stays in character, referring to himself as both 'Puck' and 'Robin'. In the final scene of Michael Hoffman's screen version (1999), however, Bottom (Kevin Kline), on his way home late at night from celebrating the triumph of the mechanicals' play, walks past a street-sweeper whose back is turned to him. The sweeper turns to camera and proves to be Puck (Stanley Tucci), still with the horns and inhumanly protuberant ears he has worn throughout the film. He puckishly draws attention to the horns and speaks the epilogue in a tracking shot, in part direct to camera. This takes the actor, at least to some extent, out of his role as he asks, knowingly, for the applause of a cinema audience, which will almost certainly, such is the contemporary convention, not give it in any literal sense. Even if it did, Puck/Tucci would obviously be unable to appreciate it, confined as he is to celluloid or digital medium.

At the end of *As You Like It*, the actor playing Rosalind, speaking prose, steps almost out of her role to speak a flirtatious epilogue. Teasingly making explicit the actual gender of the Elizabethan boy actor who would have played the part, 'she' says, 'If I were a woman I would kiss as many of you as had beards that pleased me ...' This both complements and brings to a wittily appropriate conclusion the performance of gender, which has been an intrinsic part of this play, because this Elizabethan boy actor playing the woman Rosalind has also played the boy Ganymede, Rosalind's disguise during part of the play. The epilogue is therefore manifestly an interface between the world of the theatre and the actual world to which the audience is on the point of returning. In Kenneth Branagh's film version (2006), after a few brief closing credits following a wedding dance, Rosalind (Bryce Dallas Howard) speaks the epilogue direct to camera as she walks to her trailer. Followed by a visible microphone boom, she starts to take off her costume as she moves through a film crew, caterers, security people, dressers and so on amid their clutter and cars; we even catch a brief glimpse of Branagh himself. On the final words of the soliloquy – 'when I make curtsy, bid me farewell' – she shuts the door of the trailer behind her and in the final shot we see that it's labelled not with Howard's name but Rosalind's. On this threshold, the theatrical–cinematic illusion briefly persists in the form of an appropriately wry joke. This actor, divesting herself in a meta-cinematic gesture of the costume that has been one of her disguises in the film, appears to become her character again as she enters a trailer from which, however, we are permanently excluded by the door she shuts in the camera's face.

Cinema has been comparably experimental with soliloquy-prologues. Whereas many theatrical productions omit the prologue-sonnet to *Romeo and Juliet* (beginning 'Two households, both alike in dignity ...'), movies have been generous to it, as if grateful for a distancing frame for, or lead-in to, the action. Both Renato Castellani's version (1954) and Franco Zeffirelli's have famous theatrical knights as soliloquizing Chorus. In the former, John Gielgud, rather absurdly made up as Shakespeare in an Elizabethan ruff, turns from his book and speaks with magnificent mellifluousness direct to camera. In the latter, Laurence Olivier speaks in voice-over, anonymously: his name does not figure in the film's credits, although many viewers will recognize the voice. In both cases, it seems almost that *Theatre* itself is speaking – or, in Zeffirelli's case, that *Shakespearean Film* is speaking too, since his opening crane shot appears to echo the opening panorama of Olivier's *Henry V*. Gielgud was also already associated with Shakespearean film, having played Cassius in Joseph Mankiewicz's *Julius Caesar* (1953), and he was later to play Henry IV in Orson Welles's *Falstaff (Chimes at Midnight)* and Prospero in *Prospero's Books* (1991), Peter Greenaway's 'adaptation' of *The Tempest*.

Almost every line of that film's script is spoken by Gielgud, in a way that makes the whole movie seem Prospero's soliloquy, at least until he abjures his magic and, in a witty conceit, the other characters, newly released from his power, start to speak in their own voices. This makes Prospero himself a kind of Shakespeare-surrogate, as he has often been understood, but rarely so emphatically, in the history of the play's reception. Interpreting Prospero like this is consistent with the fact that he himself speaks the play's epilogue. Asking not only for applause but for prayer, he appears to want to extend the play's moral or metaphysical life beyond the theatre itself. But then in the Castellani movie, Gielgud had already *been* Shakespeare. Kenneth Branagh's screen *Hamlet* (1996) pays tribute to the security of Gielgud's cinematic as well as theatrical Shakespearean credentials by including him in a brief cameo during the Player King's speech, as if to give this movie too this great actor's authoritative Shakespearean *imprimatur*. However, in a film already quite sufficiently star-studded – not to say star-surfeited – this seems one allusive walk-on too far.

In Baz Luhrmann's version of *Romeo and Juliet*, twelve lines of the sonnet-prologue are spoken at the beginning by a TV newscaster emerging from buzzy static with the legend 'Star-Cross'd Lovers' and the image of a broken wedding ring behind her. (In Part I, I noted that Olivier first conceived of direct-to-camera soliloquy in response to seeing early TV announcers address their audiences; Luhrmann almost certainly knows this.) Then at the end of the film the same newscaster, now in voice-over, speaks the final lines of the play (originally spoken by the Prince) as an epilogue, as the TV image disintegrates into static again. This makes vividly contemporary one implication of choral commentary – that everything, all human suffering, is ultimately absorbed into narrative, into the constructed stories we tell and transmit, including those formulated and fabricated by the nightly TV news. Or, even more pessimistically, that everything disappears finally into a void, a buzz of electronic interference. Presumably alluding to the Luhrmann film, the final shot of the Almereyda *Hamlet* has a TV newscaster speaking as an epilogue an amalgamation of lines from Fortinbras, the Ambassador and the Player King while a caption behind him tells us that Fortinbras has become the new King of Denmark. Inheriting this cinematic tradition and varying it, Ralph Fiennes's film version of *Coriolanus* (2011) has the well-known British TV newscaster Jon Snow speaking direct to camera not a choral soliloquy but a speech that combines a messenger's report and a fragment of dialogue, and elsewhere chairing a round-table studio discussion for 'Fidelis TV'.

In the mechanicals' play of Pyramus and Thisbe in *A Midsummer Night's Dream*, Peter Quince as Prologue speaks a parody chorus that makes fun of the whole idea of chorus. In a stumblingly curtailed sonnet, he repetitively and confusedly insists that their play is intended to give not offence but delight and that it will demonstrate the skill of its players. Their actual performance, panic-stricken and wholly inept, inevitably does nothing of the kind. Quince's speech indicates therefore how alert Shakespeare is, here as elsewhere, to the possible pitfalls of the stage conventions he employs elsewhere with such apparently instinctive command. Even so, this play-within-a-play is among the most difficult things in Shakespeare for directors and actors to get right. It can seem impossibly dull and prolix, or, when the players do their level best to resist that, too distracting in its broad comic licence. The derisive responses of the courtly audience may also seem altogether too uncomfortably close to condescension. Although they are not necessarily endorsed by the play itself, some productions make it seem that they are.

A desire to counter such a possibility must inform Michael Hoffman's decision in his film version to have Flute suddenly and strikingly abjure his high-pitched voice when speaking the final lines of Thisbe's soliloquy before killing herself over Pyramus's body. In his own voice, self-assertively tearing off his woman's wig, Flute unexpectedly grasps the truth of mortality even as he expresses it in debased parody. *He suddenly understands what he is saying*, in a way that interestingly mirrors what actors report when they say, as I noted in Part I, that sometimes, speaking on stage lines of Shakespeare that they have spoken many times already, they suddenly understand them in an altogether new, alarming and even distracting way. The courtly audience in the Hoffman film, hitherto laughing in reasonably affectionate mockery, now – clearly affected – fall silent for several long moments before applauding. Hoffman may be recalling that the situation of Pyramus and Thisbe taken from Ovid and burlesqued in this play closely resembles that of the lovers in *Romeo and Juliet*, which is of course handled with great delicacy and poignancy. Both *A Midsummer Night's Dream* and *Romeo and Juliet* were probably written in the same year, 1595. So we are led to speculate on the kind of imagination that could handle such closely comparable material in such different ways in such chronological proximity. Even given the demands on a jobbing playwright for the Elizabethan stage, this seems remarkable. Shakespeare's view of human affairs appears comprehensively or synoptically ironic, endlessly shifting perspective, aware in every experience of all the other experiences that are possible.

Julie Taymor's superb film version of *Titus Andronicus* offers a radical reinvention of the choric function – or at least this is one way of understanding a provocative variation on Shakespeare's text in a movie generally faithful to it. The film opens in a contemporary setting with a young boy (Osheen Jones) playing extremely violently, even psychopathically, with toy soldiers at a kitchen table spread with a meal. An explosion occurs outside and, as the toys become a living army whose movements seem to allude both drolly and disturbingly to the Pixar movie *Toy Story* (1995), the boy, still in contemporary dress, is transported to the film's synthetically anachronistic world, in which the Fascist Italy of the 1930s is crossed with ancient Rome. He witnesses the plot's appalling events, but stays completely silent, even though other characters are aware of him. This teases interpretative effort, but is not actually unnerving because his silence has a quality of puzzled, eerily contrastive repose.

Eventually, assuming a speaking role, the boy becomes Young Lucius, Titus's grandson, who does appear in Shakespeare's text. Shortly after the infamous meal in which Tamora eats her own sons baked in a pie – and we recall the table spread in the film's opening scene – the final, extremely lengthy shot has the boy/Lucius in an immaculate white suit carrying Aaron's baby towards an arch of the Roman Colosseum into the sunrise, accompanied by Elliot Goldenthal's lush orchestral score. The image plays with the Hollywood Western cliché of riding into the sunset and risks the sentimentality that might suggest. However, for all its allusively postmodern irony, it seems still to intend that this boy, the heir of Titus, carrying a little black baby, the heir of Tamora, delicately unites the violently opposed factions of the film, turning his back on psychotic violence and racism and orienting himself towards a more merciful, racially integrated future. This boy, haunting the Shakespearean text from beginning to end of Taymor's film, may therefore be read as a kind of silent Chorus – responding to the dramatic action not by commenting on it but by being implicitly transformed by it.

ii. Political soliloquy

In the 1965 Stratford production of *Hamlet* that I mention above, David Warner played the prince as a disaffected adolescent, a student existentialist trapped in an absurd world. The interpretation seemed to reflect attitudes to the then current, apparently interminable Vietnam War. Warner's inclusion of the audience in his soliloquies, even if originally apparently accidental, appeared to be a democratizing gesture, and the production was generally influenced by the Polish critic Jan Kott's collection of essays, *Shakespeare Our Contemporary*, which appeared in English translation the same year, with a preface by the great Shakespeare director Peter Brook. Hamlet, writes Kott, is 'a young rebel who has about him something of the charm of James Dean'. What one critic has called Kott's reading of Shakespeare 'by the searchlights of a police state' inextricably entangles the plays in contemporary Soviet-bloc politics. Warner's way of playing soliloquy – and this may well be the main reason that the style has become so prominent subsequently – also draws out an implication inherent in soliloquy in any case, and certainly in its rhetorical means and effects. Soliloquies imply a political relation or dynamic by simple virtue of being spoken by a character alone before an audience, since such a relation involves some form of self-interest, even if the interest is only that of ensuring a hearing. Soliloquy involves a rhetoric of persuasion, but the degree of self-interest varies enormously from one speech to another.

It may be determinedly manipulative, as it is in the great Shakespearean Machiavellians, Richard III (previously Richard of Gloucester, as he is also in *Henry VI, Parts 2* and *3*), Edmund and Iago, who invite, cajole and seduce audiences with perverse charm and self-promoting ingenuity. Iago's first soliloquy, beginning 'Thus do I ever make my fool my purse', at the end of Act 1 of *Othello*, is paradigmatic in this respect. He makes it seem that the decision about how best to entrap Cassio and trick Othello is being made in front of us during this very speech itself, as though we, as audience, are privileged and may therefore be expected to be partial. He ends by announcing the conception of his plot and predicting its outcome: 'I have't, it is engendered! Hell and night / Must bring this monstrous birth to the world's light' (2.1.402–3). The soliloquy itself here becomes the engendering womb of tragic catastrophe, and the sheer number of soliloquies Iago speaks – eight – proves the immense fertility of this perversely masculine womb. The ultimate irony of Iago as a soliloquist is that he *is* in fact what Othello thinks him – 'honest', that most incongruous of epithets – when he addresses the audience, but is hardly ever so when he speaks to the other characters on stage, with whom he is a monster of calculating dissimulation. It's not that we are *taken in* by Iago, but that we are obliged, while the soliloquy lasts, to see things as he sees them – obliged, because the soliloquies and asides require it by including us; by, in *this* sense, taking us in. I return extensively to Iago's soliloquies in Part IV.

The ability to charm is a function also of the sometimes almost contemptuously insouciant self-assurance and self-reliance of these characters, but the other side of this is an intense, even pathological isolation. This is nowhere more apparent than in the soliloquy – the first he ever speaks – in which Richard of Gloucester literally de-familiarizes himself after he has killed the king in *Henry VI, Part 3* and is about to threaten his own brother Clarence, whom he will also subsequently cause to be murdered in *Richard III*:

I have no brother; I am like no brother.
And this word 'love', which greybeards call divine,
Be resident in men like one another
And not in me: I am myself alone. (5.6.80–3)

The estrangement involved in the terrible dual deletion of the word 'brother' in the first line is underwritten by the alienating rhyming of 'brother' with 'another' and by the way the word 'like', which usually signifies similitude, twists away from itself in its repetition, intending only unlikeness – as does the repetition of the bluntly absolute negative 'no', twice in the first line and then four times again as it may be read inside the words 'one', 'another', 'not' and 'alone'. An even further stage of separation is conveyed by the wan chiming of 'divine' against 'alone', as if the intensity of such solitude annuls a whole metaphysical order of divine love. This speaker knows about such love, in any case, only because he has heard others 'call' it so, and they can be dismissed as 'greybeards' – old men, priests not worth bothering about. The soliloquy also inherits the style of boasting of the medieval Vice, which I discussed earlier. Richard of Gloucester is bragging here, and bragging is designed to incite envy – but no one, except another sociopath, will envy him the condition he boasts about. He is indeed himself alone, but we in the audience, who must listen to the boast, are gathered together – a group, a collective, men (and women) *like* one another. So the brag seems unutterably bleak, and we sense already what must be the only end of this aloneness. I think further about Richard's soliloquies in Part IV.

Another kind of Machiavellianism, subtler and perhaps even more disturbing in consequence, operates in the soliloquy spoken by Prince Hal at the end of Act 1 Scene 2 of *Henry IV, Part 1*. Hal and Falstaff have been joshing in the way we come to see as characteristic, with Falstaff, calling Hal a 'sweet young prince', envisaging the liberty and licence he expects to ensue when Hal becomes king. Poins enters, proposing the Gad's Hill affair, and when Falstaff leaves, Poins, effusively addressing Hal as 'my good sweet honey lord', approves with him the 'jest' they will play on Falstaff then to prove him a coward and a liar. They part affectionately, and Hal, alone on stage, speaks his first, wholly unanticipated soliloquy:

I know you all, and will awhile uphold
The unyoked humour of your idleness.
Yet herein will I imitate the sun,
Who doth permit the base contagious clouds
To smother up his beauty from the world,
That, when he please again to be himself,
Being wanted, he may be more wondered at
By breaking through the foul and ugly mists
Of vapours that did seem to strangle him.
If all the year were playing holidays,

To sport would be as tedious as to work;
But when they seldom come, they wished-for come,
And nothing pleaseth but rare accidents.
So when this loose behaviour I throw off
And pay the debt I never promised,
By how much better than my word I am,
By so much shall I falsify men's hopes;
And, like bright metal on a sullen ground,
My reformation, glittering oe'r my fault,
Shall show more goodly and attract more eyes
Than that which hath no foil to set it off.
I'll so offend to make offence a skill,
Redeeming time when men least think I will. (1.2.185–207)

Earlier in the scene, Falstaff has expressed a desire to reform, but Hal doubts his purpose of 'amendment', and, since Falstaff immediately says that purse-taking is his vocation, we must understand that he scarcely means it. But this soliloquy proves how absolutely Hal does mean it himself. Saying farewell to those who, believing themselves intimate companions, have just addressed him tenderly, he now exhibits to the audience, extremely early in the play, after the very first scene in which we see him with Falstaff, what must appear consummately cynical opportunism. The soliloquy formally enacts the transformation from Hal in company to Hal alone by moving out of the prose of the preceding dialogue – and prose is Falstaff's almost exclusive *métier* – into the ominously dangerous iambic tread of 'I know you all', where the contemptuous 'you all' levels them into undiscriminating, and incriminating, condemnation. Speaking verse here, Hal makes the very prose he speaks elsewhere seem itself a form of subterfuge and disguise, a style of slumming.

The soliloquy is cold to the point of frigidity in the calculating efficiency of its premeditated exploitativeness, and in *Henry V* Hal, now become king, permits the execution for theft of another of Falstaff's entourage, Bardolph, without demur, whereas in this play Hal even jokes with Bardolph about being hanged. This first soliloquy reveals that he is already fully capable of such expediency, as he is also of the rejecting, banishing and humiliating of Falstaff himself in *Henry IV, Part* 2, when he says, as if delighting in the revelation, 'Presume not that I am the thing I was' (5.5.55). Letting us know that his existence among low-life companions – although Falstaff is himself a knight – is a form of constantly wary espionage and subterfuge, Hal's calculation seems virtually pathological. For the sake of intending in the future to give the politically advantageous impression of reformation, Hal willingly, with wholly spurious charm, dupes people into growing fond of him and trusting him. The fact that they themselves are scarcely models of virtue or exemplary behaviour and, indeed, that Falstaff becomes less likeable the more we see of him, hardly mitigates the manipulation of this. Hal dupes them in fact to the point of extreme distress – and probably to something even worse in Falstaff's own case, because the hostess Nell (formerly Mistress Quickly) gives her opinion in *Henry V* that 'the King has killed his [Falstaff's] heart' before reporting the circumstances of his actual death. Further, Hal dignifies his opportunism as almost religious in the intensity of its commitment when he speaks of 'redeeming time', since it's St Paul who says in Ephesians 5.16 that 'redeeming the time, because the days are evil' is the responsibility of Christians, where 'redeeming' carries the connotation of Christ's own sacrificial redemption of humanity by his death and crucifixion. If this is how Hal genuinely perceives himself, is he deluded to an almost megalomaniacal degree? His reformation seems wholly worldly and politic, so is he an ultimate Machiavellian hypocrite? Is the soliloquy even testimony to a fascistic compulsion?

Knowing what Hal tells us in this soliloquy, we inevitably read everything he does subsequently in another light. He is in effect pawning his present to pay for a hypothetical future – and it's significant that both the idea of paying a 'never promised' debt and that of 'redemption' itself carry the economic imperative. We may therefore find Hal humanly obnoxious, as W. H. Auden does in his essay 'The Prince's Dog', in which he compares him to Iago (even while absurdly sentimentalizing Falstaff). Or we may decide that such calculation, or something like it, is necessary to a prince, for whom we may read a leader of any other kind too. Anyone who does think this may still be repelled, even so, by the smugness of the soliloquy's tone, by Hal's appearing so manifestly pleased with himself and his covert managerial efficiency. He is not only pleased with himself, in fact, but *knowingly* pleased with himself when he compares himself to the sun, which will eventually 'please again to be himself'. Hal is pleased again and then again with himself. This soliloquy therefore carries strong political implications and demands that we inspect our own understanding of the relationship between private and public spheres; it calls on us to scrutinize the ethics of our own judgement. When Hal says 'I know you all', then, the actor, in ambivalent apostrophe, might well turn his gaze towards the audience rather than, or in addition to, the recently departed Falstaff and his crew. The soliloquy implicates *us*, and the four plays of the *Henriad* will not let us off this hook.

In the Roman plays, matters of politics rise to the surface in fiercely dramatized debate, and a soliloquy at the opening of Act 2 Scene 1 of *Julius Caesar* presents us with Brutus disputing with, and persuading, not others but himself, that the death of Caesar is essential and that he must be party to it. The soliloquy opens:

> It must be by his death: and for my part
> I know no personal cause to spurn at him
> But for the general. He would be crowned:
> How that might change his nature, there's the question.
> It is the bright day that brings forth the adder,
> And that craves wary walking. (2.1.10–15)

He persuades himself, in effect, by a rhetorical sleight of hand in which what should be the *consequence* of self-debate is in fact its origin. If it *must* be so as the first premise of argument – even if this is Brutus tacitly quoting what has been said to him by others, notably Cassius – then what is left to debate? Even so, Brutus finds his rationale as this slithery soliloquy proceeds on its sinuously snakelike course, with its syntax of hesitation, recoil and sudden pounce appearing to imitate his own metaphor for Caesar. After working out the more orthodox, even banal metaphor of the emperor climbing 'ambition's ladder', he returns to the altogether more striking one he discovers in a form of apothegm earlier in these opening lines – 'It is the bright day that brings forth the adder' – and now perceives Caesar as 'a serpent's egg' best killed 'in the shell'. This is the logic only of prior conviction, of retrospective adjustment, spoken in the syntax of rationalization. Brutus's specious reasoning cannot hide from us the fact that his rationale depends on his claim that the potential, unproven outcome of Caesar's putative action – being crowned – is, of itself, justification for ensuring that it never happens, even if this necessitates non-judicial execution. Just eight words, repeating the verb 'may', give us the argument and its consequence in epitome: 'So Caesar may. / Then, lest he may, prevent' – eight words in which the merely postulated becomes the motive for political murder, in which 'may' becomes 'must'. So, after Brutus's servant Lucius has brought him a letter from the conspirators urging action, the soliloquy continues to its inescapable conclusion, and Brutus pledges his support, urging himself on with a further repetition of his initial verb of obligation when he says 'Now *must* I piece it out.' Whether Brutus is convinced by his own casuistry, or merely appears at this point to be so, is a matter of psychological significance as the play progresses. In Part III of this book, Harriet Walter talks revealingly about her difficulties with this soliloquy when she played Brutus, as she does also in her book *Brutus and Other Heroines*.

Coriolanus, in what is probably Shakespeare's most overtly political play, has only one full soliloquy, at the end of Act 4 Scene 4, just before he enters the house of Aufidius in Antium. Soliloquies in this play are largely supplanted by set speeches, as if any interior life in its characters has been exchanged for external relation. The speech Coriolanus makes to Aufidius in the scene immediately after his soliloquy, for instance, the self-identifying one beginning 'My name is Caius Martius who hath done / To thee particularly and to all the Volsces / Great hurt and mischief' (4.5.67–9), suggests that his identity, his 'self', is to be located or discovered only in political manoeuvre. He has become 'Coriolanus' in Rome but reduces himself once more to 'Caius Martius' in the uncertain prospect of political credit in Antium. Coriolanus's self is dispersed into dialogue, usually confrontational, rather than made available to us as established interiority. In his sole soliloquy, then – 'O world, thy slippery turns!' (4.4.12) – he utters what appears to be a universal condemnation of the fickleness and unreliability of human and political relationships, including his own – a speech in some ways resembling the Bastard's 'Mad world! mad kings! mad composition!' soliloquy in *King John*.

In fact, however, Coriolanus speaks not with generalizing satirical intent but with specific political self-interest. The soliloquy is designed to justify to himself what he is about to do – that is, to reject Rome and ally with Aufidius. So, speaking to himself, he is in effect lying to himself, because the actual behaviour of his family and friends, as we have witnessed it in the play, has proved them anything but 'slippery' – that is, unreliable or treacherous. Coriolanus needs to make them appear like this *to himself* before he can engage in such a consummate act of treachery *to them*. We may read his only soliloquy, therefore, as in fact a form of covert dialogue – a speech in which a man talks himself into the world of *Realpolitik* rather than voicing a privately constituted, identifiable self. Ralph Fiennes's film version (2011) is wholly alert to this dimension of the soliloquy when Coriolanus (Fiennes himself) speaks its closing lines not *as* soliloquy but as an address to Aufidius. This is one of the very few occasions when Shakespearean soliloquy has been made to work well as cinematic exchange. It may well be that Coriolanus's private self is what his mother Volumnia manages, uniquely, to reach in her final, at last successful appeal to her son. It's as though she has once again reached the boy he was before, as she recalls earlier in the play, she encouraged him to become a warrior – the boy he has presumably vanquished once more just before his death, when he recoils from Aufidius's insulting him with the very word 'boy'.

Shakespearean soliloquy may be political in another way too, by registering extreme private vulnerability in threateningly public worlds, by juxtaposing spaces of wholly disproportionate domination and subjection. Isabella in her desolation in *Measure for Measure* after she has been propositioned by Angelo, the acting Viennese Head of State, asks, 'To whom should I complain? Did I tell this, / Who would believe me?' (2.4.170–1). She is picking up the derisive taunt Angelo has just offered her: 'Who will believe thee, Isabel?' (2.4.153). She has no one on stage to complain to and knows that no one in the political world of Vienna will listen to her, since they can 'bid the law make curtsey to their will' (2.4.174). But her complaint is very powerfully and persuasively reaching an audience, nevertheless – the theatre audience, who will indeed respond to and be persuaded by it. The soliloquy reaches *us* in our present moment, and by doing so it reaches out from the specificity of Isabella's situation in Shakespeare's play to speak for women in succeeding states of isolation, abandonment, violation and compelled silence too – and perhaps to speak also for children fearing they will not get a hearing if they report physical or sexual abuse. 'Who will believe thee?' has been, down the years, a powerfully menacing curb on complaint.

Some soliloquies may also grow into political significance with the passing of time, as new conditions of public life project different implications on to the Shakespearean text. In such conditions, soliloquies may even make an intervention in the public moment. An outstanding case is the Scrivener's soliloquy in *Richard III*, which I glanced at in Part I. Richard, having ordered the summary execution of Hastings, ensures that a retrospective proclamation against him will be drawn up and copied out for public viewing. The copyist – this 'scrivener' – then makes his sole appearance in the play and gets a scene to himself to make it plain that he understands the exact nature of the temporal adjustment he is obliged to document. Addressing the audience, he asks,

> Who is so gross
> That cannot see this palpable device?
> Yet who so bold but says he sees it not? (3.6.10–12)

In a production of the play by Jürgen Fehling in Nazi Germany in 1937, under a regime engaged in the spurious legalizing of barbarity, the question took on added resonance and implied reprimand, especially since the deformed Richard himself was bravely played with a marked resemblance to Joseph Goebbels, the Minister of Propaganda, who had a deformed foot. In 1941, unsurprisingly, Goebbels officially outlawed the staging of Shakespeare's history plays in Germany.

A further notable instance is the way soliloquy in *Hamlet* gained new significance in Stalinist Russia. Grigori Kozintsev regarded the artist as 'a seismograph, recording the inner shocks of his epoch', and his film version of the play, with a thrillingly scarifying score by Dmitri Shostakovich, gives us a Hamlet played by Innokentii Smoktunovskii, who had been a prisoner of both the Nazis and Stalin; it was well known that Stalin loathed *Hamlet*. Kozintsev's Hamlet is often isolated, as is the film's Ophelia, behind the wooden staves of staircases and room partitions in a castle itself firmly shut off from the outside world by a strikingly shot menacing portcullis. This obviously represents the police state of Denmark, a place Hamlet tells Rosencrantz and Guildenstern is 'a prison', but it's also, by clear implication, the contemporary Soviet Union too. Not all of Hamlet's soliloquies remain in the film, largely since Kozintsev is interested in portraying a Hamlet against 'Hamletism', more active and more prominently engaged in opposition to the state, but those that survive are presented in voice-over. Apart from the 'To be or not to be' speech, though, Hamlet is not in fact alone for any of them, and is usually at the centre of a crowd, which makes it appear that even his thoughts themselves are subject to a form of surveillance.

The 'To be or not to be' soliloquy is spoken in voice-over at the sea's edge, in a way that presents a visual analogue for the 'sea of troubles', just as the sea does in Olivier's film, as I pointed out in Part I. There is, manifestly, homage in this, and since in most ways Kozintsev's interpretation is completely at odds with Olivier's this powerfully underlines what anyone interested in Shakespeare on film will quickly learn – that a community of acknowledgement and competition, in which both emulation and deviation occur, exists among the directors of Shakespeare films, not least in their ways of managing the tropes of cinematic soliloquy. Quite exceptionally for this film, then, Hamlet scowls directly at the camera during this soliloquy, as though his question is more political than metaphysical – as though, in fact, he is asking for response. Kozintsev's Hamlet, in the most famous of all Shakespearean soliloquies, appears to be challenging the cinema audience, at the time of Khruschev's ambivalent 'thaw' in the Soviet Union, to *be* rather than *not* to be.

Kozintsev used the translation of the play by the dissident poet Boris Pasternak, the author of *Doctor Zhivago*, whose versions of Shakespeare's major plays were published during the period of Stalin's purges. In 1946, Pasternak had published a poem called 'Hamlet', in which he envisages the actor playing the hero suffering stage fright in front of an audience. He is nervously conscious of being scrutinized from behind opera glasses, in a way emblematizing the poet himself or herself in Soviet Russia, subject to State control. When the American poet Robert Lowell translated this poem into English in *Imitations* (1962), he emphasized the way it derives its politics from Hamlet's reflections by adding the definition 'a soliloquy' to Pasternak's original title. Lowell's 'Hamlet in Russia, A Soliloquy' makes this contemporary soliloquy itself therefore the site of a complex political critique linking the espionage activities of Elizabethan England to both the surveillance techniques of post-war Russia and the dilemmas of an American liberal opposing his nation's foreign policy in the late 1950s and early 1960s.

iii. Soliloquy, sexuality and gender

Given that Shakespearean soliloquy is the site of the self in performance, many soliloquies are greatly taken up with sexuality and gender, those most profound indices of identity. In fact, most women's soliloquies in Shakespeare are preoccupied in this way, because in the main they are about, addressed to or oriented towards men. This is striking, perhaps even scandalous, and must be given attention in any consideration of Shakespearean soliloquy – and it's the more striking because, statistically, less than 16 per cent of Shakespeare's characters are, in fact, women, even if these include some of the most memorable women ever written, among them Rosalind, Cleopatra, Viola, Lady Macbeth, Isabella and Innogen. When wronged women condemn men in Shakespeare, they do so mainly in dialogue: Emilia in the speech to Desdemona, which includes the lines 'But I do think it is their husbands' faults / If wives do fail' in *Othello* (5.1.85–6), for instance, which I consider further in Part IV, and Paulina in her great plea and challenge to Leontes on behalf of Hermione in Act 3 Scene 2 of *The Winter's Tale*, which Noma Dumezweni in Part III says she performed as though it were a soliloquy in a Stratford production of the play in 2009.

The issue of gender is at its most electric in Lady Macbeth's soliloquy after she has read Macbeth's letter in Act 1 Scene 5. During a speech containing some of the most terrible lines in all Shakespeare, she asks the 'Spirits' to 'unsex me here, / And fill me, from the crown to the toe, top-full / Of direst cruelty!' (1.5.41–3). The implication is that to be filled with direst cruelty is to be no longer a woman, that she must be de-feminized – or newly masculinized – to be rendered capable of the crime she is about to incite and to which she will become accessory. Saul Bellow's eponymous hero in his novel *The Adventures of Augie March* says of this soliloquy that Lady Macbeth generates in it 'a call so hard, to what is so hard, that it makes the soul neuter'. Sexuality and some concept of 'the soul', if we understand that as the absolute, irreducible self, do indeed seem to be intertwined in this speech.

The Justin Kurzel screen version has Lady Macbeth (Marion Cotillard) speaking the soliloquy in a candle-lit chapel before an icon portraying devils, emphasizing its sacrilegious nature. Later in the film, in the same chapel, now without candles or icon but once more alone, she speaks the lines from Act 5 Scene 7 when she tries to wash her hands. In the text, these are delivered in front of the Doctor and an attendant, but here they are initially spoken as if in soliloquy, emphasizing the way Lady Macbeth now possesses what Macbeth subsequently calls 'a mind diseased'. As the speech ends with the words 'To bed, to bed, to bed', the camera pulls back and we see with a sharp shock that she is in fact addressing a hallucinatory child. The film opens with the Macbeths burying what we assume to be their own child, a scene given permission by Lady Macbeth's notorious remark 'I have given suck, and know / How tender 'tis to love the babe that milks me' (1.7.54–5), although no living child of theirs is evident, or even referred to, anywhere else in the play. So this 'soliloquy' confirms the movie's interpretation of Lady Macbeth – that she is suffering the trauma of losing a child, just as her husband in this film has been traumatized by battle.

Perverse and distressed sexuality find a space therefore in Shakespearean soliloquy and take us by surprise when they do, but a kind of beatific sexuality may obtain there too, in a comparably unpredictable way. In the case of a soliloquy by the heroine of *Romeo and Juliet*, this is even breath-taking in its erotic power, as a very young woman – Juliet is only thirteen – sings a hymn to 'amorous rites' couched in the dreamily urgent rhythms and repetitions of projected pleasure. Juliet here speaks her own epithalamium, celebrating her forthcoming marriage:

> Gallop apace, you fiery-footed steeds,
> Towards Phoebus' lodging. Such a wagoner
> As Phaeton would whip you to the west

> And bring in cloudy night immediately.
> Spread thy close curtain, love-performing night,
> That runaways' eyes may wink, and Romeo
> Leap to these arms, untalked of and unseen. (3.2.1–7)

The register of desire verges on the thrillingly ecstatic, but the soliloquy contains hints of where this sexual ecstasy will eventually fetch up. Phoebus is the sun god who, at evening, drives his chariot across the sky from east to west, where he sleeps. Juliet wishes that the steeds driving the chariot were not Phoebus's but his son Phaeton's so that they would career more quickly towards the night that will bring Romeo to her arms, the 'night' she subsequently addresses in part of this soliloquy. When in Ovid's *Metamorphoses* – the source of Shakespeare's allusion – Phaeton disobediently replaces his father on the chariot, his inexperience and impetuousness cause apocalyptically destructive chaos, and he himself is killed. Juliet's unalloyed anticipation is therefore clouded by Shakespeare's mythical reference, and the soliloquy supplies no single emotion and no single unqualified literary or dramatic experience. The sexual desire that flows within it eventually culminates in the death of this also inexperienced and, at least in one view (that of her parents), disobedient daughter. I return to this soliloquy in Part IV.

Lady Macbeth's and Juliet's soliloquies are extremes, then, of the perilous play of sexuality and gender in women's soliloquies in Shakespeare. Others range between these emotional poles in the degrees of their perturbation. Julia in *The Two Gentlemen of Verona* is the first of Shakespeare's heroines to disguise herself as a man; she will be followed by Portia and Jessica in *The Merchant of Venice*, Rosalind in *As You Like It*, Viola in *Twelfth Night* and Innogen in *Cymbeline*. The play of sexuality and gender in these characterizations is also a play of disguise-within-disguise in Shakespeare's own theatre, in which boys played women on stage. We have seen that these factors come into play in Rosalind's epilogue. They do also in Julia's soliloquy at the end of Act 4 Scene 4 of *Two Gentlemen*, in which, disguised as Sebastian, she examines the portrait of Silvia, the woman her lover Proteus favours over her despite the fact that Silvia is wholly unresponsive to him. Julia, played by a boy actor, disguised as Sebastian, holds up the portrait and compares 'her' face to the representation of Silvia's. The erotic complications of all this issue in the soliloquy's remarkably ambiguous exhibition of sexual jealousy entangled with obstinate self-determination, presenting in the same dramatic gesture a character both vulnerable and bold.

Such erotic confusions are pursued further in *Twelfth Night*, in which soliloquies acknowledge both the vagaries and the ineluctability of sexual infatuation. After first setting eyes on Viola, disguised as Cesario, Olivia asks herself 'Even so quickly may one catch the plague?' (1.5.287) – the metaphor derives a special potency from the fact that the actual plague was a constant danger and anxiety in the period. But what we might think the complementing soliloquy by Viola herself at the end of Act 2 Scene 3 sets the issue of gender in stark relief. This is the only instance in Shakespeare in which the heroine questions the morality of cross-dressing. This is surprising, because disguise leads to intense, if temporary, distress for several characters in the plays in which it figures; it dangerously exposes masculinity as itself performance; and its deceptiveness was one of the charges brought against the early theatre by influential forces hostile to it, including those of Puritanism.

Apostrophizing her disguise itself – 'Disguise, I see thou art a wickedness, / Wherein the pregnant enemy does much' (where 'the pregnant enemy' is the devil), Viola blames it for duping Olivia into what must be only an impossible expectation. She then generalizes on the nature of women:

> How easy is it for the proper false
> In women's waxen hearts to set their forms.
> Alas, our frailty is the cause, not we,
> For such as we are made of, such we be. (2.2.29–32)

The 'proper false' – the appealing but deceitful image of men – sets itself in the receptively impressionable hearts of women because of their innately gendered weakness. They cannot be or do otherwise, even if the lines imply some distinction between the 'we' that is women and the 'frailty' that is the blameworthy causal agent. Viola's moralizing is further complicated by the fact that she is herself 'false' in that she is disguised as a man, and further still by the fact that the actor playing Viola is a boy. In Trevor Nunn's film version (1996), these almost Russian-doll complexities are emphasized when Viola/Cesario (Imogen Stubbs) speaks part of this soliloquy after retiring to her/his bedroom, groaning as s/he unwraps her/his bound-up breasts and, in front of a mirror by candlelight, removes her/his false moustache – her/his *false* moustache. When s/he looks in the mirror, who is s/he looking at? The reflection is that of a *proper false*, and the *mise-en-scène* is a brilliant cinematic deployment of textual and dramatic implication. How much more complicated still it would be, though, if Viola was played not by Imogen Stubbs but by a boy!

Soliloquies in which women themselves further advance and perhaps further complicate issues of gender and sexuality feature in many other plays, including *Measure for Measure*, *Othello*, *All's Well That Ends Well* and *King Lear*. The end of Act 1 Scene 2 of *Troilus and Cressida* supplies an almost paradigmatic case. Cressida dismisses Pandarus as 'a bawd', but decides not to succumb immediately to Troilus's proxy propositioning of her. She explains her opportunistic motive for this – that women are far more desirable in prospect than in attainment – in what appears to be a soliloquy, despite the (entirely silent and inactive) presence on stage of her servant Alexander. The speech is a sequence of rhyming couplets on the theme, beginning 'Yet hold I off. Women are angels, wooing; / Things won are done; joy's soul lies in the doing' (1.2.277–8). Some lines are distinguished by inverted commas in both the quarto and Folio texts of the play, indicating that they have sententious meaning, and, in fact, Cressida herself defines one such line as a 'maxim'. What we appear to have in this soliloquy, then, is the play's heroine herself speaking the age's agreed prejudicial assumptions, its rhetorical *sententiae*, about cynically self-interested or manipulative female behaviour. Or, we might say, what we have is the age itself speaking its prejudices *through* the play's heroine. Cressida's soliloquy is not hers alone; she has become a quotation, her gendered interiority possessed by the assumptions of her time.

Prejudices and presumptions such as these are precisely the burdens Shakespeare's women must carry. Some, however, learn to deal with them or even manage them to their advantage during some of the plays. In a soliloquy in the opening scene of *All's Well That Ends Well*, Helena refuses the conventional filial dutifulness Lafew has just anticipated when he tells her 'You must hold the credit of your father' (1.1.78–9) – that is, she must keep up his good reputation. But for Helena, any consideration of her late father has been wholly subdued to obsessive thought about Bertram, the man she now loves. Her soliloquy is a spirited, even shocking, telling of a psychological and emotional truth, in which she explains the realities of forgetfulness and the actual source of the tears she is weeping ('his' in the second line refers to Bertram, and 'him' in the third to her father, although the ambiguity, which is initially confusing, may well be intended, and is fruitful; 'favour' here means 'face'):

> I think not on my father,
> And these great tears grace his remembrance more
> Than those I shed for him. What was he like?
> I have forgot him; my imagination
> Carries no favour in't but Bertram's. (1.1.80–5)

'I have forgot him' is alarmingly absolute. Implicitly, Helena rejects the law of the father as it operates in the comedies, even to the extent, in *A Midsummer Night's Dream*, of Theseus's threatening his daughter Hermia with death if she refuses to obey him. Helena is boldly explicit in this soliloquy about the sexual nature of Bertram's attractiveness to her, focusing in an almost appetitive way on specific physical attributes when she conceives herself drawing him – 'His arched brows, his hawking eye, his curls, / In our heart's table.' An Elizabethan *blazon*, an itemization of attractive physical parts, would do this too, but such a thing would properly be composed by a man about a woman. (Olivia makes a joke out of precisely this in *Twelfth Night* when she tells Viola that her own beauty will be 'inventoried' and then enumerates aspects of it.) Even bolder is Helena's risking blasphemy by subsequently figuring herself as the venerator of a saint. 'My idolatrous fancy / Must sanctify his relics', she says of Bertram, which draws perturbingly deep provocation from its reference to the practices of the Catholic religion, which was still, in Elizabethan England, both a personal and cultural 'remembrance' and a serious threat to the State. The striking audacity of this speech anticipates Cordelia's advising her father of the proper ratio of a daughter's love to a wife's in *King Lear* and looks forward to several soliloquies by the Jailer's Daughter in *The Two Noble Kinsmen*, a character who has no name of her own but is denominated only in relation to her father's occupation, although these speeches were probably written by John Fletcher in a play now recognized as collaborative.

*

Viola in *Twelfth Night*, as we have seen, appears to advance a tentative distinction between 'women' and the 'frailty' to which they are subject, but Hamlet makes the identification absolute in the soliloquy beginning 'O that this too too sullied flesh would melt' when he exclaims in anguish, as he thinks of his mother's marriage to his uncle, 'Frailty, thy name is woman!' (1.2.146). (Emilia in *Othello* has things to say about frailty too, though, and I return to her in Part IV.) This speech, and others of Hamlet's, are performances of misogyny contrasting starkly with Ophelia's sole soliloquy in the play ('O what a noble mind is here o'erthrown!', 3.1.149), in which she graciously grieves over Hamlet's changed nature just after he has behaved towards her with apparent loathing. The performance of misogyny in Shakespearean soliloquy is by no means confined to Hamlet, and some Shakespearean soliloquies are tirades against women.

Petruccio in the soliloquy beginning 'Thus have I politicly begun my reign' at the end of Act 4 Scene 1 of *The Taming of the Shrew* figures his courtship of Katherine as the working out of how to 'man my haggard'. This was the phrase used by the falconry handbooks of the time for taming a female hawk; but in Petruccio's application of it to Katherine it resonates also with one view of what it means to be gendered as a 'man' – the kind of man, that is, that Petruccio is proving himself to be in this very speech. Indeed, so much is he a certain kind of man of his time that he ends the soliloquy by inviting the male members of his audience to offer him any other way 'to tame a shrew' if they know of one. 'Now let him speak' (4.1.199), he says in invitation, employing the phrase used in the marriage service in the *Book of Common Prayer*, in which the woman, presumably well tamed, promises to honour and obey her husband (or her tamer). Such a direct address to the audience in the middle of a play is unusual, although not unique, in Shakespeare. Its use suggests that Petruccio finds it likely that at least a sizeable percentage of his audience will admire his method of taming a woman and may even profit from it. It need hardly be said that Katherine herself has no soliloquy in the play. She does have a notorious lengthy capitulatory speech, though, which has been performed against the grain as ironic or aggressive, or even as if she is on the very verge of insanity.

Shakespeare's final plays are deeply permeated by misogyny: their plots are sometimes impelled by it and their soliloquies burdened with it. Posthumus in *Cymbeline*, believing (wrongly) that Innogen, his wife, has had sex with Iachimo, speaks, in the soliloquy beginning 'Is there no way for men to be, but women / Must be half-workers?' (2.5.1–2), a soliloquy that veers almost out of control as he pictures to himself the specifics of the sexual encounter ('Perchance he spoke not, but / Like a full-acorned boar, a German one, / Cried "O!" and mounted'), reminding us of Iago's voyeuristic imaginings in *Othello*. As the almost frenzied soliloquy proceeds, with Posthumus crying for vengeance, the specific becomes a universal condemnation and tirade that not only ascribes all faults to women but ascribes all faults in men to women too:

> Could I find out
> The woman's part in me – for there's no motion
> That tends to vice in man but I affirm
> It is the woman's part: be it lying, note it,
> The woman's; flattering, hers; deceiving, hers;
> Lust and rank thoughts, hers, hers; revenges, hers;
> Ambitions, covetings, change of prides, disdain,
> Nice-longing, slanders, mutability ... (2.3.19–26)

As the soliloquy ends, Posthumus threatens, oddly, to 'write against them' (women, that is), although Claudio makes a comparable threat in *Much Ado About Nothing*, responding to what he believes to have been the sexual behaviour of his fiancée, Hero, who is in fact as chaste as Innogen. The threat to 'write' against them rather than merely speak against them may suggest that Shakespeare has in mind the extensive early modern literature of misogyny, the way it's enshrined in the texts of the culture, or it may even show us an author aware that what he is doing here, in his own act of writing Posthumus, is inevitably contributing to that literature too, however the ensuing action of his play in fact places and modifies, or even apologizes for, misogyny.

In Act 1 Scene 2 of *The Winter's Tale* Shakespeare certainly writes misogyny very large again when Leontes rises gradually to a crescendo of misogynistic commentary related to his wife, Hermione, as, suddenly and, it appears, wholly without reason, he is overcome by extreme jealousy. What he speaks here may be a soliloquy or a speech at least partly directed to his son Mamillius, who is present as it ends, but whom he bids 'Go play, boy, play' when it begins. The soliloquy is usually staged with Mamillius sequestered in some way, absorbed in activity; but part of any audience's reaction is the horror that this son might overhear what his father is saying about his mother. The soliloquy presents us with a self apparently wholly exposed to its most disintegrative energies, even if we suspect that an element of self-dramatizing self-pity inheres in it too, as it sometimes does in masculine loss of self-control. Abandoning himself to the luxury of repulsion, Leontes descends to the sexual gutter in a way that makes this soliloquy outrank, in the depth of its misogynistic disgust and lubricious imagining, comparable performances in *Hamlet* and *King Lear*.

So Leontes, like Petruccio, feels able to co-opt his audience. By almost baiting the married men in it with the possibility that they have wives being unfaithful to them even as they sit in the theatre – 'Now, while I speak this' – Leontes seems to go so far beyond prudence and propriety as to risk turning theatrical pleasure into the deepest domestic and sexual insecurity. It must be assumed, or hoped, that not many members of any audience will ever see it Leontes's way, since we are so manifestly witnessing a pathology. But the soliloquy is telling us, with immense power, that this is *the only way* Leontes can see it, so much so that he can even take comfort from the thought of such perversely specific solidarity:

There have been,
Or I am much deceived, cuckolds ere now,
And many a man there is even at this present,
Now, while I speak this, holds his wife by th'arm,
That little thinks she has been sluiced in's absence,
And his pond fished by his next neighbour, by
Sir Smile, his neighbour. Nay, there's comfort in't,
Whiles other men have gates, and those gates opened,
As mine, against their will. Should all despair
That have revolted wives, the tenth of mankind
Would hang themselves. Physic for't there's none:
It is a bawdy planet, that will strike
Where 'tis predominant; and 'tis powerful, think it,
From east, west, north and south; be it concluded,
No barricade for a belly. Know't,
It will let in and out the enemy
With bag and baggage. Many thousand on's
Have the disease and feel't not. (1.2.189–206)

6. The mind's construction

'There's no art / To find the mind's construction in the face' says Duncan in *Macbeth*, reflecting on the treachery of the recently executed Thane of Cawdor: 'He was a gentleman on whom I built / An absolute trust' (1.4.12–15). Immediately after saying so, he greets Macbeth, whom he has just appointed as the new Thane of Cawdor, as he arrives on stage. The following dialogue includes Duncan's elaborate praise of Macbeth, whom he calls 'a peerless kinsman', but it also contains an aside in which Macbeth expresses the 'black and deep desires' of his ambition. The painfully pointed ironies of these juxtapositions are clear. If Duncan had the art to find the construction of Macbeth's mind in his face, he would intuit his own present danger, because his murder is to be the consequence of Macbeth's ambitious desires.

Conversely, in *Richard III*, in a kind of mirror-image of Duncan's insight and immediately subsequent blindness, Hastings gets Richard hyperbolically and fatally wrong when, at the coronation conclave from which Richard has just temporarily withdrawn, he says 'I think there's never a man in Christendom / Can lesser hide his love or hate then he, / For by his face straight shall you know his heart' (3.4.51–3). This blindness is followed, in less than twenty lines, by the appalled insight forced on Hastings when Richard, returning to the chamber, orders his immediate execution for treachery – and Hastings is suddenly and dreadfully made aware that nothing at all about Richard's heart can be read in his face. He might have taken his cue from Buckingham's undeceived, sly pragmatism just a few lines earlier. When told by the Bishop of Ely that he, Buckingham, is the one who 'should soonest know [Richard's] mind', Buckingham responds 'We know each other's faces; for our hearts, / He knows no more of mine than I of yours, / Or I of his, my lord, than you of mine' (3.4.10–12). Not that the knowledge saves Buckingham himself from a fate comparable to that of Hastings shortly afterwards when he is led to execution, on Richard's orders. And, in fact, Buckingham was on stage when, earlier in the play, Richard himself, with slick duplicity, advised Prince Edward – whose murder he also subsequently arranges – that he is too young to have 'dived into the world's deceit':

> Nor more can you distinguish of a man
> Than of his outward show, which, God He knows,
> Seldom or never jumpeth with the heart. (3.1.9–11)

It may well be that the perspicacious Prince does in fact vaguely realize that this is a piece of richly hypocritical self-analysis from the uncle whose outward show never does, God He knows, jump with his heart, but, being so young, he is powerless to act on the intuition.

'Language most shows a man: speak that I may see thee', says Shakespeare's younger contemporary and friend Ben Jonson in *Timber*; 'It springs out of the most retired, and inmost parts of us, and is the image of the parent of it, the mind.' There is of course great truth in this, and we must necessarily judge people by what they say and how they say it. But Shakespeare is fascinated by our inability rightly to construe the emotions, motives and intentions of others by such means, and is fascinated too by what might lie obscured in the most retired and inward parts of us. Some of his characters – Richard III, Iago and Edmund, outstandingly – are duplicitous hypocrites, and we know them to be so by means of their soliloquies. What they say in front of an audience when they are alone on stage is not what they say to others in dialogue on stage, and may even be the very opposite. They are hypocrites, a word from the Greek *ὑποκριτής*, 'an actor on the stage, pretender, dissembler'.

An actor, then, is a licensed hypocrite, but ordinary social life makes hypocrites of us all, since it's rarely wise to speak all our mind, or to assume that others do so. Bellow's Augie March says 'When important thought doesn't have to be soliloquy, I know how valuable an occasion that is. Because to whom can you speak your full mind as to yourself?' He is delighted for once to have found – or to have thought he has found – a companion in soliloquy, someone to whom he can address his most intimate thoughts. Usually unable to speak anything like our full mind, we are all actors – and we have it on the authority of Jaques in *As You Like It* that 'All the world's a stage, / And all the men and women merely players' (2.7.140–1). How revealing it is in this regard that the Latin word *persona*, meaning 'mask', is rooted in the Etruscan *phersu*, which meant 'a masked man' – as an actor would be masked for the stage – and that in modern English *persona* becomes *person*. This etymology unnervingly proposes that our persons are our masks; they are at once what we are and what we act with. 'When acting a role,' Declan Donnellan says in his book about theatre, *The Actor and the Target*, 'actors choose not to act themselves for a while.' Or, as Richard II has it (and he should know), 'Thus play I in one person many people / And none contented' (5.5.31–2).

It's instructive, then, that the sociologist Erving Goffman's classic study *The Presentation of Self in Everyday Life* (1956) takes its method for the examination of routine social interaction from theatrical performance; its sociological principles are dramaturgical ones. Goffman gives a telling example of the recessive complexity of social performance, albeit one itself, ironically, tinged with the prejudices of its own period and place, the American 1940s and 1950s. Intelligent women were then well advised, it appears, not to parade their intelligence too obviously before men:

> when we observe a young American middle-class girl playing dumb for the benefit of her boyfriend, we are ready to point to items of guile and contrivance in her behavior. But like herself and her boyfriend, we accept as an unperformed fact that this performer *is* a young American middle-class girl. But surely here we neglect the greater part of the performance. It is commonplace to say that different social groupings express in different ways such attributes as age, sex, territory, and class status, and that in each case these bare attributes are elaborated by means of a distinctive complex cultural configuration of proper ways of conducting oneself. To *be* a given kind of person, then, is not merely to possess the required attributes, but also to sustain the standards of conduct and appearance that one's social grouping attaches thereto. The unthinking ease with which performers consistently carry off such standard-maintaining routines does not deny that a performance has occurred, merely that the participants have been aware of it.

If this young woman were to speak a soliloquy telling the truth about the way she behaves with her boyfriend, she would still be incapable of telling the truth about the other, arguably greater, act she puts on because she is unaware of it. Shakespeare's soliloquies may, if we read them aright, give us access to both the lesser and the greater part of the performance, and they also, incidentally, being historical documents, supply the grounds for judgement of the kind I have made here of what appears to be Goffman's own relatively uncritical view of the social behaviour he describes. (Probably everyone now, for instance, will make adverse judgements of Petruccio in the soliloquy I discuss above, although, if we want to understand anything of the full complexity of the speech, we would be wise to assume that such judgements were not being made, or not being universally made, in Elizabethan England. Even as I make this judgement, though, I am rebuked by the consideration that 'everyone now' in that sentence may be altogether too liberally sanguine and that the community it proposes may not extend much further than that of contemporary Western culture and may, in some respects, not extend even so far.)

So even in their soliloquies Shakespeare's characters may never truly know when they are no longer acting. And all actors are disguised as someone else, and on the Shakespearean stage all women were boys in disguise. The actor plays Iago, and Iago plays Iago too. This is one reason why Shakespeare is so fascinated by acting itself, why his metaphors are so frequently drawn from it and why he stages representations of acting, of theatrical performance and of disguise so often within his plays – why he has actors *act acting*. In *Hamlet*, the hero stages a play with the aim of gaining proper access to the mind of Claudius, which otherwise, despite the Ghost's message from the grave, he is not convinced he can truly read or interpret. Acting at this point in *Hamlet* is therefore intended to provoke a reaction beyond the control of further dissimulation; acting is intended to undo acting. But the person setting up the performance is himself not only *acting being himself* but *acting being himself with 'an antic disposition'*, to the extent that others – Claudius, Polonius – think him no longer himself and set up their own covert performance to try to discover why this is so.

Although in the case of Shakespeare's great Machiavellian characters soliloquy may give us access to intention, it does not give ready access to motive. Otherwise, we would know exactly what impels Richard III, Iago and Edmund, and we do not, because they do not fully know themselves. That is, they do not fully grasp why they behave as they do; and they do not fully understand their own nature. And soliloquy tells us this too, because all three are capable of surprising us: Richard, in his final soliloquy when he suddenly utters self-undermining terror and guilt and begs 'Jesu' for mercy; Iago, by finally refusing to give any account of himself and therefore provocatively suggesting motivation beyond anything actually expressed in the play; and Edmund, by telling us, astonishingly, towards the very end of *King Lear*, that he also has been loved – and therefore letting us know too, we assume, that he *wanted* to be, which we would not otherwise have suspected. Even more remarkably, at the point of death, he says 'Some good I mean to do, / Despite of mine own nature' (5.3.241–2) and attempts to save Cordelia from the fate of hanging he has not long since arranged for her.

Shakespeare's characters, then, may remain opaque to themselves in soliloquy too, just as they sometimes manifest self-opacity in dialogue. How self-knowing or self-ignorant is Iago's enigmatic 'I am not what I am' (*Othello*, 1.1.64), especially since Viola in disguise as Cesario in *Twelfth Night* speaks precisely the same words to Olivia (3.1.139), possibly suggesting that disguise is a form of malign mischief? Or Desdemona's 'I do beguile / The thing I am by seeming otherwise' (2.1.122–3)? She means only that she manages to appear light-hearted even while fearing that Othello, who has not yet landed on Cyprus, may not have survived a storm at sea; but some of the play's characters may choose to think that she speaks more than she knows, because we have already heard her father tell Othello that, having deceived him, she may deceive her husband too, and Iago makes capital from the same consideration later in the play. Or Hal's cruelly disdainful line to Falstaff as he banishes him, 'Presume not that I am the thing I was' (*Henry IV, Part 2*, 5.5.55)? Or Parolles's 'Simply the thing I am / Shall make me live' (*All's Well That Ends Well*, 4.3.327–8)? In Shakespeare, nothing is ever simple about the thing I am. His soliloquies let us know that this is so by performing the fact of its being so – by performing the *act* of its being so.

'Who is it that can tell me who I am?' asks Lear, and, in the quarto version, answers his own question with another: 'Lear's shadow?' (1.4.221–2).

PART III

Soliloquies in performance

Introduction

This section did not form part of my original plan for this book. I formulated the idea of it as I thought more carefully about not only what a difference the individual actor in a specific performance makes to the way we understand a soliloquy but also about how actors have conceived of soliloquies in such radically different ways over the course of the performance history of these plays. 'Thinking more carefully' involved reading monographs by Shakespearean actors, some of the essays in the Cambridge University Press *Players of Shakespeare* series and the Faber & Faber *Actors on Shakespeare* series, in which actors write revealingly and illuminatingly about what they do, and the interviews in Julian Curry's *Shakespeare on Stage*. I then discovered the Globe Theatre's *Muse of Fire* online interviews in which two actors, Dan Poole and Giles Terera, talk to numerous actors – some renowned, others relatively inexperienced – about their relationship with Shakespeare. Many of these are fascinating and compelling. Actors speak sometimes with striking insight, articulacy, humour, wit, charm, intelligence and manifest devotion about their craft and about what Shakespeare means to them. Occasionally, they discuss performing soliloquies, but not frequently or intensively enough to establish any significant contemporary performance criteria. So I wondered if, in a small way, I could do the job myself, and this is what I intend here. What follows, then, is a set of edited transcripts of what eight very fine, experienced contemporary actors of Shakespeare said to me about performing soliloquies during interviews I recorded with them on the dates indicated below.

Jonjo O'Neill's performance of Mercutio in the RSC Courtyard Theatre production of *Romeo and Juliet* in 2010 – and especially his account of the Queen Mab speech – has stayed with me as the most energetically brilliant I have seen, and he was one of the *Muse of Fire* interviewees I relished most. I asked for an interview and he agreed, with gratifying alacrity, and afterwards very kindly suggested other potential interviewees. After also agreeing, one or two proposed others in turn. Despite occasionally observing how difficult they find it to talk about what they do, these actors all seemed nevertheless keen to talk, and all do so, in my view, at least as well as the most arresting people in the *Muse of Fire* series – but specifically, of course, on the topic of performing soliloquies. I prepared a list of questions and sent it to all interviewees prior to the interview:

- Some scholars think that the convention of Shakespeare's time was that the soliloquy was understood by both actors and audience as speaking to oneself, and of course there are soliloquies manifestly intended to be overheard, notably Malvolio's. It's argued that the soliloquy was not considered to be the representation of thinking, or an act of communication with an audience. Has this 'convention' ever meant anything to you as a working actor?

- If not, how do you characteristically conceive of a soliloquy – as thinking out loud or as direct communication with an audience? Both? Or does it depend on the theatrical occasion/character?
- Do you think a soliloquist should engage in eye contact with a specific member of an audience, if that's possible in the theatrical space available? What degree of engagement is best, if you agree that there should be engagement? Does the nature of the theatrical space [proscenium arch; thrust stage] affect this?
- Is a soliloquy almost inevitably going to engage an audience's sympathy or empathy? If so, is this a danger or an opportunity?
- How do you cope with the great fame of some soliloquies and the fact that many members of an audience may know them more or less by heart? And the fact that you will probably know many other actors' stage or cinematic accounts of the soliloquy you're speaking?
- How conscious are you of verse form when you speak a soliloquy?
- Do you think of soliloquy as something quite distinct from an aside? How, in general, do you conceive of the aside? Is it anxiety or opportunity that it seems so remote from most kinds of contemporary theatrical convention (apart from pantomime)?
- Do you think an actor will conceive of soliloquy quite differently for a film or TV rather than a stage performance? Do you think the convention of speaking direct to camera in close-up or with voice-over an outmoded or clichéd one?
- It seems to me that the performance of a soliloquy might be the cause of particular debate between actor and director. Would you like to comment?

In some interviews, we mainly kept to the list; in others, we strayed a little from it. In the interest of readability, and to avoid repetition, I excise my questions themselves from the transcripts that follow. Although this may occasionally make transitions seem a little swift or even abrupt, it also has the not undesirable effect of giving these statements, in their own way, the aspect of ruminative soliloquies too. Most interviews lasted an hour or so and took place over lunch or coffee or in dressing rooms before performances. I showed my transcripts, which I intend should preserve the relaxedness of their conversational origins, to all interviewees. One or two revised or added to them slightly, and all have approved them. I am immensely grateful to these actors for their time, patience and courtesy.

*

Almost certainly of most fascination in what follows for the student of Shakespearean soliloquy is the way these actors speak about performing specific soliloquies in specific plays, many staged in renowned productions in notable spaces, including the open-air Shakespeare's Globe in London and the Royal Shakespeare Theatre and its smaller sister theatre, the Swan, in Stratford-upon-Avon. In some cases, the actors recreate in conversation the thought processes involved, taking us through a specific soliloquy as they remember playing it, revealing the complex psychology of necessarily on-the-hoof decision and discovery. In this respect, what may also seem notable is the variation in performance possibility, the way individual actors read themselves into a role or write their own signature upon it, finding personal opportunity where there has been initial anxiety or trepidation.

However, although these are all individual voices articulating individual decisions with compellingly individual inwardness and personal voice, certain matters recur frequently as preoccupations, and some discursive means are also held in common. It may be worth cataloguing these in a preliminary way, as a point of entry into what follows.

For all these actors, soliloquy is a matter of engagement with an audience. This dynamic seems axiomatic, although we must remind ourselves that it has not always seemed so to actors in the past, and has certainly not been so in some of the ways described here. The metaphors used for the relationship between actor-soliloquist and audience – and it's worth reminding ourselves that these *are* metaphors, since the audience is in fact the usually silent witness to theatrical performance – are consistently those of 'conversation', 'dialogue' and 'argument'. These imaginative hypotheses about inter-relationship may seem required by the painful isolation and aloneness of the character speaking a soliloquy at this point of the play's plot, which will sometimes be a matter of almost despondent extremity; but they are required even more – necessitated, even – by the urgency of the demand that the actor-soliloquist find a way of speaking these words on this stage, *now*, and again *now*, and *now*, and *now*.

So, within these overarching metaphors, the audience may, for the actor-soliloquist, variously and at different times, be figured as any of the following: mirror, shadow, energy, point of focus, recruit, subject, judge, conscience, another character in the play, the location of the next thought to be discovered. The conversation or argument may itself be figured as the asking of questions and the receiving of answers, or the making of a call and the receiving of a response, although the actor-soliloquist must posit the answers or responses for himself or herself and then respond to them in turn, since – apart from one notable case we hear about – the audience does not (of course) *in fact* answer or respond. The actor-soliloquist may conceive of himself or herself as seducing, or flirting with, the audience, or as inviting them into the 'globe' of the brain; but he or she will be aware too of speaking truth to an audience (as he or she may well not do, or not always do, to other characters in the play). The actor-soliloquist will also, however, tend to trust an audience, just as necessary relationships of trust must obtain too with the play's director and with its linguistic and formal material, blank verse itself, if soliloquy is to be properly managed. In fact, the fully adequate speaking of the verse, the placing of reliance in it – which is a capacity acquired only with great difficulty and much practice – may of itself appear to organize and direct the course of the soliloquy's argument or set the terms of its dialogue.

The actor-soliloquist must be immediately present to – must be wholly *in* – the moment of performance, but succeeding in this is no easy matter. Acquired and perfected technique will be enabling, but the actor-soliloquist must constantly guard against appearing to be *making a speech* or, even more witheringly, *doing some acting*. In this regard, metaphors of spontaneity – in which the soliloquy is perceived as, variously, journey, route, invention, recognition, realization, surprise, fright, jazz music, mathematics, a Bob Dylan imitation, and a permanently revelatory discovery or 'epiphany' – will help. Conceiving of the soliloquy as fluidly unfixed, to be arrived at anew in every performance, may also mitigate the anxieties of repetition, influence and belatedness, but this involves willingly engaging in danger and risk and in knowing, exactly and crucially, what is involved in 'timing'. The acknowledgement of theatrical power will, similarly, be accompanied by scruple about its potential abuse.

Famous precursor soliloquists and occasions of soliloquy sometimes induce anxiety, but reliable mentors – directors, voice coaches, verse counsellors – are gratefully acknowledged, in a way that cogently evokes dependably supportive traditions of community and continuity in Shakespearean production and performance, even where radical experimentation is also being celebrated; indeed all of these actors are themselves, at times, advisers, teachers and counsellors in their turn, either casually or professionally, as coaches and tutors in drama schools. Shakespearean continuities will sometimes appear to the actor-soliloquist in strongly political terms – perhaps particularly in relation to women's soliloquies – but may also seem almost transcendental, prompting a quasi-religious understanding of Shakespearean theatre or a strong sense of this poet-playwright's universalism. The sense of having adequately performed a Shakespearean soliloquy will result in the experience of something 'joyous'.

The moment of joy, to which many of these transcripts testify, is itself the product and consequence, as they also amply attest, of great labour. To be a successful 'player' is also to be a successful worker, even though the success of the playing depends wholly on the concealing of the working. This is one implication, I think, of the various points in these transcripts at which actors hesitate between first- and third-person personal pronouns, between 'I' and 'he' or 'she', when attempting to define, with precision, what they do as soliloquists. I identify these hesitations with the punctuational sign of ellipsis, three points (...). This may be regarded as the punctuation of performance itself, in which the ego of the actor momentarily contracts in self-recollection in order all the better to leap forward into ... what, exactly? From the 'I' of self to the 'he' or 'she' of 'character' or 'role', certainly, but from actor to soliloquist too, breaking the dash of 'actor-soliloquist'. The ellipsis marks the journey from conception to performance, which is in turn sustained in being and motion by the audience's – by *our* – fascination, by the quality of our regard, by our needy response to the neediness of the soliloquist's appeal, in the enduring traffic and transaction, the permanent allure, of the Shakespearean stage. So Puck, speaking his epilogue-soliloquy at the end of *A Midsummer Night's Dream*: 'Give me your hands, if we be friends ...'

*

The soliloquies discussed in what follows are, in the main, those of well-known Shakespeare plays. The exceptions are *Henry VI*, *Part 3* and *King John*. A word or two about these might be useful.

Henry VI's soliloquy beginning 'This battle fares like to the morning's war' occurs in Act 2 Scene 5, set at the battle of Towton during the Wars of the Roses. Henry is a weak king whose war is in effect being fought on his behalf by his wife Margaret and 'lieutenant' Clifford. Henry has retired from battle and romanticizes a notional world of bucolic fulfilment opposed to his own perturbation as monarch; he sits on a molehill to do so. Immediately after the soliloquy he overhears two others, by a Yorkist son discovering that he has just killed his Lancastrian father and by a Lancastrian father discovering that he has just killed his Yorkist son – a correspondence emblematic of civil war. Henry soliloquizes further, pointing the moral and expressing the depth of his guilty grief.

King John follows the fortunes of the medieval king, ambiguously both hero and villain, in his lengthy contention with the French. Early in the play he settles a dispute between the Faulconbridge brothers, recognizing the elder one, Philip, as the bastard son of Richard I and knighting him. Philip the Bastard subsequently defends chivalric values, winning significant military victories for the king, but is, even so, self-serving. In his 'Commodity' soliloquy at the end of Act 2 Scene 1 he blames others for failing to fight for honour, but ends by pledging himself to the god of 'gain'. The word 'composition' used in the soliloquy's opening line has lost the meaning it had for Shakespeare, which is usually glossed as 'argument' or 'compact', and probably includes the sense of 'compromise'. It therefore connects with the word 'commodity' itself, usually glossed as 'advantage' or 'self-interest'.

*

1. Noma Dumezweni, Royal Court Theatre, Sloane Square, London, 3 November 2015

FIGURE 1 *Noma Dumezweni as Paulina,* The Winter's Tale, *2009*

Noma Dumezweni has performed in RSC productions of *Antony and Cleopatra*, *Macbeth* and *Much Ado About Nothing*. Here she focuses on *The Winter's Tale* (RSC Courtyard Theatre, 2009) and *Romeo and Juliet* (Courtyard, 2010). She refers to Greg Doran, the current Artistic Director of the RSC and Rupert Goold, former Associate Director at the RSC and current Artistic Director of the Almeida Theatre.

A lot of the time English teaching at school was having to put it into your head before you get it out of your mouth. But doing *Shakespeare for Kids* in schools was just that immediate heartbeat. With Shakespeare, and especially the soliloquies, I have to say it first and start feeling what it wants me to say, my version of it.

When I was working at the RST in Harriet Walter's *Macbeth*, Greg Doran said *Shakespeare's a guide; you then find it out for yourself, you hit the rhythm first, but the answers are all in there.* I don't like being over-directed; I can't feel it. I do body first and then it makes sense to do the head. I once dried monumentally as Titania because I hadn't put the rhythm inside me. It's got to be yours, and it's your version of yours. Let's just *play*; Shakespeare's there to be played with, and that's why we're 'players'.

Paulina doesn't have a soliloquy in *The Winter's Tale*, but she has a major speech (3.2.172–211), which I always thought of *as* a soliloquy. Soliloquy has to be done *to* someone, some thing, some other; there is a point of focus. We have those moments in day-to-day when I am talking to myself, trying to figure things out, but there has to be a point of focus. So I pick one person in the audience that's going to be your mirror, as it were. Wherever that shadow, that darkness, is, you know that there is a body, an energy coming towards you. We don't do it in a void; any spoken stuff is not in a void, and especially with the soliloquies.

I do think theatre is the closest thing we have to church for someone like me, because as soon as people go into an auditorium and the lights come down, we are in church. There is a complicity; we've made a commitment – it's as simple as that. You are not absent; no one is absent.

Greg Hicks was wonderful playing Leontes' soliloquies. He knows how to talk to himself and the audience at the same time. Years and years of practice, years and years of trust, and it's trusting your story-telling, knowing where you want that story-telling to go.

Yes, I am talking to myself but I am so aware that you're there and you are maybe the voice in my head and the energy that's going to be there.

I really haven't read that much Shakespeare. I want the parts to come my way first; I want the thing to be new writing for me. I take away the pressure of what other people's versions were. I received permission for this from Rupert Goold when we were doing *Romeo and Juliet* – *Do you know what? You don't need to go before, because this is the moment now.*

For me, the audience is *it*, and I'm one of those actors who loves looking at the audience when I'm talking, and particular members of the audience if someone's there. Some people find it *very* uncomfortable and some people love it and some hold your gaze. An audience is an individual. I've said to young actors, *Find out what the character of the audience is; you can feel it …* When you're doing a part, you think, *I don't need your love because I'm loving this character*. It's an exciting power, and it's a dangerous power because it becomes intoxicating.

In cinema the camera chooses when you get to look; the camera has the absolute power. So I want close-ups if you're going to do soliloquy because that's what the joy of film is. You go into those eyes, and the thing the camera makes you do is to go internal. Voice-over really bores me; I want to see the face speaking.

Trust that it will meet you and you will meet it. Trust the language and within that it will do what you need; don't over-act it. What's the word? Say the word and see what the next word gives me. Don't try and pre-empt it. The language gives us an anchor and shows us where the story has to be. Hear those sounds, let them vibrate within your body and then see what happens. Feel the freshness, the truth of the present moment, be in the moment with it.

I talk about the 'story' when I talk about plays. It's like reading my eight-year-old daughter a bedtime story and I go, *Ooh, I'm going to play all the characters*, and she goes, *No, mamma, don't do the voices – just read me the story*. It's that. You know, that's because actors are going, *What's* my *character doing in this story? I don't quite know what the whole plot is, but I'll hold on to that.* When actors in Shakespeare's day were only given their own parts – Oh God, can you imagine how exciting and terrifying that would be? You'd be so *present* with it, because you have to absolutely acutely *hear* to hear a play that way.

If you've done your work well, you will be healed, because you know that you have told the truth. You have told the truth and it has been received, and by it being received you have felt the acknowledgement come back, and it's an extraordinary feeling. It becomes a thrill, the thrill of an audience commenting; they are absolutely *there*. There is an answering call to what you are doing.

2. Mariah Gale, Bloomsbury, London, 10 February 2016

FIGURE 2 *Mariah Gale as Juliet,* Romeo and Juliet, *2010*

Mariah Gale has played such significant Shakespearean roles as Hero in *Much Ado About Nothing*, Viola in *Twelfth Night* and Portia in *Julius Caesar*. Here she talks about playing Isabella in *Measure for Measure* (Shakespeare's Globe, 2015), Ophelia in *Hamlet* (RSC, 2008) and Juliet in *Romeo and Juliet* (RSC, 2010, directed by Rupert Goold). She refers to Patsy Rodenburg, who taught at the Guildhall School of Music and Drama and has written books about verse speaking; John Barton, the Shakespeare scholar and director, associated prominently with the RSC; Giles Block, Globe Associate in charge of text and author of *Speaking the Speech: An Actor's Guide to Shakespeare* (2013); and Mark Rylance, the actor and the first Artistic Director of Shakespeare's Globe (1995–2005). 'Minnie' is the name by which Mariah Gale is usually known in the life beyond her professional designation.

I'd worked on Isabella's 'To whom should I complain?' (2.4.170–86) at drama school with Patsy Rodenburg and I thought, *O God, that's the famous bit that I'm trepidatious about.* But in rehearsals it just poured out of my mouth because I felt so propelled by her need to speak, and that it was the audience I was speaking to. I never questioned that instinct because it felt so strong. Angelo's words – whether he's *physically* violent or not – are shockingly violent. When you experience it as an actress, it can be terrifying, and when he leaves the room this horrible feeling of aloneness was so powerful that I felt this *massive* urge to connect with just anybody who was there – the director, the other actors, the stage managers. So I always thought I'd go, *O God, here comes this famous speech*, and the first time I got to it, it was just like the floodgates opening, and I *needed* those other people in the room for a very concrete reason. It's incredible the way Shakespeare has created this need at certain points.

She's somebody searching for an ally anywhere. Previously she's been looking for God and she's turned away from the world. And she's been forced back into that world and been met with perhaps what she was expecting – brutality and darkness. The first scene with Angelo is a marvellous chess game, she absolutely wipes the floor with him, and the second one ... she's gone back to the convent, but he's been thinking, *How do I get what I want?* And he does indeed back her into a horrible corner where she's faced with this awful dilemma. Sometimes in the Globe I'd see the sky and think, *Can I go up there, can I go to God?* But she doesn't reach to God. The way she speaks, she's reaching out – *Is there anybody here in this world who feels my pain?* Even more practically than that, *Is there anybody out there who can help? Is there anyone who's going to believe me?* She needs an *army* against this guy who's saying, *It's my word against yours.* Isn't it wonderful that, because there's no other character on stage she can go to, the play bursts its banks? It bursts the fourth wall; it bursts the fictional world of the play; it bursts out into reality. There's nothing more dramatic than that, you feel how that stage ... how *fiction* is literally thrust out into your space, and you're *so* part of it. It was such a discovery that that speech just had to pour out.

The wonderful thing about delivering a soliloquy in the Globe is, you think you have to re-orientate all the time, but actually in one glance you can go from the upper gallery ... you can flick your eyes down and there's somebody in the groundlings who's only maybe even a *metre* away, and it's an electrifying feeling. And it was really interesting the responses you'd get because you can see people's faces *so* clearly, they're in daylight, and sometimes you'd see people weeping and other times ... I saw a bunch of lads in the groundlings once *laughing* hysterically and I was *metres* away, and I really *felt* that one. I thought, *We're still in a world where this is dividing people's emotional response so massively.* And somebody said, *Thank you so much. I work with women who are raped, and people are still put in positions of power, this is very much going on today.* Shakespeare taps into issues that run deep and are universal and timeless, and it's really unfortunate that that issue is timeless, or appears to be, and I think it's great to plug into the equivalent contemporary scenario. So in that soliloquy I just felt so driven.

I think there's something more exposing about the soliloquy than there is about dialogue because ... with that one, she's just throwing herself open in a very delicate and feminine way ... it's full of questions, and questions are tender. But then it gets to the point where she says *These things are certainties to my brother, he will feel this way I do*. And the tragedy is that what she offers up to the audience as certainties are then turned on their head.

What I love about Shakespeare is he doesn't seem prescriptive. You can watch some theatre where you're being fed somebody's take on life and a set of morals or opinions. *Measure for Measure* shows even in the title that he's going, *What do you think? You decide. I'm going to throw you the toughest web of moral dilemmas* ... By having these soliloquies, he's not feeding you his opinion – he's just throwing everyone into a spin and deliberately saying, *Come on, think! What would you do? Who do you think is in the right?* That to me is the beauty of it, and to have characters delivering soliloquies is almost like they're taking the floor, saying, *Come on, you've got to be on* my *side*.

With Ophelia (3.1.149–60) it felt like a similar outpouring. You've had a scene beforehand that's heart-breaking, and it seems to be an immediate response to seeing Hamlet in a terrible state. The thing I really love Ophelia for is that her thoughts burst out about *him* ... she worries about *him* first and then she says, 'And I, of ladies most deject and wretched' ... you know, *I don't feel too good either*. She *loves* him. And it's another moment of feeling utterly alone. When we did it, my 'remembrances' were letters I'd given back, and he tore them up and poured them over my head like ... a snow globe, and as Polonius and Claudius were delivering those lines over my head – 'You need not tell us what Lord Hamlet said – / We heard it all' (3.1.178–9) – just so glib and reductive ... I would gather up all the pieces – and that's what that soliloquy came out of. That felt similarly that there was no one else to turn to – she has to burst through to appeal to the audience.

Patsy Rodenburg used to talk about circles of attention. First circle is your world, second circle is where you're in dialogue and third circle can be vast, there can be millions of circles. With Juliet's 'What's in a name?' (2.2.38–49) you feel it's going to a different place to 'Gallop apace, ye fiery-footed steeds' (3.2.34) – that's endless, it's way more expansive and going to a different target. So some of them feel like they're stream of consciousness and thinking out loud, and others feel more like a direct personal appeal, and then some of them go up to the gods. Each soliloquy has a completely different kind of action and a different target. Juliet's invocation in that speech is different from her adolescent bitch about the Nurse ... they've got different parameters.

I was fearful of the balcony scene because you think, *O my God, it's the most famous love scene in recorded history*. Me and the guy playing Romeo [Sam Troughton] had a chat with Rupert about our preconceptions and fears. You think *It's got to be a love scene and it's got to be so passionate and sexy and all these things that we have in our heads about what love scenes are.* And then I just thought *No, it's a conversation between a man and a woman, or a boy and a girl* and you're just in that rehearsal room with that actor and those words, and we started to break the scene down. Is it again a chess game? And if you just play that game, all the humour and passion, all this other stuff starts happening without you having to invent it. Just discovering it – asking, *what am I trying to change, what do I see in Romeo? Do I see a Romeo who's going to love me and leave me? And I need to test – to sound – him to see how true he is.* Then it becomes immediate and present, and all of those other fears dissolve, and there's a joy, an incredible freedom that comes with shedding that anticipatory anxiety and giving yourself over to the moment.

When you ditch the iconic idea of this wallflower looking pretty on a balcony sighing in a lovesick way and you go, *Well, okay, let's see what's going on in her mind, what's the argument, what's the problem, why does she need to speak?* it really hit me how politicized she is and how much of a rebel she is, like Isabella. You could transfer that to so many divided cultures around the globe. When you're forbidden to marry a certain person, that's when your experience of love becomes politicized. I just see a girl blowing apart a closed-minded culture where she's sat outside her parents' house saying *Okay, if the problem is that he's called Romeo Montague, let's just explode that word, let's explode the name. What is a name? It's not any physical part.* And she just so cleverly explodes all these restrictions and just *takes apart* all these received ideas she's been fed ... and she's fourteen.

If you speak the poison soliloquy ['I have a faint cold fear thrills through my veins ...', 4.3.15–58] out loud, you start from where she's trying to reason, and she speaks herself into a completely other state where she sees Tybalt. Just speaking it out loud does it to you – just rhythmically, and the imagery. She's got no friends left and she says 'I'll call them back again to comfort me. / Nurse! – What should she do here? / My dismal scene I needs must act alone.' That's so heart-breaking. She thought the Nurse was her ally and she just deserts her. She's almost going to have another dialogue, and she goes back into soliloquy. Something I found very sweet and touching about Juliet is that sometimes she seems like such a woman and other times like a girl, and in that speech she's so lonely; she's a prisoner in her own home. It's not a *mistake* that she meets Romeo and rebels; it comes *out* of a desperate need that's already there, and in that speech in particular – but she does it elsewhere in the play too – she personifies objects. 'Come, vial', she says, and 'Lie thou there' to the dagger. The dagger becomes her friend, and objects in her room become ... *people* that she talks to.

The beauty of all of these parts is that there's no one way of delivering them or experiencing them. When they shine through who *you* are, my Juliet will be completely different to yours. There's nothing concrete, and every night you can find a different path through, and I found that especially with Juliet. You have to let it ... well, you don't *have* to do anything, but I had so much more fun in the productions where I could see where it wanted to go that night, when you're on stage with actors who are similarly fluid. Greg Hicks said, *Wherever you're at, is your point of entry.* So Minnie on a Wednesday night in 2016 playing Juliet is going to be different to Minnie in 2013 on Saturday night at the Roundhouse.

When we were doing 'The clock struck nine' (2.5.1–17), Rupert said, *Don't tell them off, they're your friends*, and it really unlocked so much for me. Don't tell them off, let them in, they're your friends. It takes the fear out of it ... especially Press Night playing Juliet at the RST, I remembered his words when I went out there that night.

I've gone through various phases with blank verse and met different practitioners who've been really influential. I talked to John Barton a lot when I was rehearsing *Romeo and Juliet*. He put a notice on the notice board at the RSC saying if anyone wants to come round to mine to do sonnets. So we did sonnets, and he kicked our arses and pointed out why you were doing it all wrong, and some people went *Oh, I'm not going back there*, and I thought *No, he's the man.* And he put another note up saying *Anyone who wants to do any work on anything, you know where I am*, and I was one of the only people that got in touch with him, and I spent *hours* at his house talking about Juliet, and we did a lot of the soliloquies together and we unpicked them. He connected me to what was going on in her viscerally, through the language. Giles Block at the Globe helped me with *Measure for Measure*. He was really interested in how Shakespeare's writing style evolves – pointing out how you might finish a thought mid-line and a new one starts mid-line or another character will complete it, and he was very interested in the first and last strong syllable of a line. I found that very helpful for that play and that character. When I looked where Shakespeare was pointing, it unlocked such a lot, and it wasn't about hitting that word over the head with a hammer – it was to do with that word maybe having more room, or tickling that word or ... you could do all sorts of things to it. It was like lightbulbs would flick on in my head about the sense of my argument, and sometimes words landing on the end of the verse line would really surprise me and I'd go, *Oh God, that's not what* I *would have paid attention to*, and then the more I spoke it the more these moments of revelation came. I like doing a lot of work on my own, just giving texture to those words, so that when I get back into the rehearsal I can play. It's like a musician learning a piece of music – you learn the phrasing *so* well that when you come to play it you don't have to think about those technical things. I wanted to know *so* well where the verse line ended that I could speak that thought – which might last several lines and then a half line – without even *thinking* of how it was laid out on the page. The structure of the verse was a way in to the psychology and the emotional life and the argument that character was battling with.

I've done so much classical theatre that it feels more alien to me that there *aren't* asides when you do anything contemporary. Isn't it more of a lie that there is a fourth wall there and that the audience aren't really in the room? To me, it feels electric and necessary and often incredibly funny. I just love the moment when Angelo says 'She speaks, and 'tis / Such sense that my sense breeds with it' (2.2.143–4) because you can just tell what he's thinking already. And that makes the audience's job much harder, because any character who sits anywhere on the sliding scale of morality is going to reach out to you and look you in the eye and say *Are you enjoying this, 'cause I am?* And people will add asides of their own at the Globe, and they *always* get the biggest laugh of the entire show. Humour is the most powerful thing you can involve somebody in ... a complicit joke. If you've got someone roaring with laughter, you've got them in the palm of your hand, and a lot of asides can do that.

I find it hard to talk about acting because it feels instinctive and physical and illogical, and every show is different. Somebody asked me *Has Ophelia slept with Hamlet?* And I just thought, *I don't know, I discovered it differently every night, and that's the whole point – it's a live discovery.* If you're fixed down too much you're not alive any more. But at the same time, when I got to the Globe I did feel knowing the score really helps. Then you can play jazz, you can stretch things and bend things. Mark Rylance described verse as jazz once and I found that really enlightening.

I've always felt that soliloquies are just a continuation of dialogue; I don't see them as *separate* – and when I have seen them as separate I've come a bit unstuck.

Rupert Goold said to me once *Don't worry – there's a really nice projection behind you while you're saying it*, but I think it was a joke.

3. Lucian Msamati, Lyttleton Theatre, South Bank, London, 25 January 2016

FIGURE 3 *Lucian Msamati as Iago,* Othello, *2015*

Lucian Msamati talks about playing the title role in the RSC Swan Theatre production of *Pericles* (2006, directed by Dominic Cooke) and the first RSC black Iago in *Othello* (2015, directed by Iqbal Khan, with Hugh Quarshie in the title role). He refers to Laurence Olivier, who played Othello at the National Theatre in 1964; *House of Cards*, the US TV political drama series starring Kevin Spacey, which began screening in 2013; *Holby City*, the British TV medical drama series that stars Hugh Quarshie; and August Wilson (1945–2005), the American playwright whose *The Pittsburgh Cycle* portrays aspects of twentieth-century African-American experience. When I spoke to Lucian Msamati he was completing technical rehearsals for Wilson's play *Ma Rainey's Black Bottom*.

Shakespeare wants us to be complicit, to invite us in to whatever is going on. Some will say that he had to keep feeding the audience information, because you've got all this mad traffic going on and you need to keep the audience as much in the palm of your hand as possible. Particularly with *Pericles*, which has its problems, he is the thread through it that we follow, so without those soliloquies there is no point.

The great trap with Iago is believing he's a master manipulator and falling into this idea of *Yes, aren't I so clever? Dance, puppets, dance.* He *doesn't* know what he's doing, up to a certain point. We're watching a mind working things out; we're watching him stumbling on the fact that all these coincidences just happen to fall into his lap. He's *incredibly* lucky. Iqbal was very insistent that *We've got to put this guy under pressure, we've got to feel that at any point something could go wrong*. That's far more interesting and dangerous. Without that, we have a dull play which ultimately ends up making Othello look like a complete buffoon – which has been a tendency. It's pretty obvious right from the start what his motive is, in my head. Somebody who is going to spend all that time on stage with an audience, talking stuff – that's somebody who's got a hell of a lot of baggage, he's got a hell of a lot to unburden, to try and pick his way through. But what is joyous is that you, as a performer, get a chance to implicate the audience, *really* implicate them in the darkness that he's setting in motion. What gets parlayed into myth and legend is the enjoyment of the cumulative effect that a performance has, as opposed to the danger and the immediacy of what happens in the moment. In the wrong hands, for the right reasons, soliloquies can just have no balls. There's a great deal of reverence for Shakespeare, but when you look at some of the crazy things that happen this is unbelievable. You think, *Let's push the boat out here, let's see what happens if we do this ... Oh, that's nice, but let's see what happens if we do that.*

Me playing Iago certainly made a few ears prick up and interrogated the story in a fresh way. But not in a *new* way. The relationships and themes we played with have always been there. It's one of those pieces that gets burdened with an unnecessary history for all the wrong reasons – in the right places, unfortunately. And in this case a lot of it is to do with a particularly great actor [Laurence Olivier] who 'defined' the role of Othello in a modern way, and as a result to do anything counter to that somewhere deep down inside for people still seems sacrilegious. Sometimes it's a matter of finding the *risk* again, really risk something that makes you go, *Oh, okay, it's not just because of the colour of the skin, there's other stuff.* That Iago is black doesn't change the fact that *we've served in war together and you've chosen high-flying posh boy Cassio over me* – that cuts across anything, particularly a bond of deep kinship forged in conflict.

The moment Iago asks 'And what's he then that says I play the villain?' (2.3.331–57), it's life and death; he knows what he's doing, he knows it's *nasty* – so horrible, disgusting, abhorrent. Similarly, when Pericles is about to set sail, this is *I don't know, will I ever find my loved ones again?* – it's life and death. A number-one note in the rehearsals of *Pericles* by Dominic Cooke – and it's stayed with me – was when he said *Remember, these people exist in a heightened reality, and they are communicating in poetry because it's the higher form of communication.* And so when it comes to the extremes of human emotion, it's not difficult to access; it's the bare bones of what is true and real – pure, unvarnished, unadulterated. Because of the influence of cinema we can sometimes play with *Let me feel ten but express four, let me intrigue you a little bit.* I've said to a very talented young actor, whose family is from Nigeria, doing a speech from *Richard III*, *Think of the uncle that you all love the most, he's a little bit dodgy, he drinks a bit too much, he's always the one who's passing you a fiver, think of that uncle, and do the speech again as that uncle, and just tell me, just speak to me.* And it suddenly went *phew*, and his eyes ... and he went, *Oh! Yes!* That's what it is; don't worry about, *Oh, but the caesura!*, don't trip yourself over with that stuff, that's a spice for later, but right now you're just trying to communicate.

The job of the director is to remove obstacles. The director is going *Listen, here's the map, just follow it, I've figured it out for you. You'll find hills and valleys on your own, absolutely, but here's the starting point.* I've been fortunate to have worked with directors who have trusted me and who I in turn trust. So whatever tensions have arisen have *usually*, at the period just before the end of the rehearsal process and the beginning of technical rehearsals, when you feel most vulnerable, when you're under lights, you're in weird clothes and you're not in the comfort of the rehearsal room – all of a sudden, *I don't know where I am.* It can be very disorienting. It's a bad time when the more experienced or those who have the antennae can go *Okay, let me drop two or three useful notes and then leave you be. It's not the time for me to say anything.* When it comes down to it, it's about the trust, and not being made to feel, as a performer, that you're an imbecile or a child. Sometimes you'll feel like that anyway.

The best directors and the best voice coaches and text experts are able to enthuse and educate without seeming imposing or patronizing. There's a point at which all that has to be put aside just so that you can enjoy the text, figure those things out for yourself with your fellow performers. We muddle our way through and find it. The iambic pentameter *is* here and it *is* me, and all I'm doing is making sure that I have the signposts for when it gets hard. That's where any technique comes into its own. Technique is there for the hard days; on the other days you're flying.

The direct-to-camera is wonderfully impudent and cheeky – breaking the fourth wall without breaking the fourth wall, in the most brilliant way. In *House of Cards* Spacey does that a lot. In one season he doesn't address the camera once until a pivotal moment and the audience are, *Ah!* The voice-over is a bit of a cop-out because it takes pressure away from the performer; a voice-over means that a lot of it doesn't have to be done to an audience. With Shakespeare you want to engage with somebody speaking the language. That's what radio captures, because you know that all the performer has is their voice to evoke all of these things; it's *just* a voice.

You have to embrace the medium of the aside. There's no point in trying to be clever with it; it is what it is. If you are true to what its intended purpose is at that moment you'll find a way that is true and consistent, but you cannot be embarrassed or self-conscious. There are always moments in rehearsals where you're falling about giggling, *This is just ridiculous*, but at the same time you're like, *Well, that's the story*, and people will go with us if we go with it because we all want to see what happens in the story. I am as reverentially irreverent about them as I am with most things. Let's interrogate it, let's kick it around. As much as there's a responsibility to be true and honourable to the stories, there's a responsibility to be *irresponsible*, because we cannot help the age we live in. With a smartphone, Othello could have easily gone *Let me just text where Cassio is right now.* You can't change the stories, but nothing is gospel. The less precious people are, the more exciting things we'll find. And let's be honest, there's plenty in Shakespeare that's not perfect. As Hugh Quarshie says, *Shakespeare wouldn't get past the script editor of* Holby City. Which is a fair point, you know.

I was determined to dissociate myself from the performance history of *Othello*. I needed to take my own experiences, my own faculties, my own capacity, and engage with what's in front of me. There was an article in *Intelligent Life* with all these pictures of the great Iagos of the past, and the last line was *Follow that, RSC!* My language became very colourful and I thought, *Okay, if that's how you want to play it, we'll just have to show you, we'll do it* our *way and have done with it.* The *real* competition is cultural ownership. It's not so much the colour of one's skin, what one sounds like, what school one went to. More often than not, it comes down to *Yes, but it's not really yours, is it?* To which my response is *Well, that's what I learnt in the schools on the African continent, so it is mine, and nobody can tell me how I must look at or analyse what is mine – that's up to me.* Just as much as I have no control over a 17-year-old from the Home Counties who picks up August Wilson and falls in love with it and is moved to want to produce it. Who on earth am I to say *No, you cannot*? Shakespeare *is* mine; I have understood it; I have a relationship with it which may be completely counter to what you understand, but I'm not going to break it, because it's as precious to me as it is to you. And *that* has been very interesting.

4. Pippa Nixon, West End, London, 11 November 2015

FIGURE 4 *Pippa Nixon as Ophelia,* Hamlet, *2013*

Pippa Nixon's Shakespearean roles include Titania in *A Midsummer Night's Dream*, Lady Anne in *Richard II* and Jessica in *The Merchant of Venice*. She talks here about playing the Bastard as a woman in *King John* for the RSC in 2012 and both Rosalind in *As You Like It* and Ophelia in *Hamlet* (directed by David Farr) for the RSC in 2013. She refers to Ben Whishaw, who played Hamlet at the Old Vic in 2004; Thomas Ostermeier, who directs the Schaubühne in Berlin, where he staged *Hamlet* in 2011; and Cicely Berry, the voice director of the RSC from 1969 to 2014, who has published books on voice and verse speaking.

I think the responsibility increases when you are on a thrust stage or in the round because the audience aren't *there*, now they're everywhere, you have to plant your seed everywhere. The people sitting out there and the people sitting right in front of you have to have the same experience, and that is your responsibility as an actor. You're trying to communicate with everybody and you have to think in three dimensions. Sometimes I may feel I'm shouting to someone on the other side of the Thames but the end result comes when someone who is sitting in the cheap seats up there says *You moved me to tears*, and the person sitting right there says *I was so moved*. That's when you go, *Okay* ... Again, it's part of implicating the audience – *Are you awake? Because I'm coming to talk to you, I haven't forgotten you*. The beauty is that there are plenty of people who love the fact that you're engaged with them. It *is* real, we're in this world of make-believe together, so let's go for it. Together.

Playing the Bastard as a woman, we would use the audience to bounce ideas off, which I found incredibly helpful because it made it *active*, it didn't make the soliloquies internalized. It gave them an energy and a focus, and that's what you need in soliloquy. For any audience, it's hard to get your head around the language and tune in. So as actors we can help with that by making an argument, going on a journey, through being *present* and discovering it ourselves, but also discovering it with the people in the room. That doesn't necessarily mean direct eye contact. For example, in the Swan when it's so intimate ... being able to see the people really helped to direct the thoughts, to sort of find the thoughts out there rather than just inside my own imagination.

The Bastard's 'Mad world! mad kings! mad composition!' (2.1.561–98) is a really brilliant speech that goes at such a pace and asks for so much muscle and dexterity from the actor that – probably because I didn't really know it beforehand – I had completely free licence with it; but actually I believe we should have that with any character we play.

I found the Bastard's 'A foot of honour better than I was' (1.1.182–219) soliloquy so difficult to make sense of. I would feel, even in performance, *Oh, I've not inhabited this yet*, and I really didn't feel I *did* get it until quite a long way through the run. Of course I *understood* what it meant; I just struggled to know whether we had landed on the right foot with it. I remember Jonny [Slinger] saying after six months *I've got another six months of Hamlet in me*. No actor says that unless they're still discovering. That is the amazing thing about Shakespeare; I could have done that with Rosalind actually. The language ... you just get new understandings of it all the time.

When you get your own hands on Shakespeare, there's so many discoveries. You find the nugget of truth of that character and why she does what she does; it opens up the language in a whole different way. You find a specific route that gives that speech a *necessity* for you to say, that makes you *own* the language, and for me it doesn't matter whether you've heard it a thousand times, you have to find that strand to make it live in *you*. That's the beauty of Shakespeare and why we continue to play him; it's because there's such an understanding of humanity and of language and ... spirituality, in a sense, that every actor playing those speeches can find it from a route within themselves and make it sound fresh. Because really it's about letting your own soul take fire.

Rosalind's epilogue is *specifically* for the audience; it's not about you working things through, but I love contradiction, I love this *and* this. Rosalind asks the actress to bring all of herself. So, although I didn't step out of character, it was me as Rosalind – Rosalind channelling Pippa, Pippa channelling Rosalind. So that end speech was *me* completely naked speaking the lines of Shakespeare as Rosalind, but it was also me. For me, it was a big flirt with the audience, as Pippa and as Rosalind.

A great note that a director once gave me was *Stop trying to explain everything you're doing, just speak it, it doesn't matter if the audience doesn't get it, they will get the spirit of it.* You need to, at a certain point, leave behind the responsibility of the audience. You spend a lot of time feeling responsible that the audience understand, and then you need someone to go, *Stop it, and just focus on the play.*

Sometimes you're waiting to see how someone's going to do a great soliloquy. Ben Whishaw's 'To be or not to be' was a revelation, completely different from how I'd ever heard it. He played him like a schoolboy, so there was a huge amount of grief, and there was a real fight for knowing whether he was going to kill himself or not. Rather than a philosophical argument, making the decision felt like a really present, fresh, urgent thing. Thomas Ostermeier's *Hamlet* at the Berlin Schaubühne theatre is the best I've ever seen, and I've seen loads. They did 'To be or not to be' several times. They began the whole show with it, they did it half way through sort of as a piss-take, and they did it again like for real. Shakespeare can be bashed about quite a bit, it can take quite a lot, and it can take quite a lot of *concept* too, as long as there's connection. I think sometimes you do dread the well-known speeches and you desperately hope an inspiration will come to lift it off the page. It's you as an actor going through the whole journey of that character and where that speech lands in that journey.

At the Globe you have three people giving you notes on verse speaking, so you can't help but have a little bit of self-consciousness. The more Shakespeare you do, though, the more it becomes like a language you inhabit. When I played Titania for the RSC, I got stuck in some of that verse – it's so beautiful and flowery and spiritual. I had a breakthrough, an epiphany, when I played the Bastard because we were doing something so out of context. I'd never known anybody play the Bastard as a female. It was me in 2012 speaking that language but also having done many other Shakespeare plays and having gone through countless one-on-ones with voice coaches. Only after all that did it actually start to click, and it was like the rhythm was within me and I could start to play with it and bend it slightly – but I was still sticking with the rhythm of the verse. Cis Berry says it's like jazz, and I understand what she means. There absolutely is a structure and a science and a mathematics to it, it is the heartbeat. But within that you can play and you can bend and inhabit. Taking that into Ophelia and Rosalind, I suddenly didn't feel bound by this verse, I loved it, and I was like, *yes!* Suddenly things became really obvious: you *land* on that word and you move quite quickly through to the other word, it's the contrast of it. Like learning any new language, it's really hard at first and then suddenly you become fluent in it without realizing it. Now it's just *in* me, I understand it.

David Farr asked me to make Ophelia's 'glass of fashion' speech (3.1.149–60) not a soliloquy but a monologue directed to Polonius. It's interesting, but it doesn't give you time to have that moment of *I am ruined and I have ruined the one person that I've loved* because there's something different about being on your own and speaking out loud than directing it to someone. So I found it hard to connect to that speech. But David gave me a huge amount of leeway with Ophelia in lots of ways. I think it should feel like a collaboration, but I also think the director has to say that they *know* this is the beast that we're in.

The aside is different from the soliloquy, there could be something pantomimic about it. An aside is literally sharing an in-joke or a comment directly with the audience, probably a character trying to get the audience on side. Not to belittle King John, but we found that it was the Bastard's play in lots of ways. The audience journeys through that play through the Bastard. So the asides came quite naturally – it's like *I have this special relationship with the audience that none of you lot have anyway* ... Even an arsehole character can get empathy from an audience in an aside, there is power in them. Sometimes, especially in long-running shows, the actor begins to love them more and the audience begins to love them more and before you know it they can get a bit out of control and they can draw attention away from the main scene. You have to have a certain amount of discipline because it's amazing to be loved by the audience and for them to love your character. But you can't milk it.

There *is* something powerful when you look to camera; it's like *House of Cards*. Whenever Kevin Spacey looks to camera you love it; it's awful, but it's like you love it as well. That's what a soliloquy and an aside should be. It's a flirt.

I remember Jonjo [O'Neill] saying *O God, I've given my life to Shakespeare* because he had this choice of going down the line of telly and decided he was going to do Shakespeare, and he was like *I feel like Shakespeare's just chosen me*. And that might sound a bit wanky, but there *is* something there. Not everyone does decide to do it, but if you do go down that road it does feel like that. There's something spiritual about it. I'm not equating Shakespeare to God by any means, but there is something more than other playwrights. He had this understanding of humanity that's transcended time. When you play these great characters, it asks something from your soul ... to make it truly a part of you and something that's a wonderful performance ... to make us say *I saw Jonny Slinger's Hamlet* and *I saw Jonjo O'Neill's Richard III* or *I saw Pippa Nixon's Rosalind* ... When we say those things, it's because the actor has done something more than just your normal person playing. To get it on to that plane I call 'spiritual' is because it asks for your soul, and it asks for this vulnerability and *merging* that is more than something just earthy; it connects to something that's more than just *this* time, it's been like *all* of the time. It's not to do with whether you're religious or not. It asks for something greater than the box of religion. It asks for your spirit.

5. Jonjo O'Neill, Royal Exchange Theatre, Manchester, 21 October 2015

FIGURE 5 *Jonjo O'Neill as Richard III,* Richard III, *2012*

Jonjo O'Neill talks here about playing Richard III in the RSC's Swan Theatre production of the play in 2012, Edmund in *King Lear* at the Liverpool Everyman Theatre and the Young Vic in 2008–9 and Orlando in *As You Like It* for the RSC in 2009. His other Shakespearean roles include Dromio in *The Comedy of Errors*, Mercutio in *Romeo and Juliet* and Posthumus in *Cymbeline*. He refers to John Gielgud (1904–2000), whose style of Shakespearean acting dominated British theatre for a long time in the twentieth century; to Anthony Sher's celebrated RSC performance of Richard III in 1984, the subject of his book *Year of the King* (1985); and to the intimate (340-seater) indoor Sam Wanamaker Playhouse (modelled on Worcester College, Oxford's drawings of a seventeenth-century theatre, and popularly thought to resemble the sixteenth-century Blackfriars Theatre), which was built into an existing brick shell in Shakespeare's Globe and opened in 2014. It's named after the American actor instrumental in having the Globe rebuilt.

What's a soliloquy? When someone stays onstage alone and speaks words, that's what it is. As Richard III, I come on alone and I speak to the audience. To say any more is to go beyond fact. Also, we're talking about form. We can't take any of it for granted. Shakespeare's written a happening, a piece of poetry. It's your internal world; the idea of talking to yourself reduces it. I see it as my brain being the globe, welcoming the entire audience inside. I could be taunting them, I could be asking them questions. It's externalizing the dilemma, externalizing the inner world. You're talking to the audience. Your instinct as an actor is to tell the story and to bring people through these thoughts. As an actor you realize that with Shakespeare it's not about how you feel, it's about how you think. There's no fourth wall, so the idea of talking to oneself is imposed because that springs from a naturalistic expectation.

The Gielgud kind of introspection may be an actor's choice, but I think it's a bad choice. It's imposing a style that doesn't spring from the work. There's something about Shakespeare that informs you how to do it. Doing it with an audience is what teaches you how to do it. You get on stage and that's what it's about – that, and them. That's where the power is, and if you want power as an actor, that's where it is, between the words and the audience. Would they have done this through the ages? If they wanted to get the attention of the Globe, they would have had to do it, and that's that. If you want to do it in the Wanamaker, there's different muscles involved; but how is the person at the back of the theatre going to hear the words unless you're talking to them? Shakespeare encourages actors to know they're on a stage, to know that the audience are there. I can see how someone might deliver 'To be or not to be' to themselves, but it's a bad choice because it's not as interesting as asking the audience a question. If you can make the decision in front of the audience, do it. Let them work it out as they go.

I found Orlando really hard. He's mad, mad with love. How am I going to love this character as he is? Shakespeare's taking the piss out of him for all this crap poetry. I thought, how can I do that wholeheartedly [the soliloquy beginning 'Hang there, my verse, in witness of my love', 3.2.1]? And I realized that it's me in my bedroom wanting to be Bob Dylan; that's what he is. That's the way in. So I strummed it on the guitar and it was like I was making it up. And it *is* sweet – it was about that yearning, a boy with a guitar in his room. But that was the least contact I ever had with an audience, very difficult.

With Edmund it was very much about necessity and his animal. His animal is his intelligence, his sex, not his *wit*, that's ridiculous, that's blame-brigade stuff. Edmund *is* sex, that's what he is. I delivered 'Thou, Nature, art my goddess ...' (1.2.1–22) *up*. Since then I've realized it should be to the audience, because *they're* Nature, they're *inner* Nature, and that could be both in and out. Shakespeare loves being three things at once.

I found Edmund saying he's been loved really difficult ['To both these sisters have I sworn my love ...' 5.1.56–70] because the play's going cosmic and you think *Where is that line coming from?*, and I didn't know where to put it. And of course you're dying, you know you're dying. It felt like – it smelt like – a joke to me, I didn't really understand it. What's interesting with that part is that people just *love* Edmund ... There was something very sexual about it and your relationship to the audience, and working off your wits and doing it in front of them, showing them you're lying to someone's face. They just loved it when you didn't twirl your moustache, they loved it when you just did it like that or you just did it out of necessity, they *loved* it because they know that's underneath everyone. There's something underneath Edmund – Shakespeare gives him the keys to the kingdom. There's certain characters that he just *gives*, and you feel like you're on the play and you have the power *of* the play. Mercutio certainly has that too, and the audience is just magnetized to you because Shakespeare *loves* those characters, these broken people. And then look, the one character, Orlando, who's the most full-hearted, sincere, was definitely the most boring role I've ever played.

You'll try to find different areas of the audience to connect to with different thoughts. I find clarity in Shakespeare with visualizing the thoughts in different places. One important thing with soliloquy is antithesis. That's where he gets so much of his power from – creating clear polarities, creating a language by going black, white, grey ... There's something open about the intelligence of Shakespeare that makes it infinite and capable of describing itself.

You have to keep it moving, so you're always going to have to externalize. To go in is never really that much use. It's pictorial and it's coming off the play, coming off the line. Directors will say *Stay on the line, don't do your thinking off the line, do it on the line*, and this is back to form. Rather than imposing an acting style on it, it's being educated by *it*, and sometimes it's hard to get *on* the line. The hardest one I had to do was Richard III's final soliloquy ['Give me another horse! Bind up my wounds! ...', 5.3.177–206]. It was just so clear psychologically. What you're witnessing is someone cracking apart, their realizing it with complete clarity. I felt that pressure to deliver an emotional reaction to the character's dilemma, and I felt pressure to *do acting*. Because it was very much someone alone with their thoughts. Compare that to his opening speech – that's ceremonial, he charms the audience, he forms a relationship with the audience, a pact, but at this point he's in a very different place. He's got the fear, it's very physical, and these questions, this wave of something, is coming over him, it's rising up. He unravels and realizes that he hates himself; it's an amazing piece of writing. You feel like it's your big scene, to *do your acting*. You want it to feel totally natural – what you're saying and your emotional response to be one thing. Anthony Sher seemed to have a bit of an obsession about cracking that scene. I had that. Sometimes I'd feel emotionally wild, I felt I'd got myself in the right place but then forget the lines.

I watched Olivier's Richard and I felt I was playing a game with myself, I was provoking myself. I watched five Richards. Olivier's not my kind of actor at all, but there's something of the joy ... there's something of Richard in there, a smell. I have enough confidence in myself, but also I knew what my approach was going to be. Richard was going to be me, that was my decision, *I'm going to do this as if it's me* ... To get closer to the play, to be pulled in *that* direction and *that* direction and *that* direction, to see where the high notes were, to see if they had to *be* high notes. It's a way of familiarizing yourself with the material, really, and if you see something you like, steal it. I remember I watched a BBC TV production for Edmund and he had changed a word, I can't remember which, and it was so much easier, and I thought *I'm having that*, and the director said *Where did that come from?* A little bit of that goes on; it can be useful to pull people in. It's different if it's a word Shakespeare made up.

Richard's Act 1 is kind of like a soliloquy. He does something and he talks to the audience and then he does something else and he talks to the audience. I remember Act 1 was amazing, I loved it – so exciting and joyous to have that relationship with the audience, and they *loved* it. 'Was ever woman in this humour wooed?' (1.2.230–66) – the audience just *loved* that. I turned around and said it to them.

I thrive with live happening and that's been nurtured by Shakespeare. I'm loved by Shakespeare, and I feel that Shakespeare's always asked me to do more – *Go on, get it and mean it, mean it harder*. He loves that and rewards that – *Just go on, go for it*, and that's how you trip up and get better at it. I'm not interested in strutting and fretting because it's not real, it's not what's happening. Good actors know the audience are there, and they're playing to them the whole time, they will walk with the intelligence that they are there, because they have to talk to them. Being a player, the joker face ... meaning it and not meaning it ... now you see me, now you don't, like Dylan. It's a peek-a-boo game, and Shakespeare encourages you to do it, so it's a powerful place for an actor to be, rather than stuck within a form where an audience has to agree on or buy into an idea of what we're all doing together – *We'll all watch it and be normal and agree he's good at being like a person*. There's something about Shakespeare that makes you feel good about yourself as an actor because you're working with genius, total genius, and he's encouraging you to *say it, go on, say it*.

6. Jonathan Slinger, Theatre Royal, Drury Lane, London, 11 February 2016

FIGURE 6 *Jonathan Slinger as Hamlet,* Hamlet, *2013*

Jonathan Slinger has played Florizel in *The Winter's Tale* (in which Mark Lewis Jones played Leontes), Puck in *A Midsummer Night's Dream*, Dromio in *The Comedy of Errors* and Prospero in *The Tempest*. He talks here about playing the title roles in RSC productions of *Richard II* and *Richard III* (in the Histories cycle in 2007), *Hamlet* (directed by David Farr, 2013) and *Macbeth* (2011) and also about playing Malvolio in the 2012 RSC production of *Twelfth Night*. He refers to David Warner's story about playing Hamlet for the RSC in 1965 which I recounted in Part II of this book.

When I was in the opening season of the Globe in 1997 there was speculation about what the experience was going to be like. People had a very strong idea about what they wanted, which was what they imagined to be the atmosphere and dynamic in Shakespeare's time – a very *active*, fluid dynamic between the actor and the audience, and the audience would feel free to wander in and out during the performance and to heckle and shout. But there was a lot of scepticism. People thought, *It's going to be terribly self-conscious; you'll have the odd American tourist shouting out* Gadzooks! *and cod-Elizabethan nonsense.* I was stood backstage on our first night of *The Winter's Tale*, *fascinated* to know how it was going to go down. In the scene where Paulina brings the baby from the prison and Leontes says 'Shall I live on, to see this bastard kneel / And call me father? Better burn it now / Than curse it then. But be it; let it live' (2.3.153–5), Mark, playing Leontes, took them to 'Shall I live on, to see this bastard kneel / And call me father?' and fifteen hundred people went, *Yeeees!* And he looked at them ... 'Better burn it now / Than curse it then', and they all went, *Noooo!* And he looked at them again and he went, 'But be it; let it live'. And the hairs on the back of my neck ... I had this absolute moment of epiphany, that Shakespeare wrote that *specifically* and purposefully with that in mind. There is still no doubt in my mind. It was so electric, so perfect, so brilliant ... I could suddenly chart that theatrical tradition right through to panto where it still exists today. It made me read and perform Shakespeare completely differently from that day on. That example of David Warner in *Hamlet* happened to me as well, at exactly that point [in the 'O what a rogue and peasant slave am I' soliloquy, 2.2.484–540] – 'Am I a coward?' ... and a bunch of kids in the circle all shouted *Yeah, you are!* But then of course *all* of the next bit – 'Who calls me villain, breaks my pate across?' and so on – is so *perfect* I just can't envisage it being anything else.

When I went to the RSC I started playing these bigger roles with that epiphany in mind. The audience becomes almost another character in the play. It's clearer with some characters than others. For instance, Richard III *recruits* you at the beginning; you're very much on his side, and there's a part of you that is *absolutely* willing him on, because he's so charismatic and magnetic, and it's like *Come on everybody, we're going to go on this incredible ride together and you're going to be very highly entertained.* And they *are*! What happens, around the point that he starts talking about killing children, is the audience starts to go *Whoa, hang on a minute, we didn't sign up for* this*!* It's almost as if Richard can feel them, along with members of the cast, start to melt away. So Richard's railing against Buckingham, but he's railing against you as well, he's saying, *You haven't got the stomach for this any more, have you? But I'm going to go all the way anyway*. Then the audience become his judge, so in that final soliloquy he's suddenly surrounded by the voices of judgement ... One of the most electrifying moments was 'Was ever woman in this humour wooed?' I used to find a woman on the front row and make eye contact and be absolutely asking her. And one night this woman just nodded her head in my face and the whole place went hysterical. But of course the next line is 'Was ever woman in this humour *won*?' So, even within that, there's a response to the response you're getting from the audience. Hamlet is a perfect case in point. When you really start to look into them with that frame of mind – *This is happening in my life, what do you think I should do?* – you find examples of call and response all over the place in Shakespeare's soliloquies. One reason I find the thrust stage ideal for Shakespeare is because it allows you contact with the audience that the proscenium arch doesn't give you.

The way I would play Richard II's soliloquy ['I have been studying how I may compare ...' 5.5.1–66] is, the audience are the people in the world that I can't contact. I'm in this prison. They're *there* and he's talking to them, and they become a sort of sounding-board for his thoughts. It's almost as if the audience has ultimate knowledge. There's a sense of, *As I am ... as Richard is ... having these moments of epiphany ...* 'I wasted time and now doth time waste me' ... it's almost as though he's going, *I wasted time, and you* knew *that, didn't you? You knew all along. If only I'd been able to listen to* you, *or the various other people in my life ... John of Gaunt ... that were telling me that ... Richard II* for me is the ultimate play of a journey into self-awareness. It's a character who begins with no self-awareness at all and as he loses everything he thinks important he gains this extraordinary self-awareness: 'whate'er I be, / Nor I nor any man that but man is / With nothing shall be pleased till he be eased / With being nothing'. It's like this extraordinary Zen Buddhist realization just before he's killed. That's what's so beautiful about this play. But the audience knows, right from the beginning ... they're sitting there going, *This awful, superficial, shallow, vain, self-obsessed man ...* So this soliloquy's not active in the way that in other soliloquies characters are *definitely* going, *What am I going to do? I don't know what to do*. It's more that they're silent observers of his epiphany, and he *is* talking to them, but there's a sadness within how he talks to them because they're not actually in the room. He's absolutely on his own, and he has that line at the beginning, 'I have been studying how I may compare / This prison where I live unto the world; /And, for because the world is populous ...' That's the world that *they* inhabit, which he's not in, so he's sort of talking *beyond* the prison walls to the people. I always used to imagine that the prison walls are at the edges of the stage ... those are my *walls*, but it's almost as if he can see *through* the walls to the people beyond, where he would love to be, ideally, but ...

The minute you go *Nobody's going to understand this*, you're done for, they're done for, the production's done for. It's very important that you never put that constraint on yourself, ever. I have a romantic theory that in Shakespeare's time people would have understood dense textured thought much more easily than we do now, that in some way what we have gained in our ability to communicate at long distances very quickly, directly proportionally we have lost in our ability to communicate one-to-one very complicated ideas. The challenge for the modern actor is to *forensically* understand every single beat of what you're saying because if you don't have *absolutely* every single minute thing understood then the audience has not a hope in hell. I think one of the reasons people don't get Shakespeare is because a lot of actors doing Shakespeare don't understand what they're saying – not forensically, with absolute minute detail. A lot of actors get the gist – they 'get the gist' – and think *If I do it in a nice voice and I say it poetically, that's all that's needed.* The best directors don't mind spending a hell of a lot of time sitting around *absolutely* mining it. It takes time to be able to even *think* with that level of complexity, never mind articulate it. So you have to go through a period where you are *spelling out* every single word that needs its emphasis, and everything just completely slows down whilst your brain gets its head around that. And then, over the course of the next few weeks, it's a question of thinking it that quickly and then being able to speak it that quickly. The whole process takes a long time, and that's the challenge of Shakespeare.

I – rather controversially, compared to some actors, academics and directors – pay very little attention to the rules. Greg Doran is a master at the techniques of verse speaking and he will entertain and educate for hours about how all these rules 'help' you to do it. There's some very interesting stuff in there, but one of the other things that can stop an actor being able to deliver Shakespeare in a comprehensible way is coming at it with a rule-based approach. What can happen is you can start to *hear* the metre. The minute I hear the metre I just switch off completely. If you can come in from the rule-approach side to verse speaking and then get *through* that so that we can't hear any of that any more, great. But unfortunately it's very difficult for a lot of actors to jettison it. So I always say to people *Approach it as if it's a modern piece of text and you want to make it as comprehensible to me as you can. Forget the verse, forget the structure and make it understandable to me.* What's interesting is that once you connect with the emotion, the verse takes care of itself. My theory is that Shakespeare wasn't really *thinking* about it in that way; he was thinking about the character's dilemma, what the character's trying to say, the emotion of the character, their relationship to the other people on stage. First and foremost was, *What's the drive of this thing?*

Malvolio, albeit on his own, still had a relationship with the audience … a slightly distrustful one: *Are you on my side? Or are you with that lot?* So there's an element of having an image that he wants to desperately believe in, but he's aware that certain people are not wholly on his side or believing of that. So that speech is all about trying to prove to himself that he's worthy of Olivia's love and that she could possibly be in love with him. Part of that was him trying to boost himself, but for me it also became, *I'm convincing* you *as well, because you might be sitting there thinking this is complete nonsense.* So that dynamic I still held on to. And of course as he grows in confidence, finding the letter, suddenly the *idea* becomes something that could actually work out for him, then the relationship with the audience becomes even more triumphant – like, *For all you doubters out there … You* see, *you* see*?* … My Malvolio wore a wig, he was a bald man with a toupée, so I used to come on for that speech and look around to make sure he was on his own – quite weirdly – but when he realized he was on his own … I had a picture of a mirror, and he straightened the toupee. So it's an interesting thing about soliloquies: *Am I on my own? Am I not on my own?* And then, *I'm on my own, but I'm not on my own, because there are three people hiding behind the bar. I'm on my own so I can be vulnerable, but then I'm going to talk to you …*

I also find with soliloquies that you can dip in and out of your awareness of the audience. I found with 'To be or not to be' that there were stretches that were completely to himself, but then he'd … I'd come out of that moment of being on my own and notice everybody and then deliver a little bit and go *It's amazing, isn't it, because life is like this?* So it can be very fluid, and I don't think you need to say *I'm going to address the audience at all times with every single moment of this speech*. You can be very into yourself and then there are moments which … 'Thus conscience doth make cowards of us all' … *Us all, all of us in this room. You know what that means?* It came out of a moment of self-realization and then it became more expansive.

Singing the Ken Dodd song 'Happiness' before 'To be or not to be' was my idea; not the most popular choice in the world … I remember going through a period of questioning it with David [Farr]. We explored it in rehearsal and it was fun, it gave us something, and he was adamant. There was a good and specific reason for it which didn't have anything to do with wrong-footing the audience. Just before he enters, Polonius says, *I hear him coming*, and we were thinking, *What does he hear? I suppose it could be footsteps or … is it whistling, is he humming?* And that led to, *Maybe he's singing something*. Hamlet thinks he's coming to have a chat with Claudius, so he's very much in his antic disposition at this point. So we put the two things together. Polonius hears him coming in some way, Hamlet's coming expecting that Claudius is going to be there, so whatever mood he's in will be tailored for that meeting. He isn't expecting to walk in and see Ophelia sitting there, so we came up with this bonkers idea that he was in his antic disposition singing a song which was very much in juxtaposition to how he was actually feeling. That was the thought.

The fame of the soliloquies is an anxiety. The way you get around it is by making the impulse to say that speech your particular impulse in your particular production and your particular characterization – to make that as specific to you as you can. With 'To be or not to be' we chose to have Ophelia sitting in the room because in the text she doesn't leave. It's often purely a soliloquy. So he walks in singing, expecting to see Claudius; Claudius isn't there; he sees Ophelia, and, having expended energy appearing to be happy, everything wells up in him about his position, his desperation, everything … and having her there helped that. So the moment of desperation, finding that impulse to say those lines, coming out of a moment of pretending to be something else, helped me to find the specificity of that moment. The other choice I made, which made the beginning of that speech specific to me again, was to stress 'that *is* the question' rather than '*that* is the question', which is more traditional, because I thought, *Hamlet's an incredibly bright person, are we really expected to believe that somehow this is the very first time he's ever thought about that?* – which is what I think is implied if you say 'To be or not to be, *that* is the question.' It just didn't seem to me to strike very true. So that line became, *I've thought about this time and time again, and the thing I always come back to is the simplicity* of 'To be or not to be, that *is* the question' – *it's the only question.* So that was another way of slightly taking the curse off, because I made it extremely specific to me and to my own characterization.

With Macbeth's 'Is this a dagger' soliloquy (2.1.34–64), it helped me to anchor it in my awareness of an audience because I could go *I think I can see that, can you? Am I going mad here?* To me, that takes it into a more ... portentous world. You're a bit more limited when it's just you, your mind on your own. Unlike Richard III, who recruits you, with Macbeth the audience becomes the character's inner life. Richard III starts with incredible confidence and then that relationship with the audience becomes more fractured and they become the judgement at the end. With Richard II, the audience are his subjects, they reflect his innate sense of superiority over the world: *You will bow down before me because I have the ultimate knowledge.* By the end, he realizes he doesn't have the ultimate knowledge and they become the people in his own brain saying *Well, this was never going to end well, was it?* Macbeth *knows* right from the beginning that, if he goes on this course, the chances are it's all going to end terribly for him. He says it right at the beginning and then repeats it at various times, for instance in the soliloquy 'If it were done, when 'tis done ...' – *If we knew now that we wouldn't go to hell for this, then we'd do it in a heartbeat, but chances are I will* ... So the audience are then reflective of that, it's like they're the ones sitting there going, *This isn't a good idea, Macbeth*, in the same way that his conscience is already doing that.

Probably because I cultivate a relationship with the audience very strongly I don't think the asides are that different from soliloquies. Soliloquies are the character's truth; whatever the truth of the character is, is revealed within a soliloquy, in so far as they know the truth at that particular point in the play. Asides are exactly that – they're just snatched lines within a scene, the only difference being that there are other characters on the stage; but they serve the same purpose, because there are moments in a scene where the character steps out of the scene and speaks truth to the audience. He doesn't want the others to hear, because he doesn't want them privy to that truth.

Who owns a soliloquy? Within the context of a production, the character owns it. The character is a collaboration between the actor and the director, and the best experiences I've had have been very collaborative ones, which is why I liked working at the RSC so much. So ownership of those choices is between actor and director – and designer, I guess, to a certain degree. Within that evening out that people come and see, that character owns that speech, but ultimately the playwright owns it. And what's fascinating once you really start analysing a playwright's work is recognizing how much personal ownership that particular playwright has over that soliloquy. I was talking to a friend of mine about Hamlet and Hamnet, Shakespeare's son who died when he was eleven, and how much the play is in some way a sort of exorcizing of that particular thing in his life. We know frustratingly little about Shakespeare and so it's very difficult for us to *know* really what was in his mind at any point writing these plays and how much of these soliloquies were personally motivated. The question's very often asked *Which of Shakespeare's characters is most like him?* It's an impossible question to answer, but it's an interesting game to play when trying to imagine who this person was and which of his lines, which of his soliloquies, which of his characters *he* is speaking through. Very often with plays you get a real sense of the *author* speaking through certain characters. I'm thinking about George Bernard Shaw and some of his problem plays, where with some of the characters you can hear him going *This is what* I *think and* I *believe*. Maybe that's the genius of Shakespeare; you can hear him in everybody. There isn't one character where you can go, *Well, that's clearly Shakespeare*, because the universality of his voice seems to resonate through all of his characters.

7. Alex Waldmann, Richmond, Surrey, 4 November 2015

FIGURE 7 *Alex Waldmann as Orlando,* As You Like It, *2013*

Alex Waldmann has played Sebastian in *Twelfth Night*, Horatio in *Hamlet*, Bertram in *All's Well That Ends Well* and Troilus in the 2008 Cheek by Jowl production of *Troilus and Cressida*. He also played the King in the 2012 RSC production of *King John*, in which Pippa Nixon, who talks about it above, played the Bastard. Subsequently, he played the Bastard himself in the Globe production of the play in 2015, and he talks about that here, as he does also about playing Orlando to Nixon's Rosalind in the 2013 RSC production of *As You Like It* and Henry VI in the 2015 Rose Theatre revival of the John Barton-Peter Hall *Wars of the Roses*, an adaptation of the first Histories tetralogy staged by the RSC in 1963. He refers to Declan Donnellan, who co-founded the Cheek by Jowl theatre company with Nick Ormerod in 1981; Donnellan's book *The Actor and the Target*, first published in Russian, appeared in an English edition in 2002.

You always look for the human way in; what is it that drives him as a character? I'm always fascinated by what the received wisdom is. It's not as if I go out and deliberately do something different, it's just that all my work in Shakespeare is inspired by Declan Donnellan and Cheek by Jowl. It transformed my life ... *really* looking at what's in the text ... and as those words get filtered through my imagination, it's often quite different to the way people think it should be.

My way in to any soliloquy is always a conversation, so the audience is absolutely another character in the play. It's a unique conversation because they don't have any lines back, but it's still a dialogue, so I as an actor fill in the gaps of what I think they're saying in between, which makes me want to say the next line. So, for example, as Orlando I'm looking like an idiot at the RST for being tongue-tied in front of this gorgeous woman. I wanted to pretend, like, *Usually I'm great with the girls, this is just a one-off, I've just gone twelve rounds with Charles the Wrestler, usually I'm brilliant, my tongue physically doesn't work*. You've got to look at them and think *I know what you're thinking, but I want to change the way you think about me*. So automatically you're having a dialogue by contradicting what you know they're thinking about you. It's always active; it's always about the other person. They never, I hope, feel they're just watching a speech.

The other thing that affects soliloquies is that in life we're acting all the time – we put on armour, public faces. We're different speaking to our parents, to our children, to our old mates ... Romeo's different in every scene – with the Nurse, with Juliet, his language is different. In soliloquies it's important to think *How good are these characters at covering up the way we really think and the way we really feel?* Or what you're not prepared to admit to yourself ...

What's beautiful in the Globe is that you can see a thousand faces ... I'd much rather be able to see people's eyes. You talk to one person for a bit, then the whole audience will get that. I think that's the way to make soliloquies come alive, if you can see them. There's something so obviously theatrical about the nature of that space ...

When as the Bastard in *King John* I said 'composition' [in the 'Mad world! mad kings! mad composition!' soliloquy, 2.1.561–98], I pretended I was expecting them all to go *O yeah, of course,* 'composition', but that's the reason I had to say the word again, as written ... 'tickling commodity' ... *come on, you all know what I mean*, 'the bias of the world' ... and what I'm getting back from the audience makes me go on to the next thing, and then I was able to play with the audience. This is something Pippa did that I thought I could take further as a bloke – 'old men, young men', I picked on, like a recall in comedy ... 'maids', so I pick on maybe a slightly older woman who probably isn't a maid, so the audience feel involved. If there was ever a part that was written for the Globe, playing the cheap seats, the people standing in the yard, against the expensive seats ... So he really is *I'm the man for everyone, the groundlings are mine, I'm only pretending to be with you guys*. The audience love being addressed directly, there's no doubt about that. It's very deliberate; Shakespeare wants the audience to be seduced by those characters. You don't have to like what the Bastard is doing, but to understand what's driving him is vital for an audience. To have that interaction, that's what Shakespeare gives us that modern playwrights don't.

King John has Shakespeare's shortest soliloquy – three words, 'My mother dead' (4.2.182). He's left alone on stage. Talking about having a relationship with the audience, those three words were always influenced by the audience that night. So my general approach would be, *This woman, that person that gave you life, who you looked up to for everything, is no longer alive in this world. What does that even mean for me? I'm now an orphan* ... three words that could mean so much, but there would be nights when someone just there, where you're sitting, would be that close to me on stage ... I remember someone went and rustled some sweets or something and I went up to him *And you doing that and my mother's just died; my mother's dead.* And another night there was a little boy sat with his parents holding his mum's hand, and I went in front of him and I was like, *You know, it must be nice having a mum 'cause my mummy's dead.* You can do so much based on being open to what the audience is bringing you; and even if it's three words, it's still a conversation. I'd rather interact with an audience than just be observed *doing some acting*.

With Henry VI [in the 'molehill' soliloquy, *Henry VI, Part 3*, 2.5.1–54], I thought *I'm going to take this moment to speak to you directly – you've all caught me running away from battle with my hands over my ears; so you're looking at me in a certain way, so I'm going to try and explain what this battle is.* So the way it's written, the rhetoric of it ... it's a beautifully written speech, and it comes at a climactic moment in the play and the whole cycle. But Shakespeare's done all that work for me with the rhetoric and I don't need to overdo it. I just wanted to have a conversation with the audience, *Look, I'm sorry, I'm taking up your time, how can I explain this battle to you?* It's like, 'This battle fares like to the morning's war, / When dying clouds contend with growing light' ... *That hasn't worked, let me try this analogy about the sea fighting ... It's going nowhere.* I look round and then I get an idea out of nowhere – *Oh, there's a molehill, I'll go and sit down.* I took my slippers off, I took the *weight* of this crown off and then explained, *Just in case you hadn't realized, you know, quite embarrassingly, Margaret and Clifford* 'chid me from the battle, swearing both / They prosper best of all when I am thence'. So that makes me think *God, I wish I were dead*, and as soon as I say 'Would I were dead' it makes me think *It's up to God*, and then, now I've mentioned God, I think 'O God!' *I tell you what* ... So the audience for a second are watching me having a direct conversation as a Christian man ... and he thinks about 'a happy life / To be no better than a homely swain', who I sort of mentioned earlier ... and then I suddenly think *Wouldn't it be nice just to be a homely swain, and then* 'to sit upon a hill'? *O God, I'm sitting upon a hill, that's what swains do, and just* 'To carve out dials quaintly, point by point' ... and then out of nowhere you interrupt yourself and invent the idea *If I did that, I could* 'see the minutes how they run' ... and then I think, *O my God, I could just divide up the days.* So I couldn't overplay the rhetoric; it's just a series of things as I was imagining this. But the whole way driving through it was *I promise you, all you guys living out there, as much as you think being a king must be great, I'd take that any day.* It goes for *all* soliloquies – when you ask a question, even though you know you're not going to get an answer, you ask the question as you would anyway to *try* and get an answer. To me, there's no such thing as a rhetorical question. So when I ... when Henry asks 'Gives not the hawthorn bush a sweeter shade ...?' I'm waiting for an answer. Then *Yeah, give me an answer*, so I'm going to have to tell *you*. So I almost did it like a modern panto – 'O, yes, it doth' – and then actually it's not a joke, it made me quite upset ... and to conclude, it was like *I promise I won't be keeping you for much longer,* just so you make it clear that you're dealing with treachery and people want to kill you, where as a shepherd you just deal with your daily life. *All* Shakespeare is rhetoric in a sense, because it's all about an argument; it's all about *I think this, I want you to think this, or I'm not sure what I think, what should I think?* ... I let the audience hear that for themselves rather than me doing it as a set speech. It's all invented each night, by timing ... and that's the one time Henry gets to say it directly; other times he speaks to God and not to the audience.

The genius of Shakespeare is that in this cycle he's dealt with fathers losing sons and sons losing fathers and then he thinks *What happens if a father discovers he's killed his own son and a son discovers he's killed his own father? If the grief at losing someone isn't bad enough, let's have a look at how this affects them.* And then you've got the king in the middle of it. Literally, *I've got blood on my hands. I can choose not to fight, but I'm directly responsible for these people losing their lives. And so three men in pain* ... I'd never have to act it; I'd just be there listening to that and I'd always be crying by the end of it ... these three men grieving in their own worlds ... Extraordinary writing, my favourite scene to do in the entire play.

8. Dame Harriet Walter, Hammersmith, London, 26 January 2016

FIGURE 8 *Harriet Walter as Lady Macbeth,* Macbeth, *2001*

In an extremely distinguished theatrical career, Harriet Walter has played a remarkable number of major Shakespearean roles in productions for, among others, the RSC, the Royal Court and the Royal Exchange. These include Ophelia, Imogen, Viola, Isabella, Beatrice, Lady Macbeth and Cleopatra. She talks about some of them here and – a recent departure – about playing Brutus and Henry IV in the Donmar Warehouse all-female productions of *Julius Caesar* (2013) and *Henry IV* (2014), directed by Phyllida Lloyd and set in a high-security women's prison. After this interview, later in 2016, she added to these the role of Prospero in *The Tempest*, and all three plays were staged at the King's Cross Theatre, London, as the Shakespeare Trilogy.

John Barton was my mentor at the RSC and his whole thing is that nothing is set in stone. There are guidelines and clues in the text as to how to play Shakespeare but no hard-and-fast rules. It's all about helping the actor to communicate to an audience, not about some mystique. So there is no real rule about soliloquy. Each one is different and they should be treated case for case – in terms of where it comes, what needs to be said, who's saying it. A soliloquy is a person voicing private thoughts, but it's not just an interior monologue that you speak out loud; you're actually bouncing off the audience. When you talk to yourself, who are you talking to? You're talking to another person who is you, who argues with you or reinforces you, and that person is basically a friend. So as an actor you're using the audience as a composite other you, a confidante who's not involved in the play. They're not in the same danger you are, they're not in love like you are, they're safe and other and beyond the crisis, so you can step out of your world and share something with them. Shakespeare and his contemporaries were making up the rules of theatre as they went along. They weren't naturalistic like us so there was no problem with someone suddenly talking to the audience from within the play. Before the theatre took off in England in the sixteenth century people would talk to God or a priest, but in Shakespeare's more humanist times maybe this was the beginning of man questioning himself: *Am I right in doing this, or am I not?* or a more desperate plea to the audience. *Did you* see *that?!* – 'to whom should I complain?' And also it's used humorously, like Viola saying 'How will this fadge?' (2.2.33). She's in a predicament, but she's allowing the audience to see the ridiculous side of it. So they're a sounding-board. Usually we do it rhetorically, but occasionally you can electrify an audience and put them on their mettle by *really, really* saying *What? Tell me, tell me.* You know, 'Am I a coward?' Hamlet asks ... and truly tempts the audience to reply, but of course they would have to be answering their own question: *Am* I *a coward? What would* I *do?*

For this generation of actors who watch such truthful, interior acting on film and TV it's a struggle to believe themselves when they do something as heightened as a soliloquy in blank verse on stage and they feel naff, but you have to get over that and not fall into the trap of mumbling or looking at the floor as that looks naffer and also self-indulgent. You have to share with the audience – that's the point. Cicely Berry helped us track our way through a soliloquy by getting us to think of it as an argument, with your two heads going at one another, so there's an animated dialogue, an energy that pushes you through to a conclusion, so the action doesn't stop while you tell the audience what you already *know* you're thinking, you're working it out as you go along and surprising yourself or frightening yourself and you're in a different place at the end of the speech than you were at the beginning. It's dynamic.

It's very like the direct-to-camera speech in film. You're looking at a camera lens, and each one of the people watching thinks you're talking privately to them, and that's what we should achieve in a theatrical soliloquy. With a live theatre audience someone told me it's better to fix on individuals in the audience and directly address each of them than to rove your eye around in a more general way. Somehow that direct look has the effect on the whole audience that you are really latching on to them as individuals or that you might suddenly switch to them. They think I'd better be alert. A general roving kind of leaves people off the hook. At the same time you need to change from person to person so that your head is lifted. They become very aware of the other people in the audience. But the actor has to stay in character even if they are allowed to be a bit personal or cheeky in a soliloquy. You can come out of the play but not out of character. You feel awful if you slip out of character; you feel you've almost betrayed everybody. They've willingly suspended their disbelief and you've completely broken it for them.

But then you get Lady Macbeth, who's alone on stage talking [in the 'unsex me here' soliloquy, 1.5.38–54], but she's talking to the spirits; she's not talking to the audience. That feels different. She doesn't have an ally in the audience, and the only people supporting her are, she thinks, the evil spirits 'that tend on mortal thoughts'. Macbeth has more of a philosophical and moral debate with the audience, and as he gets deeper in shit he talks less and less to them because he can't confront his thoughts any more. That's so key, isn't it, because it shows how much our discourse with ourselves keeps us moral and sane, and we can't do that anymore with something we've lost – that sanity or integrity. I just felt Lady Macbeth was isolated, with not a lot of discourse with herself, and that's why she goes mad, in a way. Maybe life has done it to her – she's asking the spirits to help her narrow herself down and become this sort of gall-filled, effective person.

Viola is tender, vulnerable, self-deprecating. She can enlist the audience's friendship but she starts off a bit tentative. She is not as confident as Rosalind, who knows she can charm them. Her epilogue in *As You Like It* is borderline soliloquy, because it's a stepping out of character, but it is the actor stepping out of the role as well.

Isabella is desperately coming out of a terrible situation and ... you know that thing when something happens to you and you just *wish* someone had been there to see it? So Isabella is calling the audience to be her witness. She's putting them on the spot: *You saw what he did. You heard what he said.*

So soliloquies have many different purposes. Your relationship with the audience is your *character's* relationship to the audience, and you can't step out and be Harriet. In fact, I found it very difficult rehearsing *Twelfth Night* because Viola's most concrete relationship is with the audience. So at rehearsal I couldn't really *get* her. She was forced into a relationship with Olivia; she wanted a relationship with Orsino, but it wasn't the one she got; so the only person she could really express herself with was the audience.

Being given a soliloquy is like being given a close-up in a film. Or having the camera look at the world from your point of view. This happens far less for women for various reasons – partly because they are not usually the main protagonist, but they do have more secrets sometimes, precisely because they don't get to say so much within a scene. Still, it is often frustrating as an actress when your character gets no private moments with the audience to express herself.

I've been lucky to have the chance to play some male characters in all-female performances of *Julius Caesar* and *Henry IV* at the Donmar directed by Phyllida Lloyd. I played Brutus and King Henry. I didn't have difficulty getting into the head of a male character. It was no bigger leap to think like a Roman general than the Empress of Egypt. But I did have problems with Brutus's first soliloquy, 'It must be by his death' (2.1.10–34), when he tries to convince himself that Caesar has to be assassinated. I found it really difficult to motivate because it seemed that he was saying the wrong thing for that point in the story. I even suggested to Phyllida that the speech should be in a different place, because it's about a much more infant stage of Caesar's dictatorship than the one we've reached in the play. Shakespeare *really* didn't help me there. I didn't *want* to say those words, I wanted to say something else! But Shakespeare has me say stuff about 'young ambition' and 'Caesar may' and 'lest he may, prevent' and talks about him as a 'serpent's egg' – always the infancy of tyranny, not the full-fledged dictator that he historically was.

I thought you don't kill somebody who might *one day* turn into a tyrant, or anyway Brutus wouldn't. There is an aspect of Brutus who doesn't quite face up to the truth about himself, and I know I was in danger of trying to avoid Brutus's faults, but I felt that it would just be such a negative play if there's nobody with any moral compass in it at all. And he is the only character who can really make it clear to the audience that Caesar had become a tyrant and that everyone in Rome was living under a dictatorship and that all the ideals of the Republic had been betrayed. There were so many things I *did* want to tell the audience and this speech just wasn't it. It felt wrongly placed, as if Shakespeare had written it for an earlier draft or had it in his bottom drawer and wanted to fit it in somewhere.

In the all-female *Henry IV*, we conflated Parts I and II and put the King's very beautiful 'sleep' speech (3.1.4–31) earlier in the play just before he gives Hal a dressing down and after the Lady has sung in the Glendower scene. In our prison production Lady Percy sings a beautiful modern song and the other 'prisoners' sing along and one by one curl up to sleep on the floor. Suddenly out of this singing comes this totally isolated person, the King, up high on a balcony looking down on them. He has no sympathy from the audience because they're very aware of the women left behind after their husbands went off to war on one level, and prisoners sleeping on a cold hard floor on another. And there's this man going *I can't get to sleep and here are all these groundlings with no problems who can nod off anywhere.* It's very often where a speech is *couched* that gives you the energy to say it, and while the Brutus soliloquy didn't feel to be at the right place, this re-positioning of the sleep speech wound up feeling like it was nestled in the right place, and you felt the audience was ready for something quiet and you could say 'in the calmest and most stillest night', and it was very very quiet, and it just gives you that little glimpse of sympathy for Henry. You could read Elizabeth I, Obama, into him, people coming to the end of their term wanting to leave a legacy of having healed rifts, and his reign was riven with factions. He doesn't really talk to the audience in that speech; he talks to Sleep, this person he can't conquer who seems to have abandoned him: 'How have I frighted thee?' So I thought of Sleep as a woman, him coming tip-toeing up to her and saying *What have I done wrong?* And then getting a bit cross with her and saying *Can you do that for all those people? This boy on the ship's mast with a howling gale, are you going to let him sleep, and you won't let me sleep? It's ridiculous.* But then he gets philosophical. It's a king telling the audience *What's the point of power? I don't have power over my own body, my sleep rhythms.* So there is a little bit where he does talk to himself and the audience and says 'Then happy low, lie down! / Uneasy lies the head that wears a crown.' It's Shakespeare telling the audience *Think about it from his point of view, just for a second.* I didn't know how the audience reacted because I was on a balcony above them, looking out to Sleep, who was up there somewhere, or looking out to the top of the mast. But you do sort of get feedback. Of course if something is funny you get a laugh, but even in serious stuff you can sometimes tell by the quietness, the attention or a little sigh of recognition or something, just a little expiration that tells you they're with you ...

A character never lies to the audience in a soliloquy, so that's a helpful guideline. They may not be entirely in touch with the truth, but they will tell the audience the truth as far as they know it. Benedick [in *Much Ado About Nothing*] skirts the issue; he's aware the audience are judging him: *I know I said that, but I didn't know it was going to be like this.* And it's delightful, because the audience feel he's projecting on to them a kind of judgement that perhaps they're not even feeling. And then it's funny the way he tries to wriggle off the hook and all the time they can say *O come on, you love her, for God's sake!* But he's never going to get there himself because he's too proud. And that's a great use of soliloquy, because the audience is absolutely at that place where they're being talked to, but they know more than he does.

The fame of soliloquies really is difficult. It's all to do with momentum. It's like an orchestral piece where everything that's gone before leads to this and provides a springboard to a place where you've just *got* to say this thing. There are other times where that momentum doesn't quite come, and you just force your mouth to say it because it's the time. It's to do with setting yourself up and being in the right emotional place and finding the need that night to *say that thing.* You have to con yourself and the audience that this is the *only* time this is going to happen – it's never happened before and it's never going to happen again. It's part of the energy and commitment you give the performance. Don't try and be different for the sake of being different from some other actor – there really aren't too many ways of saying 'To be or not to be'. The context is all, and that will vary in different productions as to whether they support you in building up to a speech and placing it right or if they make you work uphill on your own. Anyway, audiences don't care if they hear their favourite bit over and over again. They go to the opera and hear that aria over and over again. They still look forward to it. In fact, when you know something slightly, it sends more tingles down your spine than when you don't. Or sometimes you don't know something as well as you thought you did, and something surprises you. You're always in a context – you have a different chemistry with the other performers, the set's different, your clothes are different, it's a Tuesday not a Wednesday.

Some characters are given the chance to soliloquize and others aren't, and it gives them a great advantage. Cressida doesn't get to explain herself; Cleopatra gets one moment when she's not acting up for the other people on stage. There are soliloquies that are missing. As a character, you want your chance to say *No, but* my *story is* ... You know, *Hamlet* is the worst – Gertrude, I've turned down quite a few times. You're told 'Look here upon this picture, and on this', *how can you compare these two men?; you're too old to have sex anyway; and how can you possibly have done it?* and he never lets her answer ...

Ophelia's was the first Shakespeare soliloquy I delivered. The context we did it in was very shocking. Jonathan Pryce played Hamlet brilliantly and terrifyingly. He really attacked Ophelia once he realized he was being set up. Hamlet storms off and the king and my father have been eavesdropping on the scene and seen the violence of it and don't seem to care and go off to talk about it, leaving Ophelia absolutely shaking, broken. I used to end up a crumpled heap on the floor and try to build myself up to standing slowly by means of the soliloquy. I used the soliloquy to kind of get me back together again, to recover my sanity, but not for long. By playing the soliloquy as if she's beginning to crack, I gave the audience a glimpse of the madness she would give in to later. She's trying to tell the truth, desperately clutching at phrases – 'noble mind', 'the glass of fashion and the mould of form' – these are all things that have been said of him but they go against what she has just experienced, so this is a soliloquy that is not appropriate or true to what we have just seen because you want her to say *How dare he behave like that? What's got into him?* She can't admit that he is at fault in any way, so she just says he's lost his mind and that is the least hurtful way she can explain it, though she is devastated: 'O woe is me to have seen what I have seen, see what I see'. So there's a disconnect from reality beginning. And she is sort of describing herself when she talks of Hamlet, as if she's saying My *noble mind is here o'erthrown* and I'm *a discordant, cracked instrument*. Her mad scene is a sort of soliloquy. In our rather terrifying police-type state of Elsinore I was suddenly free to say the unsayable. Or at least hint at it. You have quite a lot of freedom as an actor as well, to think up the story behind your cryptic images of owls and bakers and cockle shoes and rue and rosemary and cabbages and kings. You can invest these seemingly sweet ramblings with any amount of bitterness or accusation. She doesn't directly address the audience like in a conventional soliloquy, but she's like a dissident who has defected from the world of the play to tell us the truth in code and her suicide is a continuation of that soliloquy and speaks volumes.

PART IV

Soliloquies in play

Introduction

We tend to remember soliloquies primarily as unique dramatic or cinematic events or reading experiences, but in fact they work in concert with other soliloquies within Shakespearean plays or – as with *Henry VI, Part 3* and *Richard III* – even across different plays, as they create and maintain expectations but also modify and sometimes even defeat them. Soliloquies in Shakespeare *accumulate* meaning in individual plays, and part of the pleasure to be taken in them is the interpretation of their inter-relationships. The consistencies and ruptures among Richard III's soliloquies; the imagery, attitudes and emotions, both shared and divergent, of the lovers' soliloquies in *Romeo and Juliet*; and the strange convergence of the soliloquies of Iago and Othello, together with the provocative divergence of Desdemona's one tiny soliloquy and a great monologue by Emilia in *Othello* all project or suggest structures of more general meaning too. The soliloquies in these separate plays also invite consideration in different overall perspectives: rhetorical development or sophistication in *Henry VI, Part 3* and *Richard III*; Shakespeare's own literary critique – to do with the conventions of Elizabethan Petrachism and sonnet form – in *Romeo and Juliet*; and the provocative play's complex literary reception in the case of *Othello*.

I have chosen these plays for close attention for several reasons. They provide the opportunity to discuss at some length several great, well-known soliloquies; they are generically varied; and they are all available in remarkable film versions that handle soliloquy in stimulating, provocative and influential ways. In addition, actors speak illuminatingly in Part III of this book about performing some of them, so that section of the book and this one may be thought to engage to some degree in a kind of dialogue between performer and critic and between performance and text. Finally, these plays considered in succession offer the opportunity to think about the development of soliloquy in Shakespeare, from the gradual sophistication of rhetoric in the early tetralogy of history plays to the astonishing and endlessly surprising inwardness and complexity of the major tragedies.

1. Richard in *Richard III*, with *Henry VI, Part 3*

Richard III is one of Shakespeare's earliest plays. Probably written in 1593–4, it completed the sequence known as the 'first tetralogy', being preceded by the three parts of *Henry VI*. All four plays deal with the Wars of the Roses (1455–85) between the houses of York and Lancaster, an extremely bloody period of dynastic and internecine conflict in English history when, as the Duchess of York, Richard's mother, characterizes it, 'the conquerors / Make war upon themselves, brother to brother, / Blood to blood, self against self' (*Richard III*, 2.4.62–4). There is disagreement about whether Shakespeare planned the plays as a tetralogy, partly because the first part of *Henry VI* appears to have been written after the other two, but they are sometimes performed in adapted form as a trilogy, most famously that staged by John Barton and Peter Hall as *The Wars of the Roses* at the Royal Shakespeare Theatre in 1963 and produced again under Trevor Nunn's direction at the Rose Theatre, Kingston-upon-Thames, in 2015. (This is the production in which Henry VI was played by Alex Waldmann, who talks about performing that character's best-known soliloquy in the previous section of this book.) Richard of Gloucester, who eventually becomes Richard III, first appears in *Henry VI, Part 2* and begins to dominate the action from about the mid-point of *Part 3*, in which he ultimately murders the king. The tetralogy is sometimes thought to exemplify what has been called the 'Tudor Myth': that the English civil wars of this period were God's punishment for the deposition of the Yorkist Richard II by the Lancastrian Henry IV – the material Shakespeare subsequently shaped into *Richard II* – and that the operations of divine grace may be seen in the eventual triumph of Henry Richmond over Richard III at the battle of Bosworth, which ends the wars, unites in marriage the houses of York and Lancaster and brings to the throne the first Tudor monarch, Henry VII. *Richard III* culminates with that battle.

The Richard of Gloucester who stepped alone on to the stage of the Elizabethan playhouse at the beginning of *Richard III* to speak his first soliloquy beginning 'Now is the winter of our discontent ...' therefore trails a long history behind him. He has already been represented by actual historical accounts by such writers as Hall, Holinshed, Polydore Vergil and Thomas More, in which he figures as a manipulative Machiavellian monarch, and probably, at least to the most discerning members of early audiences, as an element of the Tudor monarchy's ideological self-representation. And he also appears as a character already represented in and familiar from pre-existing plays, not only Shakespeare's. So his opening soliloquy contains at least a sketchy element of exposition, situating the initial action at a time of peace following on devastating civil conflict.

The fact that Richard speaks a soliloquy to open the play also suggests continuities with what has gone before, in several senses. As we have already seen, opening a play with a soliloquy – and this is the only time Shakespeare does so – is virtually to declare an affinity with the Senecan tradition of theatre Shakespeare found already adapted in the work of Kyd and Marlowe; and Richard of Gloucester inherits a great deal especially from the figure of Barabas in Marlowe's *The Jew of Malta*. Like Barabas, Richard speaks many soliloquies – eight – during the play, and in the previous section of this book Jonjo O'Neill, discussing his performance as Richard, talks about conceiving of the whole of the play's first act as Richard's soliloquy. We do indeed feel, in that act, almost as though we are brought to perceive everything in the play's action through Richard's eyes or mind, as he tells us in soliloquy what events he intends to set in motion, sets them in motion and then comments, again in soliloquy, on their consequences.

The effect is underlined in Laurence Olivier's 1955 film version by the way Richard speaks many of his soliloquies direct to camera in front of casement windows and open doorways, which give on to scenes of dramatic action. Once, he even impudently extends his arm towards the camera, as if beckoning us in to the action. In a film directed by Olivier, then, Olivier's Richard appears to be directing us to see things as he sees them – to see with his eyes. This seems wholly appropriate to the way the soliloquies work in Act 1, as they reveal Richard's smoothly manipulative manners. In one, he condescendingly apostrophizes his brother Clarence, who has just been taken to the Tower where he will be executed on Richard's orders, although Clarence does not realize this. Richard's perverse wit operates in the pentameter's pauses: 'Simple, plain Clarence, I do love thee so *[pause]* / That I will shortly send thy soul to heaven *[pause, for the almost ashamed-of-itself audience laugh]* / If heaven will take the present at our hands *[further pause, for the incremental wit of the joke to sink in, and for its blasphemous nature to be fully appreciated]* (1.1.118–20). In another, we get the brazenness of Richard's response to his seduction of Lady Anne over the corpse of Henry VI, whom he has himself recently murdered, in which the malevolent comedy of the pause required by the line-break is exquisitely managed. Richard invites us to admire the quality of his performance while he himself relishes the roguishly cynical self-satisfaction he derives from it: 'Was ever woman in this manner wooed? / Was ever woman in this manner won' (1.2.230–1)?

Accompanied by Richard's insinuatingly ingratiating asides, these soliloquies put him magisterially in charge of the play's action in its first act, in which he is the master of ceremonies whipping the circus animals of his plot into line. In fact, however, the entire play is framed by his first and final soliloquies, which are, as we shall see, as different in matter, rhythm, syntax and psychological effect as it's possible to imagine. So *Richard III* itself may be read through the variant moods and registers of its hero's soliloquies – until, of course, fatally for this hero, the world refuses to see things as he does, and we perceive Richard's way of directing things as a form of monstrous self-delusion. That Henry Richmond's prayer-soliloquy at the end of the play inevitably seems colourlessly insipid compared to Richard's soliloquies – especially his last, which is in fact a form of prayer-soliloquy too – makes it no less the utterance of new, possibly divinely instituted power. Its comparative dramatic ineffectiveness, however, may reveal the difficulties of writing Tudor propaganda as Elizabethan theatre; political power has no necessary relationship with, and may even neutralize, theatrical power.

If we know the earlier plays of the tetralogy, we might almost anticipate that Richard will open the play named for him with a soliloquy, because speaking soliloquy is so prominently what Richard of Gloucester does in *Henry VI, Part 3*. We might even conceive of Richard as almost genetically programmed to speak soliloquy since, as we saw in Part I of this book, one of the first great soliloquies in Shakespeare is spoken by Richard's father, the Duke of York, in *Henry VI, Part 2*. Indeed, the moment we first recognize the Richard of Gloucester of the *Henry VI* plays as indisputably the Richard of *Richard III* is when, in Act 3 Scene 2 of *Henry VI, Part 3*, he speaks the soliloquy beginning 'Ay, Edward will treat women honourably'. At seventy-one lines, this is the longest soliloquy in Shakespeare, and the first to give adequate formulation to an entirely credible subjectivity, both self-defining and self-analytical.

Richard has just been outraged by his brother Edward's choosing a wife for reasons of ineluctable sexual desire rather than political expediency, and this soliloquy begins in angry, anti-fraternal contempt. Letting us know that he is himself unlikely to find satisfaction in sex (to 'make my heaven in a lady's lap') because of his gross deformity – which Shakespeare seems to have exaggerated beyond his sources – Richard pledges himself alternatively 'to make my heaven to dream upon the crown'. 'Crown' is repeated at the end of another line too, as though Richard will gag on the word itself until he possesses the thing it names. Predicting the subsequent progress of his ambition, he also articulates an almost inchoate sense of motive. Both self-knowing and self-opaque, therefore, these baffled lines offer one of the great moments in early Shakespearean soliloquy:

And yet I know not how to get the crown,
For many lives stand between me and home,
And I, like one lost in a thorny wood,
That rents the thorns and is rent with the thorns,

> Seeking a way and straying from the way,
> Not knowing how to find the open air,
> But toiling desperately to find it out,
> Torment myself to catch the English crown:
> And from that torment I will free myself,
> Or hew my way out with a bloody axe. (3.2.172–81)

This is Richard becoming himself and recognizing exactly what he is becoming – becoming it, indeed, in the acts of cognition and articulation themselves. But he is articulating not only the becoming but the compulsion behind it; not only the decision, but the murk of impulse behind the decision, which, especially in the line 'Seeking a way and straying from the way', sounds, in its sibilance and repetition, both hopeless and hapless. It's as though he is impelled by the urgent necessity of an ungovernable desire that he is as powerless to resist as his brother is to resist what Richard considers the wrong woman in the wrong marriage. This dream of a putative 'heaven' seems not so much the alternative to sexual possibility as its only conceivable fulfilment. So the passage is constructed from a tiny nucleus of repeated words – 'thorn', 'rent', 'way', 'find', 'torment' (which rhymes with 'rent' and figures as both verb and noun), 'myself' – making it appear that Richard is being whirled, or is whirling himself, in a vortex of obsessive desire.

The imagery of wood and way is coincidentally almost uncannily close to that of the opening of Dante's *Divine Comedy*: 'Nel mezzo del cammin di nostra vita / mi ritrovai per una selva oscura, / che la diritta era smarrita' – 'Midway in the journey of our life I found myself in a dark wood, for the straight way was lost.' In Dante, the poet-pilgrim's journey through the wood, during which he is conducted by benevolent guides, eventually culminates in his knowledge of the nature of eternity and the appropriate means to salvation. Richard's thorny wood is the site of a virtually contrary, entirely self-willed journey towards depravity and damnation; his progress in *Richard III* has a marked theological or metaphysical dimension. As we have already seen in this book, the characterization of Richard draws to some extent on the Vice figure in medieval morality plays, and *Richard III* realizes an *Elizabethan* morality in which the hero takes on aspects of the satanic, whether we read the play under the auspices of the providentially determined terms of the 'Tudor Myth' or not. We might also regard Richard here, or Shakespeare himself, as struggling free of the wood of Senecan rhetoric, just about, as the passage's single sentence works its resonant way over the end-stopped lines – although the final line undoubtedly retains the true Senecan swagger.

These lines also almost plead to be read psycho-sexually. The existential 'torment' of Richard's condition is sadomasochistic, as he represents himself as at once rending and rent with the wood's thorns. There may be an almost blasphemous element in the imagery of Richard's simile, since the words 'crown' and 'thorn' reiterated in such proximity subliminally suggest the crown of thorns forced on Christ's head before his crucifixion. The 'home' from which Richard is at present divorced figures the longed-for haven of the English throne, but the word has other metaphorical resonances too. These make it appear that what Richard lacks, and half understands he lacks – 'Love forswore me in my mother's womb', he says earlier in the soliloquy – is something more essential and absolute than the crown, something for which, indeed, the crown may be only an almost fetishized substitute. His relationship with his mother, as we discover it in *Richard III*, is an entirely unloving one, and this passage of the soliloquy has been read as an evocation of the process of birth itself, in which 'home' may be understood as 'womb'. Finding no home where he should, Richard divorces himself entirely from his family in a subsequent soliloquy in the play:

> I have no brother; I am like no brother.
> And this word 'love', which greybeards call divine,
> Be resident in men like one another
> And not in me: I am myself alone. (5.6.80–3)

I discussed this passage in Part II as an example of the relationship between soliloquy and 'intense, even pathological isolation'. In the context of Richard's Act 3 Scene 2 soliloquy, it takes on an added significance. It's as though Richard is here authoring or engendering himself in distinction to the loveless engendering he presumes for himself. Regarding himself as 'myself alone', he gives birth to a self-conception that is also an opportunity – since, being the product of a 'no' and a 'not', the traumatized consequence of a negativity, he can then become anything he chooses to be.

This is why the Act 3 Scene 2 soliloquy ends in Richard's apparent boast about how he can 'frame [his] face to all occasions' (3.2.185) by playing the parts opportunistically suitable to him at any one time; he can, he says, outdo Nestor, Ulysses, the Machiavel and others in the skills for which they are best known. This context underwrites what I also said in Part II: that the passage offers testimony to Richard's rhetorical and histrionic competences, to his hyperbolic self-dramatization. He is a consummate *actor* and a consummate *hypocrite*, a word whose etymological origins lie in the Greek word for acting, as we saw in Part I. The element of theatricality, the exuberant flamboyance with which Richard engages and cajoles us in his soliloquies, is a force hard to resist, and, far more than the *Henry VI* plays, *Richard III* is itself preoccupied in its plot as well as its speeches with the nature and effectiveness of theatre itself – most notably when Buckingham, who, he says, can 'counterfeit the deep tragedian', stage-manages Richard's acceptance of the crown in Act 3 Scene 5, in which Richard himself brilliantly plays the part of someone having to be reluctantly persuaded to do so. This is yet a further reason why soliloquy seems so essentially

Richard's true mode of discourse. Himself alone, he performs himself best by speaking only to and of himself.

However, we must wait until the final soliloquy in *Richard III* to hear again the note of distress sounded in the soliloquy in *Henry VI, Part 3*. When Richard steps on stage at the beginning of the play, what impresses us, rather, is the apparent serenity of his self-confident command, as his smoothly polished pentameters and rhetorical figures are marshalled to conjure the state of the nation before they eventually turn decisively to articulate the state of a self:

> Now is the winter of our discontent
> Made glorious summer by this son of York,
> And all the clouds that poured upon our house
> In the deep bosom of the ocean buried.
> Now are our brows bound with victorious wreaths,
> Our bruised arms hung up for monuments,
> Our stern alarums changed to merry meetings,
> Our dreadful marches to delightful measures.
> Grim-visaged war hath smoothed his wrinkled front;
> And now, instead of mounting barbed steeds
> To fright the souls of fearful adversaries,
> He capers nimbly in a lady's chamber
> To the lascivious pleasing of a lute.
> But, I, that am not shaped for sportive tricks,
> Nor made to court an amorous looking-glass;
> I, that am rudely stamped, and want love's majesty
> To strut before a wanton ambling nymph;
> I, that am curtailed of this fair proportion,
> Cheated of feature by dissembling Nature,
> Deformed, unfinished, sent before my time
> Into this breathing world, scarce half made up,
> And that so lamely and unfashionable
> That dogs bark at me as I halt by them –
> Why, I, in this weak piping time of peace,
> Have no delight to pass away the time,
> Unless to see my shadow in the sun
> And descant on mine own deformity ... (1.1.1–27)

This soliloquy virtually repeats some of the material of the 'Ay, Edward will use women honourably' soliloquy, as Richard harps again on the way he must find an alternative to sexual fulfilment in excessive and relentless dynastic ambition. For an audience aware of the earlier soliloquy, the repetition seems wholly appropriate in conveying an obsession; this is the dark matter that Richard cannot leave alone but is compelled more than once to drag up or manipulate into the light of articulation. In fact, recognizing the similarity, some productions of *Richard III* mix lines from the two soliloquies: Olivier does so in his film version, and so do Ian McKellen and Richard Loncraine in theirs forty years later, in 1995. Given the repetition of topic from the previous play, it seems apt that this soliloquy is itself constructed from a rhetoric of repetition, or rhetorical anaphora and epistrophe ('But I, that am ... I, that am ... I, that am'); from the verbal repetitions that constitute alliteration, sibilance and assonance ('summer / son / bosom / buried / brows / bound / clouds / loured / our / house', and so on) and from a syntax of repetition or return too.

The famous opening lines – 'Now is the winter of our discontent / Made glorious summer by this sun of York' – force the reader/listener to do a double-take across the line-break, because we must wait for the first word of the second line, which is the complement to the verb, to recognize that Richard is saying the opposite of what he appears to be saying in the first line. Even so, many people who know the play's opening line think that its syntax is completed with the word 'discontent', so that Richard is thought to be making a declaration that *this present time* is the winter of our discontent. On the contrary, he is saying that the winter of our discontent – the long duration of civil war – is now over, and we are in the glorious summer, the post-war peace, of the sun of York. The syntax is therefore comparable in its doubleness to the punning on the word 'son' itself, which turns the universal, natural agency of summer's warmth into the political expediency of the new monarch, Richard's loathed brother Edward, the eldest son/sun of the house of York. The syntax of the lines catches us up short and makes us revise our understanding as we realize that we must accommodate ourselves to the speed of Richard's wit. However, what the soliloquy immediately goes on to let us know, so that we must revise our understanding yet again, is that in fact our misreading or mishearing of the opening line was in one significant sense a true reading, and one possibly even intended by Richard – because in fact this *is* now very much the winter of *his* actual discontent and he intends to disrupt this summer as soon as he can by treacherously grasping after his brother's crown. Furthermore, in the soliloquy's closing lines he even spells out helpfully for us the way he intends, at least initially, to manage this, and we subsequently witness the acting out of what he himself here calls the 'plots' he has 'laid', those 'inductions dangerous' that set the play's own plot in motion. Richard is acting here, therefore, as a kind of Prologue to his own play.

This, rather than the more immediately psychologically suggestive soliloquy in *Henry VI, Part 3*, is the one Freud focuses on when he discusses Richard in the first of his three essays entitled 'Some Character-Types Met with in Psychoanalytic Work' (1916), in which he finds a reason for our attraction to Richard despite his being so clearly 'evil' a character. And Richard has indeed, since Freud wrote, been read often enough as a fascist leader: Bertolt Brecht partially appropriates him for *The Resistible Rise of Arturo Ui* (written in 1941), his play based on the rise of Hitler, and Ian

McKellen's cinematic Richard adopts quasi-Nazi uniform and regalia after his coronation. Discussing types who proclaim themselves 'exceptions', Freud says that Richard is 'an enormously magnified representation of something we can all discover in ourselves. We think we have reason to reproach nature and our destiny for congenital and infantile disadvantages; we all demand reparation for early wounds to our narcissism.' What the 'Now is the winter of our discontent' soliloquy is saying, says Freud, is 'Nature has done me a grievous wrong in denying me that beauty of form which wins human love. Life owes me reparation for this, and I will see that I get it. I have a right to be an exception, to overstep those bounds by which others let themselves be circumscribed. I may do wrong myself, since wrong has been done to me.' Making universalizing sense of Richard in this way genuinely, it seems to me, aids an understanding of our attraction to him, but Freud's essay also revealingly demonstrates modern psychoanalytic techniques being put into operation not on an actual human being but on a literary character who is, at this early stage of Shakespeare's writing life, created partly out of highly artificial rhetorical devices. In addition to the valuable local analysis, then, Freud's account makes clear the intense psychological acumen with which Shakespeare can, in soliloquy, engage Elizabethan rhetoric with a view to enabling the performance (or simulacrum) of credible characterization.

Richard's opening soliloquy is prospective, though, as well as retrospective, effecting an almost musical introduction to motifs that will figure recurrently in the play. Ideas of theological determinism are suggested by the word 'determined' if we read it as a form of pun proposing that Richard, whatever he thinks, does not actually plan what he does but has it planned for him towards a specific end (his eventual downfall), in a way completely outside his own knowledge or control. Connecting with this possibility, the forms of prophecy, witchcraft and magical thinking more generally, including the prophetic power of dreams, are frequently alluded to in the play. In fact, the word 'dream' or one of its cognates occurs more often in *Richard III* than in any other play of Shakespeare's. Dreams have high significance in terms of both psychology and plot, notably in Clarence's astounding prophetic dream of his own murder just before it happens, in Stanley's dream of the boar and in Hastings's 'unquiet slumbers'. These dreams culminate in Richard's nightmares, acted out on stage, on the eve of the battle of Bosworth. In these, the ghosts of those he has murdered appear to him reiterating their hope that Richard might 'Despair and die', while they also appear, in rhetorical parallel, to Richmond, advising him, conversely, to 'Live and flourish'. Richard's final, distraught soliloquy is then spoken when, the stage direction tells us, '*Richard starteth up out of a dream*':

> Give me another horse! Bind up my wounds!
> Have mercy, Jesu. – Soft, I did but dream.
> O coward conscience, how thou dost afflict me!
> The lights burn blue. It is now dead midnight.

Cold fearful drops stand on my trembling flesh.
What do I fear? Myself? There's none else by.
Richard loves Richard, that is, I am I.
Is there a murderer here? No. Yes, I am.
Then fly! What, from myself? Great reason why?
Lest I revenge. What, myself upon myself?
Alack, I love myself. Wherefore? For any good
That I myself have done unto myself?
O, no. Alas, I rather hate myself,
For hateful deeds committed by myself.
I am a villain. Yet I lie; I am not.
Fool, of thyself speak well. Fool, do not flatter.
My conscience hath a thousand several tongues,
And every tongue brings in a several tale.
And every tale condemns me for a villain.
Perjury, perjury, in the highest degree;
Murder, stern murder, in the direst degree;
All several sins, all used in each degree,
Throng to the bar, crying all, 'Guilty, guilty!'
I shall despair. There is no creature loves me,
And if I die, no soul will pity me.
And wherefore should they, since that I myself
Find in myself no pity to myself?
Methought the souls of all that I had murdered
Came to my tent, and every one did threat
Tomorrow's vengeance on the head of Richard. (5.3.177–206)

We might start thinking about this soliloquy by pondering the curious information offered in Part III of this book that actors playing Richard III find it exceptionally difficult to manage. Jonjo O'Neill says that Richard's 'cracking apart' and realizing it with such 'complete clarity' seems to demand that an actor '*do acting*' in response; that is, that the actor must attempt to rely on the learned adequacies of technique rather than expect fully to interiorize the character's dilemma at this point. In his film *Looking for Richard* (1996) – an interestingly if not always successfully hybrid kind of documentary about filming some scenes of the play in contemporary New York – Al Pacino confesses to comparable difficulty. Olivier's film omits most of the soliloquy, although it includes Colley Cibber's addition, 'Richard's himself again', presumably to suggest that the self that Richard has apparently lost at this point has been found again before the play ends. Ian McKellen does perform the soliloquy, still lying down after waking. He weeps and is comforted by Ratcliffe, played by Bill Paterson as an ultra-loyal military batman kept ignorant of Richard's true nature and consequently deeply moved by his present plight. In the annotated text of the screenplay McKellen says that it's sometimes difficult to play this soliloquy on stage because it can easily get lost in the turbulent battle preparations. He thinks it gains its proper importance in cinematic close-up, and his own distressed performance of it in the movie has great power.

The soliloquy is a difficulty for actors, then, for reasons of characterization and setting, but also, I think, for reasons of form. A Richard III cracking apart in panic, anxiety and dread seems almost unrecognizable as the Richard who opens the play in insouciantly self-confident control. *That* quasi-directorial Richard, inviting us to applaud a performance, evaporates here into the self-address of exclamation, query, contradiction, cancellation, repetition, self-castigation and the startling, apparently almost frenzied reiteration of his own name in hesitantly groping attempts at self-definition. The pentameters of Richard's early soliloquies are imperturbable in their movement – stately, developmental and progressive displays of verse form moving fluidly in harmony with syntax across line after (usually end-stopped) line. They are this even when what they are saying is corrupt or morally diseased, which makes irony in this play virtually a principle of Shakespeare's blank verse form itself, as it discrepantly advertises the ethical disaster that is Richard III. Irony in *Richard III* is hypocrisy managed with high style.

In this final soliloquy, however, the forms themselves appear on the verge of disintegration, as individual pentameter lines are disrupted – in a way that must make them difficult for an actor to speak, or even memorize – by midline breaks of various kinds, textually indicated by numerous marks of punctuation: dashes, points, question marks, commas, exclamation marks. In *Year of the King*, his book about playing Richard, Anthony Sher says of this soliloquy that 'it's as if T. S. Eliot has thrown a speech into a Shakespeare play', and Ian McKellen thinks that, compared to the regular rhythms of most of the rest of what Richard says in the play, it's as bleakly modern as the writing of Samuel Beckett. The disruption of the iambic register is what sounds harshly modernistic to the ear and strangely discordant to the mind of anyone who has followed Richard up to this point. Even so, we might think that it's also as if Christopher Marlowe has thrown a speech into a Shakespeare play, because the disintegrative rhythms of Faustus's final soliloquy as he is damned in *Doctor Faustus* seem to inform Richard's cadences too.

And yet what we have in this soliloquy is in one sense Richard coming into his own, since, if every tale condemns him for a villain, he has now succeeded in what he sets out to do in his opening soliloquy, where he is 'determined to prove a villain'. He has by now all too adequately proved his determination, but he may well also now be subject to theological 'determination', since the 'Tudor Myth' would have it that God, who is addressed in Henry Richmond's prayer-soliloquy, ensures Richard's fate. This soliloquy also lets us know, though, exactly what it is to be 'myself alone' – it's a form of hell. In its twenty-nine lines the personal pronouns 'I' and 'me', the possessive adjective 'my' and the reflexive pronoun 'myself' occur thirty-four times. 'Richard loves Richard, that is, I am I' is a statement entangled to the point of despair. Some editions of the play prefer the reading of the first quarto, 'I and I', which makes the near-schizoid disintegration more apparent. The split self objectifies itself and names itself as others name it – 'Richard' – and says it loves itself but then immediately acknowledges that it fears itself so much as to believe it might kill itself, since that is what it would mean to exact revenge upon oneself. And, indeed, Richard's death at the hands of Henry Richmond is sometimes played, as it is in the McKellen film, as a form of suicide. Identity – 'I am I' – lies in self-love, but this self – 'I and I' – hates itself, equally and oppositely; so the self in guilty despair is a self in the profoundest distress of self-antagonism. This is the ultimate consequence of Richard's at first apparently confident but always altogether perilous self-generation. The peril as well as the generation is manifested in a soliloquy in which the 'I' speaks and the 'I' is spoken about.

That the true panic of Richard's plight lies in the fact that he is entirely self-aware about it is plain from his identification of the nightmare from which he has just awoken as the form taken by his own guilty conscience: 'My conscience hath a thousand several tongues, / And every tongue brings in a several tale, / And every tale condemns me for a villain.' There is a near-personification of 'tongue' here that intrudes a sudden, almost surreal element into Richard's metaphor – appropriately so for the evocation of a nightmare. Regarding himself as everywhere spoken against, Richard is also, in at least one of the several antagonistic voices that speak in this very soliloquy, speaking against himself. The tongue that condemns him as a perjurer and murderer is very much his own; and Richard remains himself alone by refusing pity to himself just as he has refused it to others and as he knows others will refuse it to him. This is psychological hell, but, in the Christian-metaphysical system acknowledged by the play, it's also the form taken by eternal damnation. Which is one reason why *Richard III* has often in literary history been read as comparable to, or as precursor of, *Macbeth*, with its also knowingly self-damning hero.

*

When Sylvia Plath opens one of the greatest of her late *Ariel* poems, 'Nick and the Candlestick', published in 1965 – a poem that attempts to rally itself with gestures of self-consolation among what appear to be the ruins of its own despair – she remembers the Richard of this soliloquy waking to the blue light of his small-hours-of-the-morning candles:

> I am a miner. The light burns blue.
> Waxy stalactites
> Drip and thicken, tears
>
> The earthen womb
> Exudes from its dead boredom ...

It's a startling accommodation of the Shakespearean nightmare and of the jagged modernity of this soliloquy to an extreme contemporary distress.

2. *Romeo and Juliet*

Act 3 Scene 2 of *Romeo and Juliet* opens with Juliet speaking a soliloquy whose risqué nature led to its being radically cut in performance, or even entirely suppressed, between the Restoration and the early twentieth century. Only one scene has intervened since Juliet left with Romeo to be married by Friar Laurence, but it's the scene that changes everything, because in it Romeo kills Juliet's much-loved cousin Tybalt in an outburst of uncontainable fury consequent on Tybalt's own killing of Romeo's friend Mercutio. The consequence is that Romeo has been exiled from Verona. We, as readers or audience, know all this, but Juliet does not, so her keen anticipation of her wedding night comes with all the force and pathos of dramatic irony. As we hear her speak, we know that, once Juliet knows what we do, she can never feel like this again. The unalloyed joy of anticipation is, for her, a one-off – as, it turns out, is the act of sexual consummation itself to which she looks forward so impatiently. Juliet begins the soliloquy, as we saw in Part II, with a telling allusion to the myth of Phaeton, as Shakespeare found it in Ovid's *Metamorphoses*:

Gallop apace, you fiery-footed steeds,
Towards Phoebus' lodging. Such a wagoner
As Phaeton would whip you to the west
And bring in cloudy night immediately.
Spread thy close curtain, love-performing night,
That runaways' eyes may wink, and Romeo
Leap to these arms, untalked of and unseen.
Lovers can see to do their amorous rites
By their own beauties; or, if love be blind,
It best agrees with night. Come, civil night,
Thou sober-suited matron all in black,
And learn me how to lose a winning match,
Played for a pair of stainless maidenhoods.
Hood my unmanned blood, bating in my cheeks,
With thy black mantle, till strange love grow bold,
Think true love acted simple modesty.
Come, night, come, Romeo, come, thou day in night,
For thou wilt lie upon the wings of night
Whiter than new snow upon a raven's back.
Come, gentle night, come, loving black-browed night,
Give me my Romeo, and when I shall die

Take him and cut him out in little stars,
And he will make the face of heaven so fine
That all the world will be in love with night
And pay no worship to the garish sun.
O, I have bought the mansion of a love
But not possessed it, and though I am sold,
Not yet enjoyed. So tedious is this day
As is the night before some festival
To an impatient child that hath new robes
And may not wear them. (3.2.1–31)

The half-line that follows is 'O, here comes my Nurse', and, wringing her hands, she does indeed come and – with characteristically procrastinating circumlocution – gives Juliet the news that changes everything.

Juliet's soliloquy is one of the great hymns to sexual love in Shakespeare. 'Hymn' seems the right word, because the language of erotic desire and projected ecstasy forms a kind of linguistic music in this play, in the soliloquies of both Romeo and Juliet and in their sometimes artificially stylized dialogue too. It's unsurprising that the play has inspired more purely musical responses than any other of Shakespeare's – operas by Bellini and Gounod; a 'dramatic symphony' by Berlioz; a 'fantasy overture' by Tchaikovsky; a ballet by Prokofiev; one of the great twentieth-century musicals (and musical films), *West Side Story*, with a score by Bernstein and Sondheim; and the MTV-friendly music-video style and soundtrack of Baz Luhrmann's film version.

Unlike many Shakespeare plays, however, *Romeo and Juliet* does not in fact include an actual song, even though directors sometimes give it one, as Franco Zeffirelli does in his 1968 film version, where Nino Rota's pseudo-Elizabethan 'What is a youth?', with its *carpe diem* theme, is sung at the Capulet ball; its melody then becomes the film's theme. But the play seems nevertheless conscious of its own musicality. In Act 2 Scene 2, traditionally known as the 'balcony scene' – although the word 'balcony' appears nowhere in the text – Romeo, perhaps almost aware of the remarkable exchange of soliloquy and dialogue in this beautifully orchestrated scene, which makes it appear so much like an operatic alternation of aria and duet, says, hearing Juliet call him back, 'How silver-sweet sound lovers' tongues by night, / Like softest music to attending ears' (2.2.165–6). The sibilance and vowel sounds of those lines make Romeo's point of themselves, and it's very much *our* ears as audience that attend upon this music. Again, as the lovers prepare for marriage, it's also Romeo, with a rhetorical extravagance that draws a mild rebuke from Juliet, who says he has no language for what he feels and asks her if *she* can verbalize it instead. If she manages this, he says, her breath itself will produce 'rich music's tongue', which is alone appropriate to the 'imagined happiness' they share (2.6.27–8).

Accordingly, Juliet's soliloquy offers a kind of linguistic music, as its assonance and alliteration shape their patterns in the air. In the opening few lines, for instance, the repeated 'f' sounds (fiery-footed/Phoebus/Phaeton), 'w' sounds (wagoner/whip/west/wink) and 'c' sounds (cloudy/close curtain) seem to establish a harmony finally resolved into the bass-line thrum of the repeated, almost unvoiced negative 'un' in 'untalked' and 'unseen'. Repetitions of another kind form the soliloquy's quasi-musical syntax, as the word 'Come' reiterates an imperative apostrophe to 'night' and to Romeo himself, and as it impatiently repeats itself in rapid succession in the line, 'Come, night, come, Romeo, come, thou day in night.' The urgency of Juliet's desire almost rushes across the intervening commas of hesitation and pause in a spondaic accumulation of demand. The *OED*'s first ascription of the meaning 'to have an orgasm' to the word 'come' is 1650, so it probably does not carry this sense here, even clandestinely. But the soliloquy makes us feel it should, since Juliet is voicing the very rhythm of sexual excitement itself – and Gordon Williams in his *Dictionary of Sexual Language and Imagery in Shakespearean and Stuart Literature* claims that this meaning of the word *was* in fact available to Shakespeare.

By calling Romeo 'thou day in night' Juliet is metaphorically making him an element of the cosmos itself, and, by elaborating her figure in the extraordinarily rich way she does, she underwrites the almost mythical perspective in which she views him, while also offering an erotically charged image of Romeo lying 'whiter than snow upon a raven's back'. As I have said, this soliloquy opens by alluding to the myth of Phaeton and the horses of the sun, and I drew out some of the ominous implications of that in Part II. In these lines, it's as if Juliet is countering that foreboding with another, metamorphic myth of her own, as she asks the gentle, loving night to 'Give me my Romeo, and when I shall die / Take him and cut him out in little stars …' in a way that will make him more worthy of awestruck human love than the sun itself. Juliet is not only making a star out of Romeo here – *stellifying* him, as human beings are sometimes metamorphosed into stars in Ovid – but making herself an element of the cosmos larger than ordinary human life too, by presuming to address and command night itself as an equal. She is also using exactly the imagery Romeo himself uses when he gazes at her at the opening of the balcony scene, as he conceives of her eyes sparkling brightly enough to replace stars that have temporarily vacated the heavens: 'Her eyes in heaven / Would through the airy region stream so bright / That birds would sing and think it were not night' (2.2.20–2). Juliet's tropes, then, may be read as a highly eroticized, hyperbolic form of Petrarchan commonplace. Although the erotic possibilities of Petrarchan tropes are apparent also in Edmund Spenser's 'Epithalamion' (1595), for instance, in which a personified Night is also invited to visit a mythicized nuptial scene – 'Spread thy broad wings over my love and me, / That no man may us see' – these are figures conjured by a mature man, not by a young woman; and this makes a difference.

At the end of the soliloquy, the simile that makes use of the figure of 'an impatient child' reminds us that Juliet is herself in many ways still a child too: Shakespeare reduced her age to thirteen, almost fourteen, from the sixteen he found in his main source, Arthur Brooke's narrative poem *Romeus and Juliet*. But Juliet is very much an adult, or at least an adolescent, in this scene too, with its patent eroticism, and here, by making herself and Romeo elements of a private mythology, she makes it seem that they virtually transcend the social world by which they are nominally contained. 'Nominally' is the proper word, because the inherited names 'Capulet' and 'Montague' trap them in the feud their families pursue, and are therefore the names from which both desire to be released. It's this transgressive combination of child, adolescent and transcendent, quasi-mythological being – all audible together in her soliloquies – that makes Juliet the extraordinary dramatic creation she is, permanently exceptional and unavailable to categorization.

Her stellification of Romeo is also an indication of how turned in upon itself, how self-interwoven, this play is, as it picks up and repeats figures of speech, images and figurative tropes in speeches that call across to one another as the play progresses. Juliet's putting Romeo into competition with the sun is, for instance, one of the play's many figurations of luminescence and incandescence and of the act of looking that is enabled by light. 'O she doth teach the torches to burn bright', says Romeo, gloriously, when he first gazes on Juliet, 'It seems she hangs upon the cheek of night / As a rich jewel in an Ethiop's ear' (1.5.43–5); and again at the beginning of the balcony scene, looking up at her window, he asks in sheer wonderment, 'But soft, what light through yonder window breaks? / It is the east, and Juliet is the sun' (2.2.2–3). The light breaking through the window, that is, is Juliet herself, figured as the rising sun. So if Juliet puts Romeo in competition with the sun in this soliloquy, she has put him in a kind of metaphorical competition with herself. In their mutual mythologizing, the lovers place an aura of otherworldly transcendence about themselves.

Juliet's figuration also further intensifies the vividness of her insistence earlier in the soliloquy that, in the darkness of night required for Romeo's dangerous liaison with her, 'Lovers can see to do their amorous rites / By their own beauties.' In the Elizabethan England in which the play was first staged, the dark really was dark, in a way those of us who inhabit contemporary conurbations can barely comprehend, and Juliet's imagining the luminescence of lovers' beauties as sufficient in themselves to illuminate *that* darkness is to conceive of those bodies as almost supernaturally or angelically gifted. In the balcony scene, Romeo has also already in fact perceived Juliet as a 'bright angel ... a winged messenger of heaven' (2.2.25, 27), and in the Baz Luhrmann film Juliet (Claire Danes) wears angels' wings as her costume for the Capulets' feast, conceived here as a fancy-dress ball. These make her seem, probably, more childlike than transcendent, but certainly radiant too. Juliet's hyperbolic intensity takes on a special tenderness when we remember those plays of Shakespeare's in which sex happens between people who, far from seeing by their own beauties in the Elizabethan dark, fail even to recognize their partners in it: Angelo in *Measure for Measure* and Bertram in *All's Well That Ends Well*. The 'bed tricks' in those plays are problematical exercises in duplicity, but what the men believe themselves to be engaged in is sexual conquest. What Juliet foresees for herself is virtually the opposite: a fullness of devoted gazing, for which the night is not cover but cue – 'love-performing', in fact, in her striking adjectival coinage.

But we remember all this too, with a dreadful difference, when Romeo in his final soliloquy, spoken before he takes the apothecary's poison, tells Paris, whom he has just killed, that he will bury him not in a 'triumphant grave' but in 'a lantern' – 'For here lies Juliet, and her beauty makes / This vault a feasting presence full of light' (5.3.84–6). Romeo's last soliloquy summons back Juliet's – not to nullify it, but to render its terms altogether less stable. It's as though the play's affirmative images and impulses are constantly subject to undermining revision, having an inherent capacity for both benefit and harm – like Friar Laurence's herbs in his opening soliloquy in Act 2 Scene 3, which possess both 'grace and rude will'. Herbs may be used to counterfeit death helpfully, but they may also actually kill; even when they appear to act helpfully they may still, in the end and by accident, kill. The beautiful forms and patterns of rhetoric and linguistic music can do little against the relentless onslaught of malign human will or – in some ways even more terribly – against the casual callousness of fortune or, as Friar Laurence would have it, against the design of 'a greater power than we can contradict'. The desire for transcendence may lead only to the grave.

Juliet's placing Romeo among the stars as an act of personal myth-making may also be understood therefore as a kind of counter to the fate foretold for the lovers in the Chorus's opening sonnet-soliloquy, in which the 'fatal loins' of the households of the Montagues and Capulets are said to have produced 'a pair of star-crossed lovers' who 'take their life'. Juliet cannot contest this. Her fate – that she should take her own life – is written in the stars and cannot be gainsaid. But she can still implicitly dissent from it, and this is what the stellar hyperbole of her soliloquy does. The effort of linguistic transcendence in this soliloquy opposes some other forms of human behaviour in the play: the casual homosocial misogyny of Romeo's companions; the comparable innuendo but – far worse – the cynical, irreligious opportunism of the Nurse, which leads to Juliet's disgusted abandonment of her in Act 3 Scene 5; the manipulative mercenariness of Juliet's own parents as they attempt to arrange a socially acceptable marriage for her against her will; and even, perhaps, the conceiving of love as possession, in the property-market figuration she herself employs ('O, I have bought the mansion of a love ...') – since Juliet is inevitably still at least partly imprisoned in the world her imagination longs to transcend.

This usual social world intrudes often enough in *Romeo and Juliet*, and in fact the play's very first soliloquy, as we saw in Part I, is spoken in prose by an illiterate servant. Illiteracy certainly would exclude you from the prominent discourse of this play, which is literate, allusive and rhetorically patterned to an almost baroque degree. It's a play in which the lovers themselves, and others too, speak in versions of sonnet form; Friar Laurence speaks a soliloquy in rhyming couplets; Juliet's own 'Gallop apace' soliloquy is a version of a classical epithalamium, a form written to be sung or recited on the bride's way to the wedding chamber; and the dialogue between the lovers in Act 3 Scene 5 is a version of an aubade, the traditional form in which a lover laments the coming of the dawn which must separate him from his beloved. When Juliet says 'if love be blind, / It best agrees with night', she is alluding to the blind classical god Cupid, who sometimes appears explicitly, and more often, as here, implicitly, in the play's field of allusion. Cupid is one of the properties the Elizabethan sonnet inherited from the Italian Petrarchan tradition in which love is also figured as a form of warfare. Romeo's apparent infatuation with Rosaline at the beginning of the play is conveyed, to the point of pastiche, in Petrarchan discourse, notably its oxymorons ('heavy lightness', 'serious vanity' and so on), and in Act 2 Scene 4 Mercutio actually names Petrarch and the idealized child-woman of his sonnets, Laura, in a way that would have made explicit to a knowledgeable contemporary audience the tradition the play is drawing on.

So Juliet's spiritedly independent-minded self-assurance in this soliloquy acts as an implicit rejection of that conventional literary language too – the language of the wholly male sonnet tradition – and an implicit critique of it, just as Shakespeare's own radically experimental and innovative sonnet sequence, published only after the vogue for sonnets in the 1590s was over, is too. Juliet's form of transcendence operates on an altogether different plane from that of the idealization of the woman by a male would-be lover in the Petrarchan tradition – although it should be said that the earliest English sonnet sequence, Sidney's *Astrophil and Stella* (probably written 1581–2), is itself in many respects anti-Petrarchan too, emphasizing the unavailability of the poet's love to the standard tropes. Juliet's erotic frankness, though, presents a woman fully embodied – desiring, and implicitly refusing anything less than, the mutuality of sexual fulfilment. This is certainly an implication of the word 'die' in the phrase 'And when I shall die', since 'die' meant to the Elizabethans what 'come' does for us – that is, to experience sexual climax. Juliet is therefore saying that, when she climaxes in the sexual consummation of her marriage to Romeo, the night that has been the active agent of their lovemaking must cut him out in little stars. Imagining herself in orgasm, she imagines herself seeing stars. It's hardly surprising that pre-twentieth-century productions would have had difficulty staging such a speech, and indeed contemporary susceptibilities might still quail before any such staging if the person playing Juliet were literally the age Shakespeare makes her. Those playing the part tend to be significantly older, and even the very young Olivia Hussey in Zeffirelli's film was fifteen, closer to the age of Juliet in Shakespeare's source. Even so, Hussey does not speak this soliloquy in the movie, which has nevertheless been widely regarded as reflective of the liberalization of sexual attitudes in Western Europe in the late 1960s. The dangerous edge to the soliloquy and its frank register of desire should not be underestimated – or underplayed.

There is a textual problem, however, with the printing of the word 'I' in the lines 'when I shall die / Take him and cut him out in little stars' because a variant in one of the quartos reads 'he', and some editors accept this reading. It does make sense, as the repeated 'him' of the succeeding line appears to proceed more naturally from the third-person than the first-person pronoun of the phrase. However, I favour the reading of Arden 3, and agree with the editor's justification of it, which encourages the interpretation of the lines I have offered here. If it were the third-person 'he', however, the lines would also be perfectly intelligible, as Juliet's fear, even at the moment – perhaps *especially* at the moment – of sexual consummation, that her lover must die. For the fact is that although 'die' may mean 'to experience orgasm', it does also, inevitably, mean to cease to exist. And in this sense, even more than in the others I have identified so far, this soliloquy of Juliet's ramifies extensively in the play.

For *Romeo and Juliet* is a play in which sex and death are so deeply interwoven as to be virtually inseparable, which is why structurally the play is in many respects a comedy but is generically of course a tragedy. The interweaving is pointed by Juliet's figuring the act of sex as learning 'how to lose a winning match', which is almost the opposite of perceiving it, as Angelo and Bertram do, as conquest, and it also undermines the warfare metaphor essential to Petrarchism. Juliet's apparent paradox insists that neither partner can ever lose at *this* game. Her altogether willing submission to Romeo will make it a win for both contestants, since both, being virgins (at least as far as Juliet assumes), will win by losing 'a pair of stainless maidenhoods', the implication being that Romeo will submit to her just as she will to him. The loss, being mutually agreed, is no loss at all. The figure of losing by winning also subjects to judgement those other games in the play which are fought to the death with swords – implements whose phallic suggestiveness gives rise to some of its innuendo. Indeed, Juliet's suicide may be read as a final hideous parody of the act of love when, in her last brief, interrupted soliloquy, she stabs herself with Romeo's dagger and apostrophizes it in the final line she speaks: 'This is thy sheath; there rust, and let me die' (5.3.170). The phallic dagger's sheath has become her own body; the sexual wound of the act of love has become the death wound. We may assume that Shakespeare, if not Juliet herself, would have known that the Latin for a weapon's sheath or scabbard was 'vagina'.

It's almost inevitable then that this great hymn to the anticipation of sexual love should be met by another soliloquy of anticipation, that in Act 4 Scene 3, in which Juliet trembles before the terrors of living entombment. The speech precedes her drinking the Friar's potion, which, counterfeiting death, will enable her to avoid the wholly undesirable marriage her father intends for her, which would be both bigamous and sacrilegious. It opens with a pentameter line whose monosyllabic rhythmic regularity dramatizes by almost ironizing the irregularity of the emotion it evokes – 'I have a faint cold fear thrills through my veins' – and the fear is dramatized further by Juliet's calling instinctively for the Nurse she has recently spurned. As if, disoriented by fear, she has momentarily forgotten she has done this, she immediately rejects the culpable comfort it would involve, contemptuously questioning herself – 'What should she do here?' – before realizing the inescapable reality: 'My dreadful scene I needs must act alone'. In Part III of this book Mariah Gale speaks eloquently about playing Juliet in the desolation of her loneliness here. Juliet's dismissal of the thought of her Nurse, Gale thinks, represents Juliet's heart-breaking decision to resist further dialogue by returning to the solitude of soliloquy. Her conceiving of herself as performing a scene also emphasizes the very dangerous game she is about to play. She is going to play dead, which does not seem much like playing 'a winning match', even if she has been assured by the Friar that it will, in the end, be exactly that. Beyond this, too, the theatrical metaphor introduces a riskily almost meta-theatrical moment as the woman (originally the boy) playing Juliet seems also to be proclaiming the difficulty of the scene, or soliloquy, she (or he) is about to perform, since all soliloquists 'needs must act alone'.

And then Juliet is forced to confront her anxieties in terrified self-questioning as she steels herself into drinking the potion. She wonders if the Friar has given her mortal poison and, perhaps even more terrifyingly, whether she might wake in the tomb before Romeo comes and so die of asphyxiation. At that point, her questions take on an even greater specificity and immediacy and her vision of the charnel house becomes almost as intense as Hamlet's. Indeed, this soliloquy comes to a climax as Juliet, like Hamlet, appears to see an actual ghost and conceives of herself as, like Ophelia, driven to suicidal insanity by her experience:

Or if I live, is it not very like
The horrible conceit of death and night,
Together with the terror of the place,
As in a vault, an ancient receptacle
Where for this many hundred years the bones
Of all my buried ancestors are packed,
Where bloody Tybalt, yet but green in earth,
Lies festering in his shroud, where, as they say,
At some hours in the night spirits resort –
Alack, alack, is it not like that I,
So early waking, what with loathsome smells,
And shrieks like mandrakes torn out of the earth,
That living mortals, hearing them, run mad –

O, if I wake, shall I not be distraught,
Environed with all these hideous fears,
And madly play with my forefathers' joints,
And pluck the mangled Tybalt from his shroud
And, in this rage, with some great kinsman's bone,
As with a club, dash out my desperate brains?
O, look, methinks I see my cousin's ghost
Seeking out Romeo that did split his body
Upon a rapier's point. Stay, Tybalt, stay!
Romeo, Romeo, Romeo, here's drink. I drink to thee. (4.3.36–58)

It may be that this soliloquy is omitted in some productions because Juliet here, like Richard III in his final soliloquy, sounds so little like herself, so little like the bravely independent Juliet we have come to know up to this point; Shakespeare is in fact more indebted to Brooke's poem here, with its relish for 'Gothic' effect, than he is elsewhere in his treatment of Juliet. Mariah Gale captures exactly how this must feel to a sensitive actor playing the part when she says that Juliet 'speaks herself into a completely other state where she sees Tybalt. Just speaking it out loud does it to you – just rhythmically, and the imagery.' Juliet's unlikeness to herself is the point, and is projected by the very rhythms of her speech. Terror does indeed make us different from, 'other' to, ourselves. Nothing in our experience can prepare us for it, and nothing can predict our response to it. In fact, Friar Laurence's attempt to ready Juliet for it in Act 4 Scene 1 when he offers a lengthy catalogue of the drug's effects appears almost more calculated to provoke than to allay terror when he conjures her rosy lips and cheeks fading to 'wanny ashes' and conceives of the windows of her eyes – which we know to have seen so much of erotic pleasure – falling 'like death' (4.1.100–1). Juliet's charnel-house imagining is comparable not only to Hamlet's but to John Webster's and John Donne's. The fact that all of this comes out of the mouth of a thirteen-year-old girl (or woman) is arguably far more shocking than what we have heard from her in the 'Gallop apace' soliloquy. Juliet is as outrageous in the contemplation of death as she is in the contemplation of sex.

Juliet's syntactical manoeuvres in this soliloquy – apostrophes, questions and, ultimately, her exclamation to Tybalt, or his ghost – are enhanced by the suppleness of the sinuous single sentence running from lines 36 to 54. This is propelled by the ratcheting up of three clauses introduced by the word 'where', which make the tomb of Juliet's visualizing almost concretely present to her – and to us – and then by the tremulousness with which she makes herself, with her personal pronoun, part of the dreaded scene itself ('is it not like that I ...?'; 'shall I not be distraught ...?'). The appalled reiteration of the word 'And' at the head of lines 51–3 introduces three further stages, horribly specific, in her imagined disintegration into insanity, before the sentence resolves to its dreadful conclusion. The repetition of the conjunction in this way is the rhetorical form known as polysyndeton, and it acts here as a reminder of how artfully Shakespeare manages rhetoric as an element of human emotion and psychology. The passage is rhetorically constructed, but what we perceive before and beyond the art of rhetoric is the naked terror of Juliet's conceiving of what may lie in wait for her. Despite sounding very little like herself in this soliloquy, the intensity of imagination evinced is in fact equivalent to what she displays while imagining sexual fulfilment in the 'Gallop apace' soliloquy. It's strengthened almost into something resembling the imagined experience itself, as words and forms are found for extremities of human feeling and response.

So much is this the case that Juliet's powers of visualization take on a kind of palpability in the line 'O, look, methinks I see my cousin's ghost'. To whom is this addressed, and what is it she thinks she sees? Is Juliet speaking to herself, or to us? No ghost in fact appears in *Romeo and Juliet*, but the fact that ghosts do indeed appear in other plays of Shakespeare's makes it not impossible that one might do so, especially since Juliet's 'methinks' is immediately accompanied by an exclamation to the ghost to 'stay', as if even Tybalt, whom she has just imagined mangled in his shroud, will be welcome company in this extremity of foreboding. The instruction to 'look', together with the exclamation to Tybalt, dramatizes Juliet's terror as an almost pictorial spectacle, so that the lonely soliloquy commands us too to *see* what Juliet herself does. All that can possibly remain is for her to drink the potion, or decide not to – which must seem a real possibility to anyone reading or seeing the play for the first time. She does so in the breathlessly hypermetrical shape of the soliloquy's final line – 'Romeo, Romeo, Romeo', three apostrophic gasps of the name that has been so emphasized and debated earlier in the play. Is this spoken in desperation, in longing or in the hope that Romeo might indeed appear as a kind of truly comforting alternative to Tybalt's ghost? No matter how we understand this, the raising of the vial to her lips is figured, with an irony both sublime and devastating, as if she were instead raising a loving cup at her own wedding: 'I drink to thee'.

Zeffirelli, as I have said, omits this soliloquy, and Luhrmann cuts it to the bone, but in his screen version (1954) Renato Castellani brilliantly includes it. Wearing a dress of deep blood-red, Juliet (Susan Shentall, in her unique film role) speaks, initially in the deep-focus background of a shot that foregrounds, on left screen, the wedding dress she is to wear to marry Paris hanging on a mannequin. As she speaks, she has her back to us, moving her head to one side and the other, as if she cannot confront, or permit us to confront, the terrors to which she is now subject. When she appears to see Tybalt's ghost, she turns and looks to camera for the first time, although not at eye level, and the camera retreats to set her again in deep focus in the background of a shot in which the dress is once more ominously in left foreground. We see her taking it from the mannequin, and the scene fades to black. Next morning, the Nurse finds her in bed with it on, and Juliet is put in the tomb still wearing it.

The mannequin has a protruding wicker head, which makes it resemble the surreal figure – part-mannequin, part-statue – in the left foreground of Giorgio de Chirico's painting *The Disquieting Muses*. This scene of the film is altogether disquieting, and very appropriately so. The reminiscence in Castellani's cinematography of the nightmarish surreal painting, whether deliberately intended or not, is suddenly strikingly modernistic in a film that, set partly in Verona itself, usually, and extensively, takes its visual cue from the art of the Italian Quattrocento. But de Chirico's painting also depicts an architecturally distorted Italian piazza containing both a Renaissance castle (that of Ferrara) and a modern factory. The nightmare of terror in Juliet's soliloquy thus opens cinematically into a nightmare of modernity too, in the best moment of a flawed but fascinating example of post-war Italian neo-realism.

*

Act 2 Scene 6 of *Romeo and Juliet* ends with Friar Laurence inviting the lovers to go with him to be married – 'For, by your leaves', he says, 'you shall not stay alone / Till holy church incorporate two in one' (2.6.36–7) – *incorporate*: to combine or unite into one body, making the two-in-one-flesh of the Catholic sacrament of marriage, to which Juliet herself, if not her Nurse, pays reverence. The Friar's slightly off-key pararhyme of 'alone' and 'one' may suggest the difficulty of the venture while also manifesting its possibility, and one way in which being 'alone' may become being 'two in one' is when soliloquy becomes reciprocated dialogue, as it does in the balcony scene. We have also seen some of the ways in which the lovers' soliloquies appear to share an almost uncanny transference, as images and figures are repeated across them. Romeo's final one shares things with Juliet's 'potion' soliloquy, but as he prepares to take poison in the Capulet tomb he must anticipate not the terrors of simulated death but those of the thing itself. After addressing Paris in the lines quoted above, which celebrate the tomb containing Juliet as 'a feasting presence full of light', he apostrophizes Death itself, while proleptically referring to himself as 'a dead man', before introducing yet another kind of 'light' into the play:

> How oft, when men are at the point of death,
> Have they been merry, which their keepers call
> A lightening before death. O, how may I
> Call this a lightening? O my love, my wife,
> Death, that hath sucked the honey of thy breath
> Hath had no power yet upon thy beauty.
> Thou art not conquered. Beauty's ensign yet
> Is crimson in thy lips and in thy cheeks,
> And death's pale flag is not advanced there …
>   Shall I believe

That unsubstantial death is amorous,
And that the lean abhorred monster keeps
Thee here in dark to be his paramour?
For fear of that I still will stay with thee
And never from this palace of dim night
Depart again. Here, here I will remain
With worms that are thy chambermaids. O, here
Will I set up my everlasting rest,
And shake the yoke of inauspicious stars
From this world-wearied flesh. Eyes, look your last;
Arms, take your last embrace, and lips, O you
The doors of breath, seal with a righteous kiss
A dateless bargain to engrossing death.
Come, bitter conduct, come, unsavoury guide.
Thou desperate pilot, now at once run on
The dashing rocks thy seasick weary bark!
Here's to my love. [*Drinks.*]
O true apothecary,
Thy drugs are quick. Thus with a kiss I die. (5.3.88–96, 103–20)

'Light' as radiance or illumination is not the only meaning the word carries in *Romeo and Juliet*. It also means, for instance, the opposite of 'heavy', as when Friar Laurence, in a trope freighted with omen, sees Juliet, in the terms of the stage direction, coming 'somewhat fast' and says, 'O, so light a foot / Will ne'er wear out the everlasting flint' (2.6.16–17). This is presumably spoken humorously, since even the heaviest foot will not wear out a stone that lasts forever, but it nevertheless also has the pathos of evoking a transient human body leaving, in its brief passage, hardly any imprint on the ground it treads. Earlier, in the balcony scene, suddenly frightened by the apparent rashness of what the lovers are deciding to do, Juliet says that it seems 'Too like the lightning which doth cease to be / Ere one can say "it lightens"' (2.2.119–20), which is a brilliant bringing together of the sudden swiftness of atmospheric behaviour and the brief urgency and shock of responsive human speech. Now Romeo offers one final variant on the word.

The *OED* tells us that a 'lightening' is an 'exhilaration or revival of the spirits which is supposed to occur in some instances just before death', but Seamus Heaney puts it better when he uses the word for the title of a sequence of poems in *Seeing Things* (1991) and defines it in one of them (no. xii): 'A phenomenal instant when the spirit flares / With pure exhilaration before death.' We must assume, though, that such a lightening can be commented on only by others, not by the dying person him or herself. So the first question of Romeo's soliloquy – 'how may I / Call this a lightening?' – sounds plaintively almost as though he is back in the classroom undertaking a scholastic exercise in descriptive discrimination. At the very point of death, he seems therefore very young indeed, like Juliet. His question sounds almost like the beginning of a syllogism or even a poetic metaphor and reminds us of Richard II toying with a conundrum at the opening of his great soliloquy 'I have been studying how I may compare / This prison where I live unto the world ...' – the soliloquy that also immediately precedes his death. Romeo knows that he should now feel 'merry', but how can he describe what he actually feels as that? Well, astonishingly, Juliet's beauty appears unaffected by death, and that may be a reason to feel a lightening before his own death. This syllogistic argument has no conclusion, however, and veers instead into another question altogether, which hideously conceives of Death keeping Juliet as a clandestine mistress. In the play's system of cross-reference, this trope takes up Capulet's own figure when he sees Juliet 'dead' after taking the Friar's potion, and says to Paris:

> O son, the night before thy wedding day
> Hath death lain with thy wife. There she lies,
> Flower as she was, deflowered by him.
> Death is my son-in-law, death is my heir ... (4.5.35–8)

The recursive symmetry is unnerving. The lover about to die for his beloved shares the figurative terms of the father whose violent insistence has propelled this very outcome itself – and the sexual specificity of the trope certainly sits more disturbingly in the father's than in the lover's mouth. But the symmetry makes it seem the more perturbing there too.

In any case, it's the fear that Juliet will be sexually subjected in this way that acts as the immediate provocation to Romeo's suicide. He will protect her from, as it were, a posthumous fate, a fate worse than death. At that point, the soliloquy begins to resemble Juliet's 'potion' soliloquy in its fixing on the nature of the charnel-house itself, but it goes even further than hers in its macabre figuring of the worms as 'chambermaids'. The beneficiaries of the body's decomposition are perceived as performing a dutiful service of destruction. If Juliet's soliloquy reminds us of John Donne, this seems only a step away from Andrew Marvell's great seventeenth-century poem 'To His Coy Mistress', whose almost unbearably intrusive specificity imagines corrupting worms which will 'try / That long-preserved virginity'. Marvell's is a poem of seduction, and it's with a similar correlation between death and sex that Romeo figures himself setting up his 'everlasting rest' with Juliet. Earlier in the play the Nurse, about to discover her apparently 'dead' mistress, has made an inappropriately bawdy joke out of the phrase when she tells Juliet that Paris has 'set up his rest / That you shall rest but little' (4.4.6–7) – that is, that the man about to marry her will want to have a great deal of sex with her.

Like Juliet's 'Gallop apace' soliloquy, this one of Romeo's also has a kind of music of repetition, even if this is now the music of desperation.

The vocative 'O' of succeeding apostrophes – repeated five times – sounds the note of tragic lament while reminding us also of Juliet's exclamatory 'O' in that soliloquy – 'O, I have bought the mansion of a love'. The mansion of love has now become what Romeo calls a palace, but only 'a palace of dim night', and this night is of a kind altogether different from the one Juliet repeatedly calls out to in that soliloquy. The repetition of 'O' is accompanied by the repetitions of the words 'here' and 'come', the former emphasizing the finality of the place Romeo has now arrived at, and the latter appearing almost a kind of travesty of the repeated 'come' in Juliet's soliloquy. Romeo's 'come' is addressed to the 'conduct', the poison itself, which will guide him to the death he desires, whereas hers summoned the night that would bring Romeo to her, and then summoned Romeo himself. The music of Romeo's soliloquy seems to form a sad diminuendo as he instructs parts of his own body, almost as if he is making a Renaissance blazon of them, to respond one final time to the beauty of Juliet's body: his eyes, which must look their last in a play greatly taken up with looking and light; his arms, which can hold her in a final embrace in a play prominently devoted to the embracing of lovers; and his lips, which, as the 'doors of breath', have shaped some of the play's magnificent verbal music, including this soliloquy itself, and which must also, one final time, kiss the object of their owner's love, as he dies on the word 'die' itself – just as Juliet, in a final harmony of verbal transference between the two, will herself die after a further very brief soliloquy shortly afterwards.

*

Thinking about the way the lovers' soliloquies complement one another in an almost uncanny way in *Romeo and Juliet*, we might also ponder the fact that the play's plot is itself initiated by the hero's overhearing a soliloquy by the heroine. The balcony scene opens with Romeo's soliloquy on Juliet, whom he then sees apparently talking to herself. Juliet then sighs two words to herself that we all hear ('Ay me'), and Romeo soliloquizes further, perceiving her as a 'bright angel'. And Juliet, in the play's most famous line – 'O Romeo, Romeo, wherefore art thou Romeo?' – apostrophizes him in soliloquy, believing him, as those apostrophized in soliloquy usually are, to be entirely absent from the scene of her speech (although 'wherefore', much misunderstood, means 'why', not 'where'). Her meditation on his name makes it clear that she loves him and will marry him, changing her name to his. So he asks himself whether he should listen further or speak out, and he does hear more before then telling her of his willingness to change *his* name, to be 'new baptized'. Realizing that she has been overheard, Juliet responds, and the scene's soliloquies give way to dialogue.

This sequence of speaking, overhearing, deciding to listen to, and then responding to, soliloquy makes for a beautifully orchestrated and almost operatic exchange, in which spoken aria seems to melt into duet, making the lovers appear almost already 'incorporate' before they are made sacramentally so in marriage by the Friar. But it's the knowledge that Romeo has overheard her soliloquy that impels Juliet further in her declarations of love. There is no longer any point in holding back, even if she fears that this may make her seem 'light' in yet another sense of that word: too forward or too easily available. There is no point in holding back because she knows that by overhearing her soliloquy Romeo already knows how she feels – which is why she says 'farewell, compliment', meaning that she must now reject the usual formalities of respectable social and inter-personal behaviour between men and women, the norms of her world. As soon as she knows that Romeo has heard her confess her love, the rules of that world no longer apply. And so it's Juliet, not Romeo, who proposes marriage, with characteristic impetuousness, or with utterly self-reliant spiritedness. For the ensuing action of *Romeo and Juliet*, therefore, soliloquy itself is to be blamed, or to be celebrated.

3. *Othello*

In Act 3 Scene 3 of *Othello*, usually known as the 'temptation scene', Iago has aroused Othello's suspicions about Desdemona and Cassio by appearing to speak a thought aloud almost despite himself as Cassio leaves Desdemona and the stage: 'Ha, I like not that.' When Desdemona and Emilia also leave, Iago asks Othello if Cassio had known about his love for Desdemona while he was courting her. Othello says he did, 'from first to last', understandably asking Iago why he is interested. Iago replies, 'But for a satisfaction in my thought, / No further harm.' He then slyly provokes Othello into inquiring about Cassio's honesty, and the words 'honesty' and 'honest' echo again and again throughout the play – fifty-two times, in fact, 'from first to last', and so much so that William Empson, in a famous essay on the word as it figures in the play, says that 'there is no other play in which Shakespeare worries a word like that'. Iago then implies, by ostensibly evasive question and repetition, that there is a great deal in his thought that he might say if he had a mind to. Othello, in some exasperation, demands, 'What dost thou think?' and Iago, apparently still temporizing, replies, 'Think, my lord?' Othello, now wholly frustrated, responds by repeating the question as an exclamation:

> Think, my lord! By heaven, thou echo'st me
> As if there were some monster in thy thought
> Too hideous to be shown. Thou dost mean something …
>   If thou dost love me
> Show me thy thought. (3.3.109–11; 118–19)

That Othello has thought about thought and its potential exposure is emphasized later in the play when he tells Iago that the handkerchief he gave Desdemona had been given to his mother by 'an Egyptian' who was 'a charmer and could almost read / The thoughts of people' (3.4.59–60), which resonates with the play's several dangerous or disturbing references to magic and magical thinking, including Brabantio's charge that, being black, Othello must have used 'foul charms' to attract the white Desdemona, that he is 'a practiser / Of arts inhibited and out of warrant' (1.2.78–9).

After further quibbling on the words 'honest' and 'think', Iago muses, in a way designed to derogate and implicate Cassio, 'Men should be what they seem, / Or those that be not, would they might seem none'. Othello, driven almost to distraction by Iago's hints, can endure no more:

> I prithee speak to me, as to thy thinkings,
> As thou dost ruminate, and give thy worst of thoughts
> The worst of words. (3.3.134–6)

'Good my lord, pardon me', says Iago,

> Though I am bound to every act of duty
> I am not bound to all that slaves are free to –
> Utter my thoughts? Why, say they are vile and false?
> As where's that palace whereinto foul things
> Sometimes intrude not? Who has a breast so pure
> But some uncleanly apprehensions
> Keep leets and law-days and in session sit
> With meditations lawful? (3.3.136–44)

Othello persists nevertheless in asking to know Iago's thoughts and Iago does eventually voice them – or at least he voices what he claims them to be – and both Iago's scheme and the play's tragic plot are set in motion when, as Iago knows will happen, these thoughts drive Othello mad with jealousy. There is indeed 'some monster' in Iago's thought. It is the 'green-eyed monster' of jealousy that Iago disingenuously warns Othello against in this very scene before setting it loose, turning him from Desdemona's devoted lover into her putative murderer.

The 'monstrous', like the magical, recurs in the play: Emilia, for instance, also regards jealousy as 'a monster / Begot upon itself, born on itself' (3.4.161–2) and Othello hideously sees himself, cuckolded, as monstrous too: 'A horned man's a monster, and a beast' (4.1.62). The monstrous complicity between Othello, the general, and Iago, his ensign, culminates in this scene when both kneel, Othello to dedicate himself to revenge and Iago to pledge himself to Othello's 'service' in 'what bloody business ever' Othello might demand of him, calling on the stars to witness his vow. In the final line of the scene Iago says to Othello 'I am your own for ever', and what we as audience have witnessed appears to be the plighting of a dark Mephistophelean troth between the two, in a kind of mock wedding ceremony. In the most memorable moment of the National Theatre film version directed by Stuart Burge (1965), with Olivier as Othello, Iago (Frank Finlay) takes Desdemona's handkerchief from his pocket behind Othello's turned back, tying a knot in it as he speaks the line direct to camera, as if it's the briefest of soliloquies. More directly, Oliver Parker's film (1995) has Othello (Laurence Fishburne) and Iago (Kenneth Branagh) scoring their hands with a dagger and mingling their blood in the sign of blood-brotherhood. Looking at the camera across Othello's shoulder as they embrace, Iago seems almost in orgasmic convulsion.

We know that Iago has planned the business of this scene, or something like it, because, unlike Othello, we *do* know Iago's thoughts. Not at all bound to all that slaves are free to, he nevertheless chooses voluntarily to express his 'thinkings' to us in as many as eight soliloquies – the same number spoken by Richard III. We therefore also know that the thoughts he offers Othello here are not at all what he truly thinks but what he affects to think with the purpose of promoting extreme, murderous jealousy. *Why* he does this is something he refuses to tell anyone, even at the very end of the play when Othello, although emotionally incapable of directly addressing him, begs Cassio to ask him. Iago's final words make the great, reverberating refusal: 'Demand me nothing. What you know, you know. / From this time forth I never will speak word' (5.2.300–1). The fact that Iago has willingly told us so much in his many soliloquies makes his silence here the more intensely frustrating. In several of those soliloquies Iago does offer motivation and appears to understand himself, at least up to a point. He believes he has unjustly lost to Cassio his 'place' as Othello's lieutenant, and, as we saw in Part III, that motive alone, with its implications of class distinction and social hierarchy, seems satisfactory to the first black actor to play Iago in Stratford, Lucian Msamati. Iago also thinks, or affects to think, that both Othello and Cassio have slept with his wife, Emilia, which adds to an offended sense of professional displacement one of sexual displacement too. He claims that he himself loves, or at least lusts after, Desdemona and he also seems to be disgusted by the military and sexual success of a black man – although this motive probably loses some force when he is played by a black man.

Iago's own explanations of motive, however, have rarely seemed wholly satisfactory to critics, even if they have seemed so to (some) actors, and the critical history of *Othello* displays a refusal to credit his own opinion. Most famously, Coleridge says that the soliloquy with which Iago concludes Act 1 betrays 'the motive-hunting of motiveless malignity', and many others propose alternative motives of apparently greater psychological complexity than Iago's own. Iago is a displaced artist, conceiving and executing an intricate plot, think William Hazlitt and A. C. Bradley, and as such even a kind of Shakespeare surrogate, which should make us ponder Shakespeare's ethical ambivalence about writing for the stage, although neither Hazlitt nor Bradley in fact does. He is an appalling practical joker and a parabolic figure for the pursuit of scientific knowledge by experiment regardless of ethical consideration, says W. H. Auden, influencing Jonathan Miller's controversial BBC TV production (1981), in which Bob Hoskins plays Iago. He is a repressed homosexual, think many critics over many years, and he is played as such in well-known productions. He is an 'original nothingness', thinks A. D. Nuttall, 'the dramatist of his own psyche' who '*decides* to be motivated in certain ways and then rants accordingly'.

That so many critics go motive-hunting beyond the motives offered by the play itself makes it clear that soliloquy can be as obfuscating as it is revealing. We know from his soliloquies that Iago is never, except when it serves his purposes, 'honest Iago' with the other characters on stage, but we assume that he has no reason to be dishonest with us. When, finally, he says, 'what you know, you know', however, everything is plunged into an abyss of not knowing, since this appears to imply one final time that he could tell us more than he chooses to if he had a mind to. His silence is perhaps an ultimate, triumphant expression of his power over all of us, characters and audience alike, even as he is unmasked and taken off to be tortured. But we simply cannot say that this – that Iago knows more than he is saying – is what we now know, because Iago will not tell us. We are as ignorant of his motive or motives as Othello himself – and possibly as ignorant as Iago himself too, for it's entirely possible that he cannot explain himself to himself either and must wait for the most brilliant or ingenious of his critics to do so. When he says to Roderigo in the play's opening dialogue 'I am not what I am' (1.1.64), he may mean 'I am not what I seem', as a way of convincing Roderigo of his powerful cunning – which Roderigo is, after all, paying for – but the statement goes deeper than that too in its reversing God's biblical statement of his identity: 'I am that I am' (Exodus 3.14). Iago, that is, may be offering here a statement of absolute non-identity opposed to God's statement of ultimate self-identity; being not what he is, he can be anything he seems to be. Stephen Greenblatt, in a striking reading of Iago, thinks that this witnesses in him 'the principle of narrativity itself, cut off from original motive and final disclosure'. Iago, that is, is himself only in the stories he tells, and the stories he tells are lies and deceptions whose power derives from the fact that his hearers are suspiciously eager to believe them. Othello wins Desdemona by telling stories, or so he says in his speech to the Senate in Act 1 Scene 3; Iago wins Othello by telling stories too.

In all these ways, however, we know that when Iago sententiously moralizes while appearing to ponder the behaviour of Cassio in the temptation scene, he is, with quite breath-taking hypocrisy, in fact offering us, covertly, a self-judgement. 'Men should be what they seem, / Or those that be not, would they might seem none', indeed; but Iago is the very name for not being what you seem, and it's his soliloquies that let us know so. In this long passage of the play, then, we might think of Shakespeare as actually himself pondering the nature of what soliloquy can manage, presenting us with a radical, dramatized commentary on thinking, knowing and not knowing, and on the difference between 'seeming' and 'being' made possible by the privacy of consciousness that even slaves are free to, which appears to be exhibited, but may be partly forever occluded, by soliloquy.

*

The mechanisms of the Iago soliloquy and its characteristic style are on display along with the intimation of motive in the first soliloquy he speaks, about which Coleridge made his influentially memorable remark. Like several of Iago's soliloquies, this one emerges out of prose dialogue, in this case with Roderigo, whom he is busily duping for financial gain in a way that acts as prelude to his subsequent less clearly motivated duping of Othello. Iago has had by far the greater share of this dialogue, and in any case we might read his contributions to it, which include his great cynical monologues on the nature of virtue and love, for instance ('It is merely a lust of the blood and a permission of the will'), as almost themselves forms of soliloquy, since Roderigo is such a cipher to Iago's manipulative will as hardly to have a mind or voice of his own, at least until he turns on him in Act 4 Scene 2, only to be further manipulated and then murdered by him. Before speaking this first soliloquy, Iago casually dismisses Roderigo ('Go to, farewell, put money enough in your purse') before turning confidentially to us, initially to parade his contempt even further:

Thus do I ever make my fool my purse:
For I mine own gained knowledge should profane
If I would time expend with such a snipe
But for my sport and profit. I hate the Moor
And it is thought abroad that 'twixt my sheets
He's done my office. I know not if't be true,
But I for mere suspicion in that kind
Will do as if for surety. He holds me well,
The better shall my purpose work on him.
Cassio's a proper man: let me see now,
To get his place, and to plume up my will
In double knavery. How? How? Let's see:
After some time to abuse Othello's ear
That he is too familiar with his wife.
He hath a person and a smooth dispose
To be suspected, framed to make women false.
The Moor is of a free and open nature
That thinks men honest that but seem to be so,
And will be as tenderly led by th' nose
As asses are.
I have't, it is engendered! Hell and night
Must bring this monstrous birth to the world's light. (1.3.382–403)

Roderigo thinks Desdemona can be bought by using Iago as a go-between, so we might almost agree that he is indeed a kind of contemptible 'fool'; but we come to learn that the derogation of others, and the cynicism about human nature that it entails, is entirely characteristic of Iago. Elsewhere in his soliloquies people are 'trash', 'hussies' and 'quats', and at the end of the play he calls his wife Emilia 'Filth'. This rhetoric of derogation is heavily underlined by his frequent bestializing of human beings. Roderigo here is a snipe, Othello an ass, and elsewhere Cassio is a dog and others are goats, wolves and monkeys. The sexual as well as the derogatory implications of all this are overt very early in the play when Iago tells Brabantio, Desdemona's father, that 'Even now, very now, an old black ram / Is tupping your white ewe!' (1.1.87–8) – that is, that his daughter is being made love to by Othello. The image recurs when, in Act 3 Scene 3, Iago asks Othello if he would wish to be 'the supervisor' – that is, the spectator – and 'grossly gape on, / Behold her topped.' The grossness of the metaphor and the repeated, specifying insistence of 'now', which seems designed to help Brabantio visualize the spectacle, reveal an imagination diseased equally by racism and sexual perversity. Then, just a moment later, Iago regards the act of love as making 'the beast with two backs' (1.1.115). This grotesque Rabelaisian imagining is revolting enough in itself, but the confiding nature of Iago's soliloquies seems to depend on his trusting that we will share his view, or his mind. The proposed co-option feels like a kind of uncleanness or contamination, and these soliloquies can seem things we want to shake off.

Saying 'I hate the Moor' is manifestly 'honest' of Iago, however, since he has just said this, as straightforwardly, to Roderigo, and this directness is a marked feature of his mode of address in soliloquy. It helps to secure an audience's sense that, if he is not telling the truth to the other characters in the play, he is still, as a rule, telling it to us. Even so, this very opening soliloquy raises an immediate query in our minds over his overt motivation for so hating Othello. The phrasing of the apparently explanatory sentence is peculiar: 'I hate the Moor / And it is thought abroad that 'twixt my sheets / He's done my office' – that is, that Othello has had sex with Emilia. Although this appears to propose a causal relationship between Othello's presumed sexual dealings with Iago's wife and Iago's hatred of him, the conjunction 'and' is a decidedly odd one to use to make the point. 'Since', for instance, would establish the consequential link much more firmly. If 'and' suggests, as it ordinarily does, not consequence but subsequence – this happened, and then this did – then the hatred appears to precede, and to exceed, all motive.

Comparably, the passive construction 'it is thought abroad' wholly lacks specificity, making it appear that Iago has not pursued the source of such rumour very far, or at all troubled over how much it can be relied on. The word 'office', like 'place', appears frequently in the play, if not as frequently as 'honest', although both honesty and 'honour' are also involved in the more usual meanings of 'office' and 'place': one's position, that is, in the social and military hierarchy. We already know, because Iago tells Roderigo so, that he deeply resents Cassio's securing his place as Othello's lieutenant in a way that unjustly displaces Iago himself. The sexual connotation of the word 'office' in Iago's phrase 'he's done my office' here has seemed exceptional to some commentators, although Ben Jonson uses it comparably in his 'Epithalamion: or, a Song' (no. LXXV of *Underwoods*), written in 1632, about thirty years after *Othello*, in which the newly married husband is, on his wedding night, 'master of the office' ('yet no more / Exacts than she is pleased to pay'). That the word has such a strong professional connotation too, though, suggests that for Iago, at least in his relation to Othello, the sexual and the professional are inextricably intertwined and that the conjunction may lie at the root of whatever psychological and emotional damage he suffers. And there is something distinctly offhand about Iago's willingness to entrust a matter of such grave moment to 'mere suspicion' – even if 'mere' then meant 'absolute' or 'complete' – rather than to proven truth, especially since, if one's wife is adulterous and known to be so, this would be a 'cuckolding', a profound humiliation for a man in this patriarchal society. This makes it clear why so many, following Coleridge, think that Iago is searching, rather than accounting, for motivation here, and elsewhere in his soliloquies too.

His plot against Othello, Desdemona and Cassio therefore comes to seem nihilistic or even, in the term the Elizabethans themselves would have understood, demonic. Iago derives in part, as Richard III does too, as we have seen, from the Vice figure of the medieval morality plays, and in the soliloquy beginning 'And what's he then that says I play the villain?' in Act 2 Scene 3 he appears to address Satan as 'Divinity of hell!' and says that 'When devils will the blackest sins put on / They do suggest at first with heavenly shows / As I do now' (2.3.346–8). 'Suggest' means 'prompt' and 'heavenly shows' are the disguises a devil might assume to prompt people to evil, so Iago is here making a clear correlation between his own mendacity, duplicity and hypocrisy and the powers of evil as they were understood by the Christian religion. This is one of several signs, in fact, that just below the surface of *Othello* we can detect the trace of the medieval *psychomachia*, which I discussed in Part II as an influence on Elizabethan soliloquy. This trace rises to the surface, as so many things do, in Act 3 Scene 3, when Othello personifies his desire for revenge and apostrophizes it: 'Arise, black vengeance, from the hollow hell ...' (3.3.450), which also has strong Senecan overtones. When such things become explicit, we might become more than usually aware that within Othello's name lies the word 'hell' itself and within Desdemona's the word 'demon'. When Iago says that he intends to 'plume up [his] will / In double knavery' in his opening soliloquy, then, he is voicing the motives of pride and assertive disobedience that are the prerogative of Satan himself, the fallen angel, in Christian and English-medieval dramatic tradition. *Othello* is not a medieval morality play or an allegory of salvation and damnation, but it draws some of its energy from such submerged sources, even for audiences no longer able to recognize them for exactly what they are.

When Iago asks himself (or us), 'How? How?' and begins to deliberate ('let's see'), he initiates the most consistent process of his soliloquies as they succeed one another. Inviting us to join him, as it were, and as if improvising, he designs his plot – what he calls here his 'purpose' – explaining it stage by ensuing stage, commenting on its progress, relishing his apparent local triumphs and encouraging himself on. It's not hard to see from these successive soliloquies how the critical tradition of Iago as malign creative artist (or practical joker) originated. The soliloquies even have their meta-theatrical moments. 'And what's he then that says I play the villain?' (2.3.331–57) is one, uttered as if in challenge to a theatrical audience, as Iago appears disingenuously aghast that anyone might find the 'advice' he has just given Cassio about regaining Othello's goodwill less than disinterestedly offered – whereas, of course, it's designed specifically to further his plot. This may remind us of the theatrically self-conscious Hamlet asking 'Who calls me villain? Breaks my pate across?' in a soliloquy; strangely, in this soliloquy in Act 2, Iago also figures his own lies to Othello as the pouring of 'pestilence into his ear', just as the Ghost in *Hamlet* reports how poison was literally poured into his ear by Claudius. *Othello* and *Hamlet* were written not far apart chronologically, and Hamlet and Iago, both major soliloquists, may in one sense be read almost as mirror images of each other. Where Hamlet appears to struggle to find adequate apologies for delay, Iago appears to struggle to find adequate motives for the plot he himself constructs. Like Iago, Hamlet himself attempts to construct a plot – a specifically theatrical one – to entrap Claudius. The element of meta-theatricality in Iago's soliloquy is ingeniously rendered meta-cinematic in Oliver Parker's version when, on the line 'So will I turn her virtue into pitch', Iago clutches a smouldering stake, making his own hand painfully 'pitch' black, and then extends that hand over the camera lens, blocking our view of him and of everything else as the screen fades to black. Is this an Iago making ultimate directorial decisions about what we see and do not see, in a gesture of authoritative contempt that is also the product of self-induced, masochistic pain?

*

In the soliloquy in Act 1 Iago offers us an Othello likely to prove malleable to his design. Believing men 'honest that but seem to be so', as Iago tells us, Othello is almost bound to fall victim to someone whom he believes, insistently, to be 'honest' but who, we know, is exactly not what he 'seems'. The possibility of a white man so easily duping a credulous black man has colonialist and racist implications, as do other elements of the play, and some black actors find it difficult to play the role for this reason. In Part III Lucian Msamati tells us how he and Hugh Quarshie in the RSC production in some ways subversively moulded *Othello* in response to the fact that black actors now played both leading roles, but he wants to make it clear that their interpretation offered a complex take on traditional ways of understanding the play too. Issues of racism and the discourse of racial difference are so deeply woven into the fabric of *Othello* that it has become one of the crucial texts for post-colonial literary criticism and probably the most frequently performed of Shakespeare's tragedies since the 1980s, when a seminal production by Janet Suzman was staged at the Market Theatre in Johannesburg and subsequently filmed for TV, while apartheid was still in place in South Africa. In a lecture on her production, Suzman reads the play as 'a metaphor for South Africa', regarding Iago as 'the full power of the state turned upon human happiness', a sort of Eugene Terre'Blanche (the white supremacist active in the public life of the time) figure.

When he suddenly realizes in this soliloquy's final lines what his plot will be and lets us know he has done so, Iago uses a metaphor deeply implicated in the discourse that prompted such interpretations. Like others of his soliloquies, this one ends with a couplet in which Iago virtually italicizes the point he has reached in his 'purpose', almost as though he is articulating a kind of aide-memoire for himself as well as his audience. This couplet uses the metaphor of pregnancy: 'I have't, it is engendered! Hell and night / Must bring this monstrous birth to the world's light.' 'Hell and night' may represent one of those almost subliminal connections with psychomachia I have just mentioned, and the bringing of something to the world's light is a ramifying trope. Iago's plot, currently secreted in the darkness of his brain, will itself be brought to light as it works itself out in subsequent scenes of the play. But the fact that he is the one who has plotted it, which of course he intends should remain in the dark, will itself eventually also be brought to the world's light, in a way he cannot at all envisage, by the agency of his own wife. Bringing something to the world's light seems also terribly to foreshadow the lights Othello conceives himself extinguishing in the soliloquy he speaks before murdering Desdemona: 'Put out the light, and then put out the light!', which I consider further below. The phrase 'the world's light' may, in such contexts, itself recall that Christ called himself 'the light of the world', and what Iago is bringing to light in his opening soliloquy is, sacrilegiously, the deepest and most dreadful darkness, which then casts itself over the rest of the play.

But it's the metaphor of bringing a *monstrous birth* to light that resonates most deeply with the discourse of racial difference. This is in fact the play's first use of the pregnancy metaphor – of conception, generation and parturition – which is repeated during it, when it sometimes signals the fear of what may be the consequence of a union between black and white human beings in the act of copulation: miscegenation. This fear is precisely – very precisely, *now* and *now* – what Iago intends to evoke in Brabantio when he represents sex between Desdemona and Othello as the tupping of a white sheep by a black ewe. When Iago, speaking in soliloquy – with all that we know that to involve – figures his own plot as the monstrous birth resulting from a conception of his own brain, he is making himself the play's original monster too, and the origin of its monstrosity. *He* is the monster revealed to the world's light in the play's final scene as Othello's 'demi-devil' and Lodovico's 'Spartan dog, / More fell than anguish, hunger, or the sea' (5.2.359–60), where 'fell' means 'ruthless'. He is himself the human beast of his own vilest imagining.

*

Many of Iago's soliloquies, as I have said, follow on from passages of prose dialogue and, in the main, they retain the stylistic characteristics and virtues of prose rather than of heightened poetic language, which seems wholly appropriate to the gnawing little negation that Iago is, gnawing at the roots of life (as D. H. Lawrence calls Loerke in *Women in Love*, remembering the Norse god Loki), a man without any poetry in his heart or soul. In the main, they lack much figurative or metaphorical display, as they patiently spell out an intention and offer the notation of an action about to be set in train or a commentary on its unfolding and effect.

But there are exceptions. The most striking one comes in the pivotal Act 3 Scene 3 in the soliloquy in which Iago reveals how he intends to initiate the plot of the handkerchief. Conceiving again of his effect on Othello as a form of poison, which 'with a little art upon the blood / Burn[s] like the mines of sulphur' (3.3.331–2), he gloatingly points Othello out when he re-appears on stage as if he is a slowly collapsing victim – 'like a wild beast stung with the envenomed shaft of the hunter', says William Hazlitt. These are among the cruellest lines in the play, as Iago's sudden, exceptional figurative richness rises to the occasion of his despicably relished joy in Othello's pain. The third-person 'he' of Iago's contemptuous opening directive collapses into the even more derisive second-person 'thee' and 'thou', rather than the formal 'you', which scandalously breaks all the linguistic rules of master–servant relationships in this hierarchical social world:

> Look where he comes. Not poppy nor mandragora
> Nor all the drowsy syrups of the world
> Shall ever medicine thee to that sweet sleep
> Which thou owedst yesterday. (3.3.333–6)

It has been pointed out that in these lines, with their slowness of rhythm and their almost luscious expansiveness of assonance and sibilance, Iago sounds oddly like Othello. 'By heaven, thou echo'st me', Othello might well say again, if he could hear them spoken. In his book *The Wheel of Fire*, G. Wilson Knight calls Othello's characteristic form of speech 'the Othello music', defining it as 'a unique solidity and precision of picturesque phrase or image' and a 'rich harmony of words'. It can nevertheless, he thinks, become bombastic – which is the derogatory word Iago uses of it in the first scene of the play when he calls it 'a bombast circumstance / Horribly stuffed with epithets of war' (1.1.12–13).

It's true that Othello can seem pompous or grandiloquent, as when, for instance, he calls his eyes, or his eyesight, 'my speculative and officed instrument' (1.3.271). His sometimes rather orotund style, prone to repetition, seems more appropriate to public utterance than to private soliloquy, so that in the earlier acts of the play we hardly miss soliloquies from him, with their necessary exposure of interiority, especially since we are so fascinated by Iago's. (In the Janet Suzman TV production, John Kani as Othello speaks his English with a deliberate, almost alien care, since his first language is Xhosa. Kani would undoubtedly have thought of himself as speaking here the tongue of the imperialist oppressor, and rarely can the ponderousness of Othello's utterances have found more appropriate expression.) There is an extraordinary irony in the fact that even for a few lines of soliloquy Iago should sound not unlike Othello in dialogue because when, in Act 3 Scene 3, Othello himself begins for the first time to speak in soliloquy, he sounds in some ways not unlike Iago, and utterly unlike himself, almost as if he is now also ventriloquizing a voice and returning an echo. Othello seems driven to soliloquize by what Iago does to him, and what Iago does to him is to make him into something other than himself by feeding him the poison of jealousy. This apparent sharing of something stylistic in their internal reflections leads some critics to regard the play's principal characters as essentially complementary, or even as separate aspects of a single personality.

When Othello speaks in soliloquy for the first time as late as Act 3 Scene 3 he begins by commenting on Iago, who has just left the stage, before reflecting on Desdemona:

> This fellow's of exceeding honesty
> And knows all qualities, with a learned spirit,
> Of human dealings. If I do prove her haggard,
> Though that her jesses were my dear heart-strings,
> I'd whistle her off and let her down the wind
> To prey at fortune. Haply for I am black
> And have not those soft parts of conversation
> That chamberers have, or for I am declined
> Into the vale of years – yet that's not much –
> She's gone, I am abused, and my relief
> Must be to loathe her. O curse of marriage
> That we can call these delicate creatures ours
> And not their appetites! I had rather be a toad
> And live upon the vapour of a dungeon
> Than keep a corner in the thing I love
> For others' uses. Yet 'tis the plague of great ones,
> Prerogatived are they less than the base;
> 'Tis destiny unshunnable, like death –
> Even then this forked plague is fated to us
> When we do quicken. (3.3.262–81)

'The Moor is of a free and open nature / That thinks men honest that but seem to be so', says Iago in his first soliloquy, and here is Othello, in *his* first full soliloquy, proving Iago exactly right and therefore himself exactly wrong about Iago, whose knowledge of 'human dealings' is so skewed towards the malign. Beyond this echo of Iago's own words, Othello appears also suddenly to have inherited his mode of perception. A 'haggard' is a wild female hawk, and 'jesses' are the straps fastened around her legs and attached to the falconer's wrist. Figuring Desdemona like this, Othello is bestializing the human – bestializing his wife – as Iago characteristically does, and this is quite contrary to the recognizable forms of Othello's speech up to now. When he goes on to conceive of himself, comparably, as potentially a 'toad' in a dungeon and to objectify Desdemona as 'the thing', even if 'The thing I love', and to formulate the idea of her having a 'corner' for 'other's uses' – that is, a vagina for sex with other men – the Iago-like disease or corruption of the imagination is already well underway. It's as though the very forms of Iago's consciousness have begun to insinuate themselves into Othello's. Orson Welles's film version (1952) is alert to this when one shot of the dialogue from Act 3 Scene 3 presents us with Iago (Michaél MacLiammóir) speaking direct to camera as if to Othello, while we see Othello (Welles himself) reflected in a mirror facing us on screen.

This soliloquy peculiarly combines self-deprecation and apparent self-aggrandisement: self-deprecation when he conceives of his own blackness as the reason for his linguistic incompetence – which is in fact nowhere apparent in his actual dialogue, which manifests great stylistic and social competence, as we have seen – and when he regrets being so much older than Desdemona; and self-aggrandisement, when he classes himself among the 'great ones' abused in marriage. The insecurity about his own identity that may be read out of such self-contradiction has led some critics – notable cases are T. S. Eliot and F. R. Leavis – to regard Othello as egotistically self-dramatizing and, as such, psychologically and emotionally all too ready to be easily and suddenly fooled by Iago. This view was influential on Laurence Olivier's famous interpretation of the role in 1964, which Lucian Msamati, as we saw in Part III, regards as haunting actors playing it even today. In this soliloquy, there does seem something too easily, even histrionically, abject in the way Othello rushes so swiftly to read his situation as dictated by a 'destiny' and 'fate' unavoidably present in the very terms of his conception. To understand oneself as fated is, necessarily, to believe oneself worthy of Fate's notice.

Even if we believe that an element of self-dramatization is present in Othello, however, his breakdown in Act 4 Scene 1, when he has some kind of fit, still seems a nadir of nakedly necessitous distress. We may even consider this tiny speech a form of soliloquy since, as he falls into 'a trance', Othello moves into a state of unconsciousness and begins speaking as if only to himself; in fact Iago immediately afterwards speaks what also appears to be a soliloquy when, gloating yet again, he apostrophizes his 'medicine' – that is, the poison of his lies – and encourages it to 'Work on!' while he is still immediately in front of Othello. Some productions even have him kicking the prostrate hero. In Suzman's, Iago (Richard Haines) does this, with a strongly pressing political application in the apartheid circumstances of the state in which the performance took place.

Othello's collapse begins with a wholly uncharacteristic lapse from verse to prose when Iago tells him that Cassio did indeed 'lie ... With her, on her, what you will', and Othello asks himself what this might mean:

> Lie with her? lie on her? We say lie on her when they belie her! Lie with her, zounds, that's fulsome! – Handkerchief! confessions! handkerchief! – To confess, and be hanged for his labour! First to be hanged, and then to confess: I tremble at it. Nature would not invest herself in such shadowing passion without some instruction. It is not words that shakes me thus. Pish! Noses, ears, and lips. Is't possible? Confess! Handkerchief! O devil! (4.1.35–43)

This is an extraordinary moment, and quite exceptional in Shakespeare. Lear, Ophelia and Lady Macbeth go mad, and so does the Jailer's Daughter in *The Two Noble Kinsmen*, and Leontes rages with insane jealousy, 'the infection of [his] brain', in *The Winter's Tale*, but none loses syntactical control as Othello does here. The frenzy of questions and exclamations substitutes for grammatical connectives, as Othello repeats Iago's word 'lie'. This can mean 'tell lies about her' – which is of course exactly what Iago is doing – but also 'copulate with her'. That imagined act then becomes the very specific physical detail of noses, ears and lips, almost as if Othello has become a camera inspecting these facial attributes in close-up, detached from their actual context on an expressive human face. These might be regarded, the editor of Arden 3 tells us, as 'surrogate genital images', but they are surely specific enough in themselves to suggest the crazed image in Othello's head of a passionate, almost mutually consuming lust between lovers as they bury their faces in each other. Oliver Parker's film gives us at this moment, in lieu of Othello's words themselves, a rapid juxtaposition of (non-genital) parts of the bodies of Desdemona and Cassio as they have sex, presumably reflecting a fantasy of Othello's (such images occur elsewhere in the movie too). Othello's rendering of sex by simply itemizing body parts, whether genitally surrogate or not, is a kind of brief metonymic blazon as crudely detached from human context as anything in Iago's soliloquies, and when Othello asks, 'Is't possible?' he is uncannily repeating Iago's question earlier in the play (2.3.283) when he addresses Cassio about his drunken loss of self-control, a question Othello was not on stage to hear. This makes it seem that Iago is penetrating Othello's consciousness even more deeply now than he was in his first soliloquy, almost as if in some form of devilish possession. Or, it makes it seem that Othello has interiorized his own Iago. Or, again, it makes it seem that the text of this play has, as it were, started communicating with itself, as though the play has become virtually self-conscious at the point when Iago's plot makes its most savage impact yet on its victim, briefly dispossessing him first of his reason and then of consciousness itself.

*

Having had no soliloquies until the play's third act, Othello has, in Act 5, one of the most famous of all Shakespearean tragic soliloquies, as he enters the room in which Desdemona lies sleeping:

> It is the cause, it is the cause, my soul!
> Let me not name it to you, you chaste stars,
> It is the cause. Yet I'll not shed her blood
> Nor scar that whiter skin of hers than snow
> And smooth as monumental alabaster:
> Yet she must die, else she'll betray more men.
> Put out the light, and then put out the light!
> If I quench thee, thou flaming minister,
> I can again thy former light restore
> Should I repent me. But once put out thy light,
> Thou cunning'st pattern of excelling nature,
> I know not where is that Promethean heat
> That can thy light relume: when I have plucked the rose
> I cannot give it vital growth again,
> It needs must wither. I'll smell thee on the tree;
> O balmy breath, that doth almost persuade
> Justice to break her sword! Once more, once more:
> Be thus when thou art dead and I will kill thee
> And love thee after. Once more, and that's the last.
> *He [smells, then] kisses her.*
> So sweet was ne'er so fatal. I must weep,
> But they are cruel tears. This sorrow's heavenly,
> It strikes where it doth love. She wakes. (5.2.1–22)

Othello speaks this soliloquy shortly before he kills Desdemona, and it gives us access to the extremity of his perturbation, in which his emotions appear not so much ambivalent as contradictory. The repetitions of the word 'cause' at the opening are matched by the repetitions of the word 'light' a little later and seem broodingly, or morbidly, obsessive and concentrated, especially since the opening repetition is addressed to his own soul. 'It is the cause' mysteriously withholds the referent of 'it', so that we know neither *what* that cause 'is', nor what it is, or is about to be, the 'cause' of. It is as though the 'cause' is, of itself, an absolute. Presumably, Othello intends this as the 'reason' that he is about to commit this dreadful act. The fact that he says he cannot name it to the 'chaste stars' suggests, further, that the 'cause' is that of the virtue of chastity this murder will advance: Desdemona, having proved unchaste, must die for a sin against chastity, in a 'cause' espoused by her husband and virtuous killer. None of this is spelt out, though – we must infer it from what Othello does say, cryptically. The word 'cause' is itself repeated from elsewhere in the play, where it's spoken at significant moments by Iago ('my cause is hearted'),

Emilia ('You have little cause to say so' and 'I never gave him cause') and Bianca ('Now I feel a cause'). But Othello's use of the word looks back particularly to Desdemona's in an exchange about jealousy with Emilia in Act 3 Scene 4 where she says 'Alas the day, I never gave him cause', to which Emilia replies 'But jealous souls will not be answered so: / They are not ever jealous for the cause, / But jealous for they're jealous' (3.4.158–61).

Emilia's insightful and provocative refusal of causation to jealousy means that we almost hear the word 'jealousy' again when Othello so emphatically repeats the word 'cause' at the opening of this soliloquy. He needs to persuade himself that he has cause and reason for what he is about to do, but cannot convey this with any specificity. So the motive of Desdemona's lack of chastity is quickly succeeded by a motive of, as it were, social and gender responsibility or duty: 'Yet she must die, else she'll betray more men.' Othello now seems to be offering his services as a wife-murderer to the state itself, as if committing one final act of public service, and he recalls the services he has previously performed for the state in his final speech before his suicide, stabbing himself as he remembers smiting 'a turbaned Turk' on behalf of the Venetian polity, implicitly making himself now another renegade Turk deserving death and damnation. Othello seems in this soliloquy, then, almost to be hunting for a justification for killing Desdemona, in one further mirror-image of Iago's motive-hunting – that Iago who is shortly himself to mirror Othello by becoming also the killer of his wife. Part of Othello knows that there never can be such a justification. So, trying to convince himself that he is acting with justice, he nevertheless imagines the personified figure of Justice itself – a *female* figure – being almost persuaded to break her emblematic sword, an action which would thwart the murder he is about to commit.

The psychological contradictoriness of the soliloquy is clear too in the repetitions of the word 'light', which seem much more subtly self-torturing than self-dramatizing. The line in which a single phrase is repeated – 'Put out the light, and then put out the light!' – is spoken, in self-address, before we know what 'light' Othello is referring to in either case. An actor on stage will probably be handling or at least looking at a candle or some kind of lamp and then turning to look at Desdemona. We know that the candle is the reference of the first 'light' in the exclamation when he addresses it as 'thou flaming minister', a phrase with biblical resonance. But we realize only when he says 'But once put out *thy* light', addressed to Desdemona, that the second 'light' refers to her and to her life, which, like the candle's flame, he is about to snuff out. When we take in the references being made by both 'lights' in the sentence, the repetition seems more than merely repetitive. It seems cumulative, as though the putting out of these two lights will prompt a universal darkness; or as though Chaos is indeed come again; or, as Othello says, still in soliloquy after the murder, 'Methinks it should be now a huge eclipse / Of sun and moon, and that th'affrighted globe / Should yawn at alteration' (5.2.98–100). 'Put out the light, and then put out the light!' – an iambic line of ten monosyllables, four of which are repeated, it's one of those lines in Shakespeare that seem quite extraordinarily simple. Yet, like others – 'Never, never, never, never, never' in *King Lear*, outstandingly, and Charmian's mere phrase 'Ah, soldier!' in *Antony and Cleopatra* – its simplicity is devastating, appearing to concentrate into itself whole worlds of grief, sorrow and lamentation. It tells us that Othello knows what he does, and knows *not* what he does.

The 'affrighted globe' is, meta-theatrically, the affrighted Globe too, the theatre in which all of this is being spoken on the Elizabethan stage by an actor terrifying his contemporary audience. But Othello is also terrifying himself: 'Put out the light, and then put out the light!' is said as self-encouragement initially, as if the light of the candle has some kind of equivalence to the life of the sleeping woman; but in the following lines Othello educates himself in all the ways in which there is no such equivalence. Indeed, he further exemplifies this when he moves from the metaphor of light to that of the plucked rose. Initially perceiving Desdemona as possessing skin whiter than snow and as smooth as alabaster, Othello is resorting to a problematically idealizing Petrarchism in which the conception of woman as flower plays a conventional part. But Othello's very particular concentration on the effect of withering his action will have on this plucked rose brings in a wholly un-Petrarchan sensual register. 'I'll smell thee on the tree', accompanied by the recognition of Desdemona's breathing and then by the enactment of smelling and kissing, makes the embodied actuality of the woman whose body he is about to assault almost too intimately, even indecently, present to us – an effect sometimes very immediate indeed on the stage.

In this soliloquy, then, it's almost as though Othello knows, against what he regards as his better reason and judgement, that Justice really should break her sword when faced with the breathing reality of the life about to be taken. 'Be thus when thou art dead and I will kill thee / And love thee after' has a hideous, necrophiliac implication, which may register an ultimate perturbation, and 'This sorrow's heavenly, / It strikes where it doth love' is a form of self-deceiving blasphemy, since truly 'heavenly' sorrow would act not with justice but with mercy, as Portia instructs Shylock (and us) in *The Merchant of Venice* when she says that the 'quality of mercy ... droppeth as the gentle rain from heaven'. Othello, at some inchoate level of his being, knows when he speaks that in the act he is about to commit he is not serving Justice or the state, but, driven out of his mind or out of himself by Iago's poison, he is engaged in an act not only of murder but of self-destruction and self-damnation too. An actor might play the soliloquy as self-dramatizing in its opening lines, then, but not as it moves towards its end. Contained within it, almost in earshot, therefore, we can also hear the Othello who weeps in appalled self-rebuke before the play ends, conceiving of himself as 'one whose hand, / Like the base Indian, threw a pearl away, / Richer than all his tribe' (5.2.344–6). This soliloquy, contradictory in its very rhythms, is powered by the cadences of remorse as well as those of self-justification.

*

Desdemona has only one soliloquy in the play, and it's only three lines long. Act 4 Scene 2 is usually known as the 'brothel scene' because Othello treats Desdemona there as if she is a prostitute, 'that cunning whore of Venice', and Emilia as if she is the madam of a brothel. The violent offensiveness of Othello's language impels Desdemona to respond that she no longer has any 'lord' – that is, husband – when Emilia asks about him. Desdemona then asks Emilia to put her wedding sheets on her bed, ominously telling her to make them her shroud if she should be the first to die, in that macabre conjunction of sex and death that so fascinated the Elizabethans and Jacobeans and so profoundly informs the ending of *Romeo and Juliet* too, as we have seen. When Emilia leaves the stage, Desdemona utters her three lines:

> 'Tis meet I should be used so, very meet.
> How have I been behaved that he might stick
> The small'st opinion on my greatest misuse? (4.2.109–11)

It's just about possible for an actor to speak these lines with irony, meaning to blame Othello for making so much of what must be so very little; but they more straightforwardly appear to intend self-recrimination. Desdemona seems genuinely to believe that Othello is treating her as she deserves for some fault that it is her responsibility, as a wife, to discover and correct ('misuse' means her own ill-conduct).

Desdemona is an intensely difficult part to play on the contemporary stage, especially since for a large part of the play's history she was played as sweetly compliant and sentimentally passive. The scope for both defiance and acquiescence available to a woman as daughter and wife in the patriarchal society of Shakespeare's time, and any judgements about Shakespeare's own attitudes to these conventions, can be extremely hard to calibrate now, when conventions of marital relationship are so different, at least for the majority in Western European society. One of Iago's most penetratingly subtle and cruel destabilizations of Othello's trust in Desdemona is, after all, to tell him that, since she has behaved duplicitously towards her father by marrying without telling him, she is also quite capable of deceiving Othello himself, in turn, by having an adulterous affair (3.3.209–11), which is what Brabantio himself says to Othello in his parting words in Act 1 Scene 3. If we understand Desdemona's defiance of her father as bravely, even heroically, self-assertive, then how are we to judge her apparently craven acquiescence in her own murder when, with her dying words, she exonerates Othello, refusing to name, blame or shame him? 'O, who hath done / This deed?', asks Emilia, and Desdemona replies, 'Nobody. I myself. Farewell. / Commend me to my kind lord' (5.2.121–3) – that 'lord' whom she has not long previously considered to have relinquished her, who may well seem to us 'kind' only in killing her since, in a pun available in the English language of the period, 'kind' could also mean 'behaving according to nature'.

Whatever subtleties of relative self-assertiveness some critical commentators have persuaded themselves to discover in these lines, it's extremely difficult for anyone to speak them on a contemporary stage without inducing in the audience something of the extreme unease many will also feel while listening to Katherine's speech at the end of *The Taming of the Shrew*. How on earth to prevent our feeling that Desdemona is here reducing herself also, in an ultimate act of self-abnegation, to a 'nobody'? It's unsurprising that Desdemona's lines tend to be cut in contemporary productions. In the Welles film, Desdemona (Suzanne Cloutier) does speak the lines, but her face is entirely hidden from the camera by Emilia's body while she does so. Although this movie by no means presents us with a defiant Desdemona, this does diminish the potential embarrassment of the lines. In the Oliver Parker film, Desdemona (Irène Jacob) does not answer Emilia, but gazes upwards towards the camera in close-up, opening her eyes wide as if in a sort of ecstasy of anticipation.

In fact, though, *Othello* does end, as it begins, with an act of female defiance – not Desdemona's of Othello, but Emilia's of Iago. This is the more remarkable because earlier in the play she has been reduced to silence by her husband. In Act 2 Scene 1 he accuses her, in front of Cassio and Desdemona and with characteristic salacious innuendo, of using her tongue too much in their marriage – of, that is, being what contemporaries would have known as a 'scold'. When Emilia says nothing, Desdemona seems to make a point of pointing it out: 'Alas!' she says, 'She has no speech' (2.1.102). After a further insult from Iago, Emilia contents herself with 'You have little cause to say so' (2.1.108). Small wonder, then, that Iago subsequently so disastrously misreads his wife as to believe that he can compel her silence again when she realizes the truth of his plot against Othello. Now she refuses to 'charm [her] tongue', as Iago commands – that is, to control it – expressing a compelling obligation: 'I am bound to speak' (5.2.180). Shortly afterwards, in disbelief that she is about to seal his fate by saying exactly what she knows, Iago furiously says to her 'What, are you mad? I charge you, get you home' (5.2.191), and Emilia, acknowledging while refusing the patriarchal norm, says, "'Tis proper I obey him – but not now. / Perchance, Iago, I will ne'er go home' (5.2.193–4). That defiant disobedience, which every member of every audience of this play knows to be itself entirely 'proper' and finds deeply thrilling, means that this Emilia never *can* go home. Literally, she can never go home in the play, because her speaking out prompts her abusive husband to murder her. Figuratively, she can never go home, because she brings herself to a point where the social world she inhabits can no longer contain her – she exceeds its circumstances.

It seems also proper, then, to end this book with the defiance of a speech Emilia makes earlier in the play. It's not a soliloquy – and Emilia has only one, in Act 3 Scene 3, in which she informs us about the handkerchief. As with other women servants in Shakespeare, her inwardness is not required to draw attention to itself in soliloquy. The speech is made not to her husband, or to any man, but to Desdemona, and these are the last words she says to her before she is killed. We should not sentimentalize its proto-feminism, since Emilia is cynically opportunistic – or just realistically worldly – about sexual betrayal and as prejudicially hostile to the prostitute Bianca as are the men in the play. Even so, her monologue in Act 4 Scene 3 detailing the relations between men and women as they obtain in contemporary marriage, and her apportioning of an appropriate ratio of blame, seems almost cognizant of the knowledge expressed by another Shakespearean tragic character, Coriolanus, when he says that 'there is a world elsewhere'. Relevantly, we also hear in Emilia's speech the cadences of defiant complaint and plea that we hear in Shylock's monologue 'Hath not a Jew eyes?' in *The Merchant of Venice* – that Shylock who also never gets to utter a soliloquy. Emilia speaks:

> But I do think it is their husband's faults
> If wives do fall. Say that they slack their duties
> And pour out treasures into foreign laps;
> Or else break out in peevish jealousies,
> Throwing restraint upon us; or say they strike us,
> Or scant our former having in despite,
> Why, we have galls: and though we have some grace
> Yet have we some revenge. Let husbands know
> Their wives have sense like them: they see, and smell,
> And have their palates both for sweet and sour
> As husbands have. What is it that they do
> When they change us for others? Is it sport?
> I think it is. And doth affection breed it?
> I think it doth. Is't frailty that thus errs?
> It is so too. And have we not affections?
> Desires for sport? And frailty, as men have?
> Then let them use us well: else let them know,
> The ills we do, their ills instruct us so. (4.3.85–102)

'Or say they strike us' is not mere surmise, because we have witnessed Othello striking Desdemona – in public – in Act 4 Scene 1; the violence preceding his final onslaught makes the application of Emilia's charge specific. 'Frailty, thy name is woman', says Shakespeare's most famous soliloquist in *Hamlet*, written just a few years before *Othello*; and at around the same time, Viola in *Twelfth Night* says 'our frailty is the cause, not we'. But 'frailty' – moral or sexual weakness – is not gender-specific, insists Emilia, in what we might read as a striking riposte to misogyny.

SELECT BIBLIOGRAPHY

Arnold, Morris Leroy, *The Soliloquies of Shakespeare: A Study in Technic* (New York, 2013 [1911])

Auden, W. H., *The Dyer's Hand and Other Essays* (London, 1963)

Barton, John, *Playing Shakespeare* (London, 1984)

Bate, Jonathan, ed., *The Romantics on Shakespeare* (Harmondsworth, 1992)

Bate, Jonathan, *The Genius of Shakespeare* (London, 1997; rev. edn 2008)

Bate, Jonathan, *Soul of the Age* (London, 2008)

Bate, Jonathan and Russell Jackson, eds, *The Oxford Illustrated History of Shakespeare on Stage* (Oxford, 1996)

Belsey, Catherine, *The Subject of Tragedy: Identity and Difference in Renaissance Drama* (London, 1985)

Berryman, John, *Berryman's Shakespeare*, ed. John Haffenden (New York, 1999)

Bloom, Harold, *The Anxiety of Influence: A Theory of Poetry*, second edn (New York and Oxford, 1997)

Bloom, Harold, *Shakespeare: The Invention of the Human* (London, 1999)

Bradley, A. C., *Shakespearean Tragedy* (Harmondsworth, 1991 [1904])

Brook, Peter, *The Empty Space* (London, 1968)

Brooks, Cleanth, *The Well-Wrought Urn: Studies in the Structure of Poetry* (London, 1949 [1947])

Burnett, Mark Thornton, ed., *Great Shakespeareans: Welles, Kurosawa, Kozintsev, Zeffirelli* (London, 2013)

Burrow, Colin, *Shakespeare and Classical Antiquity* (Oxford, 2013)

Caines, Michael, *Shakespeare and the Eighteenth Century* (Oxford, 2013)

Clemen, Wolfgang, *Shakespeare's Soliloquies* (London, 1987)

Cooper, Helen, *Shakespeare and the Medieval World* (London, 2010)

Crowl, Samuel, *Screen Adaptations: Shakespeare's* Hamlet (London, 2014)

Cummings, Brian, *Mortal Thoughts: Religion, Secularity and Identity in Shakespeare and Early Modern Culture* (Oxford, 2013)

Curry, Julian, *Shakespeare on Stage* (London, 2010)

Danson, Lawrence, *Shakespeare's Dramatic Genres* (Oxford, 2000)

Davies, Anthony, *Filming Shakespeare's Plays: The Adaptations of Laurence Olivier, Orson Welles, Peter Brook and Akira Kurosawa* (Cambridge, 1988)

Davies, Anthony and Stanley Wells, *Shakespeare and the Moving Image: The Plays on Film and Television* (Cambridge, 1994)

De Quincey, Thomas, *On Murder*, ed. Robert Morrison (Oxford, 2006)

Dillon, Janette, *Shakespeare and the Staging of English History* (Oxford, 2012)

Donnellan, Declan, *The Actor and the Target* (2002; rev. edn London, 2005)

Duffy, Eamon, *The Stripping of the Altars: Traditional Religion in England 1400–1580* (1992; 2nd edn New Haven and London, 2005)

Eliot, T. S., *Selected Essays* (1932; 3rd edn London, 1951)
Empson, William, *The Structure of Complex Words* (1951; 3rd edn London, 1977)
Empson, William, *Essays on Shakespeare* (Cambridge, 1986)
Erne, Lukas, *Shakespeare as Literary Dramatist* (2003; 2nd edn Cambridge, 2013)
Freud, Sigmund, *Art and Literature*, ed. Albert Dickson (Harmondsworth, 1985)
Goffman, Erving, *The Presentation of Self in Everyday Life* (Harmondsworth, 1969 [1959])
Grazia, Margreta de, 'Soliloquies and wages in the age of emergent consciousness', *Textual Practice* vol. 9 no. 1 (1995): 67–92
Greenblatt, Stephen, *Renaissance Self-Fashioning: From More to Shakespeare* (Chicago and London, 1980)
Greenblatt, Stephen and Peter G. Platt, eds, *Shakespeare's Montaigne* (New York, 2014)
Gurr, Andrew, *The Shakespearean Stage 1574–1642* (Cambridge, 1992)
Gurr, Andrew and Mariko Ichikawa, *Staging in Shakespeare's Theatres* (Oxford, 2000)
Hall, Peter, *Playing Shakespeare* (London, 1984)
Harris, Jonathan Gil, *Shakespeare and Literary Theory* (Oxford, 2010)
Hawkes, Terence, ed., *Coleridge on Shakespeare* (Harmondsworth, 1969)
Hazlitt, William, *Characters of Shakespeare's Plays* (London, 1906 [1817, 1818])
Hirsh, James, *Shakespeare and the History of Soliloquies* (Madison and London, 2003)
Hughes, Ted, *Shakespeare and the Goddess of Complete Being* (London, 1992)
Jackson, Russell, ed., *The Cambridge Companion to Shakespeare on Film* (Cambridge, 2000)
Jackson, Russell, *Shakespeare and the English-speaking Cinema* (Oxford, 2014)
Jones, Emrys, *The Origins of Shakespeare* (Oxford, 1977)
Joseph, Sister Miriam, *Shakespeare's Use of the Arts of Language* (Connecticut, 2013 [1947])
Josipovici, Gabriel, *Hamlet: Fold on Fold* (New Haven and London, 2016)
Jowett, John, *Shakespeare and Text* (Oxford, 2007)
Kermode, Frank, *Shakespeare's Language* (Harmondsworth, 2000)
Kerrigan, Michael, ed., *To Be or Not to Be: Shakespeare's Soliloquies* (London, 2002)
Knight, G. Wilson, *The Wheel of Fire: Interpretations of Shakespearian Tragedy* (1930; revised edn 1949)
Kott, Jan, *Shakespeare Our Contemporary* (London, 1965)
Lanier, Douglas, *Shakespeare and Modern Popular Culture* (Oxford, 2002)
Lee, John, *Shakespeare's* Hamlet *and the Controversies of Self* (Oxford, 2000)
Lehmann, Courtney, *Screen Adaptations: Shakespeare's* Romeo and Juliet (London, 2010)
Levenson, Jill L., *Shakespeare in Performance:* Romeo and Juliet (Manchester, 1987)
Loehlin, James N., *Shakespeare in Production:* Romeo and Juliet (Cambridge, 2002)
Lyne, Raphael, *Shakespeare, Rhetoric and Cognition* (Cambridge, 2011)
McDonald, Russ, *Shakespeare and the Arts of Language* (Oxford, 2001)
McDonald, Russ, Nicholas D. Nace and Travis D. Williams, eds, *Shakespeare Up Close: Reading Early Modern Texts* (London, 2012)

McKellen, Ian, *William Shakespeare's* Richard III (London, 1996)
Maher, Mary Z, *Modern Hamlets and Their Soliloquies* (Iowa City, 1992)
Maus, Katharine Eisaman, *Inwardness and Theater in the English Renaissance* (Chicago and London, 1995)
Miola, Robert, *Shakespeare and Classical Tragedy* (Oxford, 1992)
Miola, Robert, *Shakespeare and Classical Comedy* (Oxford, 1994)
Miola, Robert S., *Shakespeare's Reading* (Oxford, 2000)
Noble, Adrian, *How to Do Shakespeare* (Abingdon and New York, 2010)
Nuttall, A. D., *Shakespeare the Thinker* (New Haven and London, 2007)
Olivier, Laurence, *Confessions of an Actor* (London, 1994 [1982])
Palfrey, Simon, *Doing Shakespeare* (London, 2005)
Palfrey, Simon and Tiffany Stern, *Shakespeare in Parts* (Oxford, 2007)
Potter, Lois, *Shakespeare in Performance:* Othello (Manchester, 2002)
Rackin, Phyllis, *Shakespeare and Women* (Oxford, 2005)
Richmond, Hugh M., *Shakespeare in Performance: King Richard III* (Manchester, 1989)
Righter, Anne, *Shakespeare and the Idea of the Play* (London, 1962)
Rosenthal, Daniel, *100 Shakespeare Films* (London, 2007)
Rothwell, Kenneth S., *A History of Shakespeare on Film* (Cambridge, 1999; 2nd edn 2004)
Seneca, *Six Tragedies*, trans. Emily Wilson (Oxford, 2010)
Shapiro, James, *1599: A Year in the Life of William Shakespeare* (London, 2005)
Sher, Anthony, *Year of the King: An Actor's Diary and Sketchbook* (London, 2004 [1985])
Slater, Ann Pasternak, *Shakespeare the Director* (Brighton and Totowa, 1982)
Smith, Bruce R., *Shakespeare and Masculinity* (Oxford, 2000)
Stewart, Alan, *Shakespeare's Letters* (Oxford, 2008)
Suzman, Janet, 'Shakespeare in the Twentieth Century – South Africa in *Othello*' (1995) in the notes to the Johannesburg Market Theatre production of *Othello* on DVD (Leipzig, Arthaus Musik, no. 103001)
Tanner, Tony, *Prefaces to Shakespeare* (Cambridge, MA and London, 2010)
Taylor, Michael, *Shakespeare Criticism in the Twentieth Century* (Oxford, 2001)
Van Es, Bart, *Shakespeare in Company* (Oxford, 2013)
Vickers, Brian, *The Artistry of Shakespeare's Prose* (London, 1968)
Walter, Harriet, *Brutus and Other Heroines* (London, 2016)
Wells, Stanley, ed., *Shakespeare in the Theatre: An Anthology of Criticism* (Oxford, 1997)
Wiggins, Martin, *Shakespeare and the Drama of his Time* (Oxford, 2000)
Williams, Gordon, *A Dictionary of Sexual Language and Imagery in Shakespearean and Stuart Literature* (London, 1994)
Williams, Raymond, *Writing in Society* (London, 1983)
Wills, Garry, *Augustine's* Confessions*: A Biography* (Princeton and Oxford, 2011)
Woudhuysen, H. R., ed., *Samuel Johnson on Shakespeare* (Harmondsworth, 1989)

INDEX